China Rising

Awesome economic growth and a more energetic foreign presence since the 1970s has led the international community to ask questions about China's future relations with the rest of the world. *China Rising* examines the extent to which China's future foreign policy may be shaped by its own agendas and constrained through interdependence and interaction with the outside world.

These chapters consider the Chinese foreign policy establishment's reactions to interdependence, the role of the army in foreign policy, the development of the navy, arms control policy, resource dependency, China's role in international trade and economic organisations, and its role in the region. They highlight three sets of questions that must shape any 'China policy': the extent to which China is a single actor in its foreign relations; the degree to which it is useful to attempt to ensure Chinese compliance with international practice; and the potential for influencing China's foreign policy.

China Rising suggests the need for strategic thinking that produces space for China on the international stage, based on multiple strategies, with both patience and tolerance, yet also firmness. It is indispensable reading for anyone with an interest in China's emerging foreign relations.

David S.G. Goodman is Director of the Institute for International Studies, University of Technology, Sydney. **Gerald Segal** is Senior Fellow for Asian Security Studies at the International Institute for Strategic Studies and Director of ESRC's Pacific Asia Programme.

China Rising

Nationalism and interdependence

Edited by David S.G. Goodman and Gerald Segal

Published for the International Institute for Strategic Studies

London and New York

First published 1997
by Routledge
11 New Fetter Lane, London EC4P 4EE

Simultaneously published in the USA and Canada
by Routledge
29 West 35th Street, New York, NY 10001

Typeset in Times by LaserScript, Mitcham, Surrey
Printed and bound in Great Britain by
T.J. International Ltd, Padstow, Cornwall

British Library Cataloguing in Publication Data
A catalogue record for this book is available from the British Library

Library of Congress Cataloging in Publication Data
China rising/edited by David S.G. Goodman and Gerald Segal. – 1st ed.
p. cm. – (Routledge in Asia)
Includes bibliographical references and index.
1. China – Foreign relations – 1976– 2. China – Foreign economic relations. 3. China – Armed Forces. 4. China – Politics and government – 1976– . I. Goodman, David S. G. II. Segal, Gerald, 1953– . III. Series.
DS779.27.C525 1996
327.51 – dc21 96-49584
CIP

ISBN 0–415–16027–8
ISBN 0–415–16028–6 (pbk)

Contents

List of tables

Contributors

Christopher Findlay is an Associate Professor in the Department of Economics at the University of Adelaide and also an Associate of the Australia–Japan Research Centre at the Australian National University. He is co-Director of the Chinese Economy Research Unit at the University of Adelaide. He is also Vice-Chair of the Australian Pacific Economic Cooperation Committee (AUSPECC).

François Godement is a Senior Fellow at the French Institute of International Affairs.

David S.G. Goodman is Director of the Institute for International Studies, University of Technology, Sydney. His recent publications include *China's Provinces in Reform: Class, Community and Political Culture* (Routledge, 1997), *The New Rich in Asia: McDonald's, Mobile Phones and Middle-Class Revolution* (Routledge, 1996) with Richard Robison, and *China's Hainan Province* (University of Western Australia Press, 1995) with Feng Chongyi.

Stuart Harris is in the Department of International Relations at the Australian National University's Research School of Pacific and Asian Studies, and is Convenor of the University's Northeast Asia Programme. He was Secretary of the Australian Department of Foreign Affairs, and then Foreign Affairs and Trade, 1984–8, while on leave from the Australian National University. He has written extensively in the fields of economic, political and strategic policies, and has recently edited (jointly) volumes on *The End of the Cold War in Northeast Asia* and *China as a Great Power: Myths, Realities and Challenges in the Asia-Pacific Region*.

Ellis Joffe is a Professor in the Departments of East Asian Studies and International Relations at the Hebrew University of Jerusalem, and a senior fellow of the Truman Research Institute. He is the author of *The*

Chinese Army After Mao (Harvard University Press, 1987) and many articles and book chapters on Chinese military affairs.

Michael Leifer is Professor of International Relations at the London School of Economics and Political Science, where he was Pro-Director in 1991–5. He is a longstanding observer of the politics and international relations of Southeast Asia and spent over six months during 1995–6 as a Senior Professorial Fellow at the Institute of Southeast Asia Studies in Singapore from where he travelled extensively in East and Southeast Asia. His most recent publications are the *Dictionary of the Modern Politics of South-East Asia* (Routledge, new paperback edition, 1996) and *The ASEAN Regional Forum* (Oxford University Press, 1996).

Gerald Segal is a Senior Fellow at the International Institute for Strategic Studies and Director of the UK Economic and Social Research Council's Pacific Asia Programme. He is also co-Chair of the European Council on Security and Cooperation in the Asia-Pacific and has been a 'fellow' of the World Economic Forum since 1995. He has written or co-authored more than a dozen books or monographs and has edited or co-edited a similar number. His most recent publications include *Anticipating the Future* (Simon & Schuster, forthcoming) with Barry Buzan, *The World Affairs Companion* (Simon & Schuster, 1996), *The Fate of Hong Kong* (Simon & Schuster, 1993) and *China Changes Shape* (Brassey's for the IISS, 1994).

Andrew Watson is Professor of Asian Studies of the Centre for Asian Studies at the University of Adelaide. He is a co-Director of the Chinese Economy Research Unit at the University of Adelaide. He is also a member of the Australian Research Council Social Sciences Panel, a member of the Board of the Australia China Council and President of the Chinese Studies Association of Australia.

Michael Yahuda is Reader in International Relations at the London School of Economics. He has published numerous articles on aspects of China's politics and foreign relations. He has published five books, including *The International Politics of the Asia Pacific, 1945–1995* and *Hong Kong: China's Challenge*, both of which were published by Routledge in 1996.

You Ji is a Lecturer in the School of Politics, the University of New South Wales, Australia. He has research interests in China's political development, economic reform and military affairs and has published widely in these fields.

David Goodman and **Gerald Segal** have jointly produced a number of books. Their most recent collaborations have been *China without Deng* (HarperCollins, 1995) and *China Deconstructs: Politics, Trade and Regionalism* (Routledge, 1994).

1 Introduction

Thinking strategically about China

Gerald Segal and David S.G. Goodman

For those with an interest in thinking strategically about modern international affairs, there is no more important challenge than to understand the nature and implications of a rising China. As this reality dawns on the public policy community, the debate has often been simplistic. The exchange seems to be between those who assert that China will soon rise to be the world's largest economy and those who argue that it cannot sustain current levels of growth. Some suggest that China will 'muddle through' difficulties, while others suggest it faces a major crisis of governance. It is argued by some that China can only be wrapped in the warm embrace of 'engagement', whereas others stress the need to 'contain' Chinese power. While the issues raised by these clusters of questions are undoubtedly important, the debates about their accuracy have rarely been sufficiently sophisticated.

As a result of our concern about the importance, and yet the relative poverty, of the debate about China, the International Institute for Strategic Studies convened a series of workshops in 1996 to assess these arguments in greater detail. In keeping with the IISS global membership, these meetings were held in Europe, Eastern Asia and the United States. A final meeting, at the Hotel Del Cornado in San Diego, brought together a team of European and Australian authors to be subject to the expert scrutiny of the fine American China-watching community. The team was chosen in order to cover a range of domestic and foreign policy questions, as well as economic, social and security issues. We were motivated by the belief that there was a special virtue in bringing together the perspectives of Americans and non-Americans in order to draw out the best of the diverse specialist communities.

The editors asked the authors essentially only one, deceptively simple, question: how much was China's rise shaped by its own agenda and how much was it constrained by interdependence with the outside world?

Embedded in this central question was an interest in understanding the extent to which China was being changed by contact with the world outside. Another embedded concern was the extent to which the world outside could help shape the rise of China in a way that suited non-Chinese interests.

It is a convention of introductions to edited books to encapsulate the arguments of the individual chapters and to engage in some 'spin control' so that reviewers and readers see more coherence and agreement in the text than might actually exist. While we will outline the central arguments in the text, it would be both unfair and incorrect to suggest that there is coherence in argument. We do hope there is coherence in the *type* of arguments, but we take some pride in having brought together differing views. We see these chapters as contributing to a more sophisticated debate about China – there is no point in pretending that there has emerged any clear consensus on an issue as important as the implications of the rise of China. What follows is an outline of the main shape of the arguments and some outline of the main features of what will have to be included in something worthy of the term 'a China policy'.

The first discussion centres on the issue of *how much is there a single Chinese actor in foreign relations*. Of course, no sensible author would argue that modern China is a single, simple actor. Certainly the editors of this book have already written and edited at length about the extent to which China is being 'deconstructed'.[1] The extent of the differences among authors has something to do with the specific topics of analysis. Not surprisingly, Ellis Joffe and You Ji, who deal with security policy, find less major disagreement among the leadership. The editors who focus on a wider range of topics see much more diversity in Chinese policy.

A second discussion focuses on the degree to which it is useful for the outside world to *ensure Chinese compliance with international rules* and norms. All the authors understand the need not only to make space for China in the international system, but also to engage with it on a broad range of social, economic, political and security issues. The debates become more heated when the question is whether and how to constrain Chinese behaviour. Michael Yahuda and Gerald Segal make more of the need for a rules-based approach to international affairs, François Godement puts the accent on the vagaries of these rules, and Stuart Harris, Christopher Findlay and Andrew Watson see much of the discussion of rules as often self-serving by the West and unconvincing to China. Michael Leifer notes the extent to which Southeast Asians tend to be closer to Chinese views about many of these 'rules' of behaviour, especially when it comes to political issues.

A related discussion, and one that was especially heated following the Taiwan Strait crisis of March 1996, *was the extent to which China's undesired activity should be constrained.* Although most of the chapters take a relatively firm line on this issue, it is fair to note that there was deep division during the discussions in the workshops about the extent to which force should be used to constrain Chinese actions. Interestingly, the disputes did not always pit East Asians versus 'Euamericans', for some of the toughest talk sometimes came from Asians and some of the most conciliatory argument often came from Americans and Australians.

One question that was never explicitly discussed, but figured implicitly in many discussions, was the extent to which China was bound to continue rising in strength. Various participants made reference to a range of deep uncertainties about the basics of continued growth and stability. It is fair to say that no one had any great confidence in the reliability of their judgements about this very fluid society. The China specialists tended to believe that somehow China would muddle through, but there were some notable exceptions. The more sceptical argument, based on worries about social, political and economic fragmentation, is evident in David Goodman's chapter. The more sanguine judgement about the robustness of the system and the party is evident in the chapter by Ellis Joffe.

Those with a more comparative or international relations perspective were also divided about the extent to which China could muddle through. Stuart Harris, as well as Christopher Findlay and Andrew Watson, were more optimistic about the ability of China and the international system to adjust to the rise of China. Michael Yahuda, François Godement, Michael Leifer and Gerald Segal were among those who argued that the challenge posed to, and by, China was huge and difficult to manage.

These, and the more numerous smaller debates embedded in this book, will not be resolved in the near future. It is clear that the debates are maturing and that they will take place in a number of different countries.[2] The evidence needed to make progress in these debates will come from both Chinese internal affairs, and the way in which it behaves and is treated in the international system. Clearly it is necessary to think strategically about China, and there appear to be four clusters of policies that, taken together, can form the basis of a coherent strategy. None of the four, in and of themselves, is sufficient to constitute an effective policy. The key is to co-ordinate among the four clusters.

The first of the four policy clusters is the evident need to make space for China in the international system. China's rise, while perhaps not likely to continue at its recent pace, and perhaps at risk of halting because of major domestic crises, will require adjustments by the outside world. China craves respect and status. The outside world seems uncertain about how much space it should make and under what conditions. There will be more confidence about granting such space if China is seen to play by the rules. The analogy might be to Japan, which has recently risen to be a major power while accepting the constraints of the international system. In an earlier century, the rise of the United States was largely according to the existing rules and was accompanied by a willingness to work within those constraints with the objective of changing the international order from the inside.

A second cluster of policies concerns the extent of engagement with China. It is hard to find anyone who suggests that there should not be a political and economic dialogue and interaction with China. Engagement is a vital, but far from sufficient, element of policy. For some people, including many Chinese who see engagement as little more than 'contact', there is a deep suspicion that talk of engagement is merely a disguised way to build a coalition to contain China. It is also worth noting that the uncertainties about the extent and nature of engagement are often most acute among China's conservative forces. They are most concerned that engagement is really a form of 'peaceful evolution' intended to transform Chinese society and politics.

Engagement also means a number of different things to non-Chinese. For some, it is indeed a way to entice China into evolving, peacefully, into a more amenable partner. For others, engagement is a synonym for 'appeasement', for there is no way in which a country as large and as powerful as China can be constrained. But no matter what form engagement may take, it is important to remember that it takes place with many actors inside and outside China, and is played out on many issues. True engagement with China is a complex process that often undermines central authority. Engagement requires multiple strategies by China and towards parts of China.

A third cluster of policies concerns the extent to which China is kept to international rules. This is, for example, evident in the vital debate about Chinese entry into the World Trade Organisation. Should China be made to agree to strict terms before it joins, or should it be allowed in with the hope that rules can be agreed after the fact? Should China be kept to agreements already reached, for example on intellectual property rights, or should great tolerance be granted because of the decentralisation of the Chinese economy and political system? Because these issues often concern the intensifying economic relationship with China, they are likely to become the most vexed in the coming years. The outside world is growing ever more concerned that engagement with China must take place with clear rules and far more transparency. While there is clear evidence that China does adapt its policies and where possible does accept externally designed rules, the process is protracted and difficult.

The fourth cluster of policies concerns the degree to which China's unwanted actions should be constrained. If China threatens to use force against Taiwan, or in the South China Sea, should it be deterred or even compelled to undo what it might have done? The very mention of this issue was, until recently, seen to be evidence of a mindset for 'containing China'. Yet there is an increasing propensity, especially after the Taiwan Strait crises in March 1996, to see a role for the constraint of unwanted Chinese behaviour. The difficulties in agreeing and implementing such a policy are legion. But there is a growing recognition of the need to tend the balance of power as well as to pursue engagement and other less antagonistic strategies.

Taken together, these four elements of making space, engagement, keeping to rules, and constraint, might constitute a policy framework for managing a rising China. While there are important policy choices to be made between these clusters – for example, must trade be based on observance of rules? – the key is that any sensible policy needs to consider all four clusters of issues. This policy of 'Conditional Engagement', or 'constrainment' or even 'enlitenment', is every bit as open to interpretation as was the strategy of 'containment' of the Soviet Union. We tend to forget just how contentious policy towards the Soviet Union was for the forty-five years of the Cold War. No one should expect policy towards China to be even as coherent as that. But the parameters of debate about, and strategy towards, China have begun to take greater shape in recent times. Given the fact that the world has never seen a power rising as fast, or on such a scale, as China is doing in the late twentieth century, there can be no more important issue for the international system. The best that we can expect from this collection of chapters and arguments is that it helps us to understand how to think about handling a rising China. But there is no point in pretending that the challenge is anything but daunting.

NOTES

1 David S.G. Goodman and Gerald Segal, *China Deconstructs* (London: Routledge, 1994).
2 James Shinn ed., *Weaving the Net: Conditional Engagement with China* (New York: Council on Foreign Relations, 1996).

2 How much has China learned about interdependence?[1]

Michael Yahuda

There are said to be two schools of thought as to how best to relate to China as a rising power so as to prevent it from becoming a cause for instability. Both recognise that because of its huge size China could destabilise Pacific Asia through the breakdown of order at home or by using its great weight to ride roughshod over the conventions and norms of international society. The first school has been characterised as 'engagement' and the other as 'containment'. The first contends that China can best be persuaded to follow the existing norms of international society by entangling it in a web of interdependencies and habits of cooperation. The intention is not only to constrain China from using force in the pursuit of its sovereign claims, but also to awaken its leaders to the concerns of others and to persuade them of the desirability of pursuing security through cooperation. The latter disputes the feasibility of that approach because of the size of the country and the character of its political system. Instead it favours a more realist approach that would focus on developing sufficient countervailing power so as to constrain China from behaving aggressively as Germany and Japan once did.

In the nearly two decades of practising economic interdependence with the outside world, China's leaders have indeed 'learned' much, but not necessarily in the way expected. In the first decade, interdependence was seen as a blessing – albeit a mixed one in view of what Deng called 'the flies and insects' (i.e. the capitalist and Western influences) that would inevitably come in through the open door. In the immediate aftermath of the Tiananmen crisis in 1989, interdependence was seen more harshly as part of a Western strategy of 'peaceful evolution' to subvert communist rule. But such alarmist views have abated as the regime survived the crisis and the policies of reform and openness were carried out with even greater vigour. But far from having changed their rather harsh realist approaches to international politics, it is precisely their realism that has persuaded

China's leaders of the necessity of developing still further the economic policies of interdependence. They recognise that the key to preserving their hold on power in the post-Soviet world is to ensure a continuous level of rising prosperity for the bulk of the people, and that requires continuing the policies of economic reform and openness. In other words, it is not that the entanglement with the outside world has tied their hands and narrowed their options or taught them the value of cooperative approaches to security, but rather that the harsh realities of the problems of maintaining their rule at home has persuaded China's rulers of the imperatives of deepening economic engagement with the outside world, and Pacific Asia in particular.

Since the realist approaches to politics are deeply embedded in Chinese culture and in the character of the communist political system, in the current context of a relatively weak Chinese leadership amid a heightened sense of nationalism, China's neighbours cannot rely on interdependencies alone to restrain China's leaders from bellicose behaviour.[2] Consequently a degree of countervailing power that can be provided only by the United States is needed if the practices of interdependence are to take deeper root and perhaps even flower once power passes from the current Soviet-trained third echelon of leaders to the next generation, which is more attuned to the demands of the modern world and the market place.

CHINESE VIEWS OF INDEPENDENCE

In their well-known book on the subject, Keohane and Nye specify that interdependence restricts autonomy and that interdependent relationships necessarily have costly effects and that is what distinguishes interdependence from 'interconnectedness'. Further, they suggest that in most cases interdependence is asymmetrical in its effects and that provides for a process of bargaining. Keohane and Nye also distinguish between interstate relations and what they call 'complex interdependence'. The latter is characterised, firstly, by a multiplicity of channels connecting societies that include informal ties between non-governmental as well as governmental elites and between transnational organisations. Secondly, the agenda of the relations is not arranged in a hierarchy of issues such as those headed by military security. The absence of hierarchy results in difficulties in coordinating governmental policy and in the generation of different coalitions within and across governments, involving varying degrees of conflict and cooperation. This leads to the blurring of the distinctions between domestic and foreign issues. Finally, they claimed that under conditions of complex interdependence 'military force is not used by governments towards other governments within the region', but they suggest that this may apply only to states that practise democracy and pluralism.[3]

China's communist leaders have always felt uncomfortable with the concept of interdependence. It challenged core values of independence, sovereignty and self-reliance. In their usage, independence (*duli* or, more fully, *duli zizhu*) has the meaning of 'maintain independence and keep the initiative in one's own hands'. Sovereignty (*zhuquan*) has the connotation of the exercise of exclusive power – as the British discovered when they sought to persuade Deng Xiaoping in 1982 that China's best interests would be served by allowing Britain to continue to administer Hong Kong after the retrocession of sovereignty to China. Self-reliance (*zili gengsheng*), meaning 'strive for regeneration through one's own efforts', is a peculiarly Chinese concept whose origins may be traced to Buddhist sources as far back as the Tang Dynasty.[4] These values draw added strength from the one abiding historical contribution of the Communist Party of China – the establishment of a strong unitary Chinese state after a century of 'shame and humiliation' in which the country had been reduced to 'a loose sheet of sand'. In so far as the modern Chinese had experienced interdependence in the late Qing and Republican periods before the establishment of China, it had been a product of abject weakness and dependence. For Chinese nationalists, interdependence is therefore associated with foreign interference. In Mao's view that was confirmed by the relationship with the Soviet Union in the 1950s when 'learning' from the Soviet elder brother involved wholesale copying of the running of the economy, the establishment of heavy industry, the organisation of cities, education, health and even the military. He depicted it as another form of dependence.

The problem for China's communist reformers, as was the case for their nineteenth-century predecessors, has been that although self-strengthening requires a degree of internal regeneration, it requires access to Western technology and know-how. A deep division runs through modern Chinese history between the impulse to close the doors that had been forced open by the predatory West, so as to uphold the integrity of China's cultural identity (whether defined in Confucian or communist terms), and the rational necessity to interact with the outside world in order to acquire the modern technology that alone will ensure defence against being humiliated once again by more modern armies. The first course promises to uphold a national cultural identity, but at the risk of becoming vulnerable to more powerful adversaries. The second may end vulnerability to external attack, but it risks undermining the cultural identity it was meant to uphold.

The Maoist approach as epitomised by the Cultural Revolution may be said to represent the first course with its attempt to renew the revolution behind closed doors. The Dengist approach since 1978 may be said to represent the second, with its emphasis on economic development through reform and openness. But tensions existed nevertheless within both the Maoist and Dengist approaches for the same reason that they existed for the nineteenth-century Chinese reformers. In practice, modern technology carries with it a complex set of values and socio-political configurations that cannot but undermine the alternative essence it was meant to serve. As Lucien Pye has pointed out, the *ti-yong (essence-utility)* formula 'had it the wrong way around, in that modernisation calls for the acceptance of universalistic values associated with the world culture, though adapted to local parochial conditions. The *ti* has to be universal values, and it is the *yong* that should be related to Chinese realities.'[5] Moreover, unlike the Confucian reformers of the nineteenth-century, the self-declared Marxist-Leninists leaders of China never could agree as to what was the Chinese essence they were seeking to preserve, as has been evident not only from the ideological struggles of Mao's day, but also from the disputes in the current reform era between conservatives and reformers. Deng's first two designated successors fell because as political reformers they had been deemed too soft on 'bourgeois liberalism'. The conservative forces had been able to prevail by accusing them in effect of having gone beyond the boundaries of where China's socialist *ti* should be drawn. Since that essence is continually modified and challenged by the process of economic development and modernisation, there is a continual tension at the heart of Chinese politics that has been used by rival groups and leaders against each other and that has militated against the development of deep or consistent international cooperation.

The resistance to coming to terms with interdependence also draws strength from the political culture of the Chinese Communist Party (CCP), with its emphasis on secretiveness and the ruthless elimination of alternative political voices and potential independent centres of power. Even though many of the totalitarian social controls have been relaxed in the course of the economic reforms, a close watch has continued to be kept on movements or individuals deemed to challenge the CCP. Thus nascent independent trade unions have been crushed and dissenters persecuted. Many of the new entrepreneurs are party members or closely tied to them, and the private and collective companies are usually closely linked to the party/state local organisations and often directly run by them.[6] There is little evidence here, at least in this early stage, of the pluralism that Keohane and Nye regard as a necessary condition for multiple interdependence.

Paradoxically, however, People's Republic of China (PRC) leaders and Mao in particular have been adept at practising interdependence in the pursuit of national security. But that interdependence involved inter-governmental arrangements sometimes only through indirect signalling and it was not designed to involve engagement between different governmental agencies, let alone inter-societal relations. Of course the interdependence was not acknowledged as such, but that was in effect what Mao practised as he bolstered his country's security by manoeuvring between the two superpowers.[7] Typically, at the time it was represented within China as a triumph of Mao's 'revolutionary diplomacy'. Although these security arrangements between governments did not involve 'complex interdependence', the contrast between the revolutionary ideology and the practice of interdependent security created problems whenever the Chinese and American systems came into close interaction.[8] However, these did not disrupt the broader security arrangements until the end of the 1980s.

The Maoist approach to the role of the international economy in China's approach to development was ironically expressed most succinctly by Deng Xiaoping himself. In his seminal speech to the UN General Assembly on the Three Worlds in April 1974, he included the statement that 'in the final analysis, political independence and economic independence are inseparable'. He added that although 'self-reliance did not mean self-seclusion, nevertheless at the present stage a developing country that wants to develop its national economy must first of all keep its natural resources in its own hands and generally shake off the control of foreign capital'.[9] Even after his return to power in 1977 after the death of Mao and the fall of the 'Gang of Four', Deng espoused what can only be considered to be an orthodox Maoist view: 'We now also accept instalment payments for machinery from abroad but only in the knowledge that we are capable of making regular payments. We must remain free from debts both at home and abroad.'[10]

By the end of the following year Deng had abandoned these positions in favour of economic reform and openness. His new approach was summed up in a considerable modification of his UN address when, thirteen years later, he declared in 1987 that 'to achieve genuine political independence a country must first lift itself out of poverty. It should not erect barriers to cut itself off from the world.'[11] Opening to the outside world was so important to Deng that he reinterpreted China's history to hammer the point home. He explained at length to his senior colleagues that the reason for China's humiliation by the West in the nineteenth century was the Ming Dynasty's decision 300 years earlier to abandon the open policy of Zheng He's oceanic voyages and to turn its back on the rest of the world. As a result

China was plunged into 'poverty and ignorance'. While Deng himself denied that China would be 'hurt' by opening to the outside world, he acknowledged that 'our comrades are always worried that undesirable things might ensue. Above all they worry whether the country might go capitalist.'[12]

In the Dengist period where, in contrast to that of Mao, economic interdependence has been positively encouraged, tension has been evident between those who have been concerned about the threat to the country's socialist identity and those who have stressed the need for deeper foreign engagement and political reform to accompany the economic reform. The conflict between the two tendencies may be said to be institutionalised between what I have called elsewhere the continentalist and maritime orientations, or the 'browns' and the 'blues', in the Chinese political system.[13] The continentalist 'browns' are represented in the core institutions of the traditional state sector, with the central economic ministries, the state-owned enterprises which account for the bulk of heavy industry and the major utilities which are still managed through complex systems of administrative directives. They are also represented in the party's propaganda apparatus. Their outlook has also been described as 'neo-conservative'.[14] Recognising the need for access to foreign investment and technology transfers as well as for the operations of a market, they seek to control and administer such processes. Opposed to further political reform, they seek to uphold the Communist Party's monopolistic hold on power, to consolidate the central position of key state enterprises, and to limit the penetration of foreign influences which they tend to regard as generally disruptive and subversive. The 'blues', by contrast, are represented by the growing maritime dimension of the coastal provinces and the more entrepreneurial groups and peoples. They are also to be found in the state's central representative institutions such as the National People's Congress and the Chinese People's Political Consultative Conference. They seek to establish a better legal system and to intensify the growth of the embryonic pluralism evident within the Chinese system. In short they recognise the need for political reform and seek deeper engagement with the outside world. Some organisations, such as the modernising military, may include within their ranks both brownish and bluish tendencies, and indeed some personalities may encompass the two, leaning sometimes in one direction and sometimes in the other. The most notable may be Deng Xiaoping himself who has been the most ardent advocate of economic reform and openness even to the extent of wanting Guangdong Province to model itself on the smaller tiger economies, while simultaneously being the most belligerent and obdurate in upholding dictatorial party rule.

In the early years of the Dengist era, interdependence, like political reform, was positively encouraged, especially in 1980 and 1981. But following the campaign against 'spiritual pollution' and the constant warnings against 'bourgeois liberalisation', Deng became more cautious. Although Deng recognised the need for economic reform and openness (*kaifeng*) in the pursuit of rapid economic growth, there was nothing in his approach that suggested any compromise towards the possibilities of complex interdependence. His main strictures were less against foreign influence than domestic deviations by either the 'blues' or the 'browns'. To this end he argued both before and after the Tiananmen killings that the state apparatus was sufficiently 'powerful to deal with any deviations'.[15] In the immediate aftermath of 4 June 1989 he agreed with others that there was a Western strategy to subvert Communist Party rule by peaceful evolution, but he did not allow the leftists (or browns) to use that to restrict his agenda for rapid economic development. His comments on the collapse of East European communism and the 'betrayal' by Gorbachev recognised the pressure of the strategy of 'peaceful evolution': '. . . all enemy attention will be concentrated on China. They will use every pretext to cause trouble, to create difficulties and pressures for us'. But what China needed was 'stability, stability and more stability'.[16] After the demise of the Soviet Union itself Deng explained that one of the principal differences between China and the former socialist motherland was that the Chinese people had experienced rising prosperity as the result of rapid economic growth and that it was this, combined with communist dictatorial rule, that provided the necessary stability.

The official version (i.e. the one endorsed by the leadership as a whole) of Deng Xiaoping's talks on his southern tour (*nan xun*) of early 1992 makes very clear that in the view of China's rulers the country remained stable after the 4 June crisis because of the policies of reform and openness that promoted economic growth and raised living standards.[17] The talks reaffirmed the significance of the Special Economic Zones and the importance of economic engagement and learning from the capitalist countries. As understood in the West, all these policies involve the development of economic interdependence.[18] Indeed according to Chinese official figures, the GNP in 1995 came to 5,773 billion yuan and that of foreign trade to 2,419 billion yuan ($280.9 million).[19] Although these figures undoubtedly exaggerate the significance of foreign trade in the Chinese economy, they nevertheless are important as they suggest a readiness to acknowledge a high degree of dependence on foreign trade. Moreover, the relative value of the state-owned sector of the economy continued to shrink as it now accounted for less than 35 per cent of the total gross value of industrial output after accounting for 95 per cent in 1978. Yet China's leaders continued to claim that the state or publicly owned sections of the industrial sector controlled the commanding heights of the economy and that this situation not only ensured its socialist character but also limited the degree of influence on the Chinese economy that could be exercised by the international economy or by the forces of capitalism. Consequently, China's rulers were able in effect to argue that far from being damaged by the continued economic engagement with Pacific Asia, their socialist system positively needed that interdependence if they were to remain in power.

CHINESE 'LEARNING' AND INTERDEPENDENCE

It has been suggested that a sharp distinction should be drawn between the concepts of 'learning' and 'adaptation' as applied to the capacity of the Chinese leaders to respond to the implications of their deepening engagement with international society. With the example of Gorbachev in mind, it has been argued that 'learning' involves a fundamental change of assumptions and approaches, whereas the latter requires no more than adjusting to changing circumstances while retaining the existing *Weltangschauung* intact.[20] While analytically neat, it is not clear how the distinction can be observed in practice given the implication that the immense economic, social and ideological changes that have taken place in China have had but a minimal impact on fundamental politics. Moreover, in the case of Gorbachev, his learning arose from the recognition of the impasse that the Soviet Union had reached as a result of its manifold problems rather than from any lessons that the outside world may have taught him. In the case of China, perhaps a longer-term perspective is needed in order to appreciate the degree of change that has taken place. It would be difficult to sustain an argument that little of substance has changed in the conduct of foreign and security policies since the Maoist period even if the attachment to realism remained central to the Chinese outlook. As has been argued, the fact that the economic engagement with the international economy is regarded as essential to the maintenance of CCP rule is in itself a change of profound significance.

China's leaders have in effect accepted economic interdependence while attempting to reject its political implications. That may be seen as another variant of Deng Xiaoping's policy of promoting economic reform while rejecting political reform. Nevertheless, as a result of the devolution of a good deal of economic decision-making and the deeper involvement of foreigners and overseas Chinese in the Chinese economy, combined with

Chinese attempts to secure even better access to the international economy, the Chinese government has come under greater pressure to establish a better and more transparent legal and regulatory system not only for the economy, but in many aspects of social policy too. Thus the Chinese government has not only produced a plethora of legislation to cover foreign economic relations that at least in part has drawn on international practices, but it has also attempted to establish a regulatory framework for aspects of social welfare and insurance policies that has been based largely on foreign experience. The development of expertise in these fields has come from the training of experts abroad and from the acquisition of direct experience through the participation in international bodies. One major study of China's participation in the major global international economic institutions claims that this has prompted significant changes in policies, policy processes and organisations within China.[21]

A good deal of 'global socialisation' has taken place as a result of Chinese participation in a very wide range of international institutions and processes. This is evident from Chinese behaviour in arms control and disarmament, UN peacekeeping, environmental matters, human rights, science and technology, global information, etc. Moreover, China's leaders recognise that there are corresponding benefits to be had and prices to be paid for international norm-enhancing and norm-defying behaviour. They have sought to use their country's international weight, the perceived potential of its market and temporary international coalitions to prevent their norm-defying behaviour from being defined as such. The dominant character of Chinese behaviour in international organisations has been described as 'state enhancing functionalism'.[22] Essentially, China's leaders hope to gain the benefits of international economic interdependence without paying the political cost of accepting a penetrated political system. In this sense the 'learning' is conditional and partial.

Yet it is true that the available evidence and the analyses of others suggest that Chinese 'learning' about the significance of interdependence is very much circumscribed by a neo-mercantilist realist approach that rejects many of the cooperative and transnational implications that others regard as intrinsic to the subject. Thus at one of the high points of the Chinese practice of interdependence in 1988, Deng Xiaoping revived the old Five Principles of Peaceful Coexistence with their 1950s emphasis on sovereignty and non-interference in internal affairs as a guide for inter-state relations in the new era. In fact it was a ploy to deflect Western criticism of his regime's human rights record. Interestingly, by 1992 even the Chinese government quietly dropped its insistence that human rights was exclusively a domestic matter by publishing a white paper on the subject and building a coalition with other Asian governments to argue their case in international fora. That may be seen as a more sophisticated way of participating in international processes to obtain the same result. In fact on substantive matters the Chinese official position has been to make demands on the international community, such as international organisations (including the World Bank) and various Western countries, for economic transactions on favourable terms that can be granted only if those concerned followed international norms and principles of obligation that the Chinese government has been unprepared to have applied to itself.

Chinese approaches to foreign relations have been based on a relatively narrowly defined notion of self-interest, as is evident from three recent studies of different facets of Chinese international behaviour. An extensive analysis of China's conduct of international economic relations described it as basically neo-mercantilist.[23] After a careful survey of China's diplomatic practice spanning the late 1980s and including the Gulf War of 1991, Samuel Kim concluded that its government followed a *maxi/mini principle* in the conduct of multilateral diplomacy – maximising China's rights and interests and minimising China's responsibility and normative costs. He described it as 'an unprincipled quest to make the best of all possible worlds'. [24] Chinese arms control policies in the 1980s and 1990s were found by Iain Johnston to be based on newly acquired expertise. But, nevertheless, China's leaders continued to exhibit their previous similar tendencies to free-ride on the back of the obligations undertaken by others to constrain their development or deployment of particular arms while avoiding as much as possible the assumption by China of similar obligations.[25] Moreover, because of their perception of the country as a victim of historical wrongs, China's leaders have developed what might be called a diplomatic culture of entitlement, as may be seen from their expectation of favourable treatment from Japan by invoking war-time guilt or from the United States by demanding generosity as of right.[26]

China's narrow, self-interested, realist approach is usually explained with reference to its political culture of traditional realism allied to that of its communist political system that is dominated by considerations of hierarchy, power and the calculations of *guanxi*. More broadly, it is additionally attributed to the way in which China's contemporary international identity has been defined and developed as the successor to both the historical territories and peoples administered by previous dynasties, and the Qing in particular. That has not only confirmed the myth of China as a special victim of modern international history, but it has imbued Chinese claims for 'lost' historical territories with a claim that eschews reference to principles of self-determination, as is the case for example with regard to Tibet or Taiwan. This complex identity has been subsumed within a contemporary Chinese nationalism that has acquired greater salience and that has been expressed with greater vehemence as communist ideology has lost its appeal in China. Indeed the original promise of establishing a new China, imbued with a moral socialist basis for unity, on which China was founded in 1949, has long been tarnished, and nationalism has emerged as the only unifying ideology for the Chinese people. Ever since Deng began his new course, the Chinese communist leaders have been trying to wrap the CCP in the flag of patriotism. Arguably this has made them even more inflexible and intransigent in the pursuit of national interests, especially with reference to any matters associated with sovereignty. In practice, however, the question as to whether the nationalism that is projected is confident or assertive and even aggressive depends very much on the degree of perceived vulnerability and on the character of the factional in-fighting in Beijing.[27]

Consequently, the Chinese political system may be said to be more open and accessible to outsiders than in previous years, but that still falls short of the conditions of openness and interactions envisaged under the conditions of 'complex interdependence' as outlined by Keohane and Nye. The greater ease of interactions with foreigners has yet to be translated into a greater transparency of Chinese institutions or into the development of a more open diplomatic style. Thus in one form or another British and Chinese representatives have been negotiating over Hong Kong more or less continuously since 1979, yet the cultural gaps between the two sides remain to be breached, especially on the Chinese side, which has time and again shown a poor appreciation of British motives and interests. No camaraderie developed between the two sets of negotiators and there was little evidence of real bargaining.[28]

Even in an area where the Chinese may be said to have fulfilled some of the requirements for the 'learning' of interdependence in officially approved institutional settings, doubts remain as to how much has been 'learned'. The Chinese government now has access to a wide range of advice from Chinese experts who have been educated to the highest levels provided by the most famous centres of learning abroad, many of whom have acquired experience in international organisations and some of whom have even participated in some of the consultative regional organisations of the Asia-Pacific. But it is not clear whether as a result of their advice the Chinese leaders may be said to have developed a better understanding of the outside world and the operations of different political systems. Studies of their approaches to the United States and Japan have revealed a dearth of understanding.[29] Indeed since the Tiananmen crackdown in 1989 and the emergence of a weaker leadership following the physical decline of Deng Xiaoping since 1993, expert advice has been less sought and consulted than was the case during the tenure of Zhao Ziyang.[30]

More recently, Jiang Zemin has been reported to have ordered the establishment of a special study group to report on the workings of the United States Congress. Much as this is to be welcomed, coming some twenty-five years after working relations with the American government were first established, the failure to do so earlier suggests an enormous gap of understanding by China's leaders that must be seen as a major constraint on interdependence taking root in China. Chinese leaders have tried to use the lure of their market for bargaining purposes, but such attempts should not be seen as part of the bargaining processes of complex interdependence. Attempts to reward the capitalists of some countries for the 'good' behaviour of their governments or to punish others for alleged misdemeanours, as evident from the differential treatment of Germany, France and Britain in 1992–3, may be seen as traditional, not to say old-fashioned, diplomatic practice implying that governments could run the market and that in capitalist countries big firms could dictate government policy. A further indication of this was Chinese use of Boeing and other firms with large business interests in China to pressure Washington on MFN in 1994; but when the issue shifted later in the year to the Intellectual Property Rights, the Chinese found themselves empty handed.

In sum, despite possessing a system of government that involves a good deal of complex bargaining within and between different bureaucracies,[31] the Chinese government has shown a reluctance or an inability to adapt to the practices of interdependence beyond the confines of realism. The one area where interdependency could be said to have developed involves China's relations with the Chinese overseas, including those of Hong Kong and Taiwan. But these informal economic ties, which draw on common ethnicity, culture and custom, do not conform to the concept of interdependence as developed by Keohane and Nye as they do not directly involve inter-governmental relations and they do not provide a basis for cross-border bargaining between common institutions. Nevertheless, they are an important part of China's greater opening to the outside world and, as will be argued later, they could yet serve as a bridge towards interdependence involving China and Pacific Asia.

CHINA'S GOOD NEIGHBOURLINESS

Chinese behaviour within Pacific Asia has seemingly demonstrated a more cooperative pattern than the previous characterisation might have suggested. This has been particularly true since the ending of the Cold War and the demise of the Soviet Union when the leaders of China have for the first time been free of the fear of military attack by either of the superpowers. In fact in the 1990s China has enjoyed considerable strategic latitude within Pacific Asia. Yet far from deliberately exploiting its new-found geopolitical advantage within the region, China has cultivated what its foreign minister described as its 'traditional policy of good neighbourliness'. In this new period China has systematically sought to reach agreements with all the neighbours with which it shares land borders so as to settle or at least diffuse outstanding disputes in a policy that a senior military figure described to me in Beijing in 1994 as characterised by 'restraint'. This has been true of relations not only with smaller and relatively compliant neighbours such as Burma and the Central Asian republics, but also with larger countries such as India and Russia which, according to some Chinese analysts, could yet constrain China's freedom of manoeuvre in the future. Moreover, in the 1990s China has joined APEC, the ARF and participated in a variety of other multilateral regional institutions and gatherings.

The new cooperative approach may be said to stem from a redefinition of the main threat to Chinese security in the new international strategic environment. If in the bipolar era the key threat had been primarily military, in the new era the threat had become mainly political, concerning the survival of Communist Party rule. Since that was best addressed through rapid economic development, the need for improved relations with neighbours and for a stable regional environment was self-evident. The disengagement of the region from superpower rivalry also gave China's leaders the opportunity to develop a regional policy for the first time, and the opportunity was provided by the reluctance of countries within the region to follow the Western lead of imposing sanctions on Beijing in the wake of the Tiananmen crisis. Beijing was also fortunate in that its new orientation towards the region coincided not only with a phase of more intensive intra-Asian economic relations, but also with the development of multilateral IGOs in the Asia-Pacific of a consultative kind that China could join without being encumbered with formal obligations that would limit its autonomy.

The way in which Beijing developed relations with the Soviet Union after Tiananmen and then with Russia after the demise of the Soviet Union is instructive of the new style of cooperation. Conscious of the significance of the impact of domestic developments in the Soviet Union/ Russia on Chinese society and politics, China's leaders deliberately drew a sharp distinction between domestic and foreign matters in their response. They continually and openly cultivated friendly relations with Moscow, while behind the scenes their propaganda first vilified Gorbachev and then drew the attention of domestic audiences to the chaos that followed the fall of the communist order as a warning not to destabilise the communist regime at home. Inter-governmental relations were used to control and limit the consequences of interdependence. Indeed the process was so successful that Chinese and Russian officials were able to develop reciprocal confidence-building measures initially through unilateral initiatives that were then followed by reciprocal measures and then by more formal agreements. Yet throughout the period important elements and interests in both societies openly voiced deep suspicions of the other side. Currently, 97 per cent of the once disputed borders has been settled by agreement. There have been exchanges of high-level visits by civil and military leaders. Economic relations have developed at both national and local levels, so that by 1993 China ranked as Russia's second most important trading partner and Russia ranked as China's seventh, with the value of bilateral trade reaching $7.68 billion. Since then trade has slipped, in part because of the incompatibilities of their respective trading regimes and Russian sensitivity to the vulnerability of the Far Eastern provinces. Close relations have developed between the ministries of defence of both countries. Russia has also sold China advanced aircraft and its experts have helped upgrade domestic Chinese military industries.[32] Nevertheless, the relationship corresponds more to that of relations between countries observing the Five Principles of Peaceful Coexistence than those practising interdependence. Although at the border a whole variety of informal and often illegal practices have developed, these reflect the weakness of government controls, for at the state level relations are 'correct' and there is little sign of the inter-governmental bargaining associated with interdependence.[33]

The furthest that China has gone to date in the development of multilateral institutional arrangements resulted less from the entanglements of economic interdependence and more from the new politicised concept of security. On 26 April 1996 the state leaders of Russia, China, Kirghstan, Kazakhstan and Tadjikistan signed a joint border agreement that committed their countries to establish collectively a range of confidence-building measures in the military field in their adjacent border areas. This was buttressed by a separate agreement signed with Russia the previous day which included a section entitled 'On Security and Cooperation in the Asia-Pacific'. Interestingly, it stated that both sides 'believe[d] that stability in social and economic development is an important factor for ensuring regional security and stability'. It also committed them to 'stand against stirring up national, ethnic and religious conflicts'.[34] In effect, China was seeking to use its new political and economic weight in Central Asia not only to tie its neighbours to supporting its attempts to develop the economy of its far western region of Xinjiang, but also to ensure that they would not assist their ethnic and Moslem religious brethren in that region who were defying Chinese rule.

At the heart of China's new regional policies of improving relations with neighbours were the needs to safeguard domestic stability, to ease China's economic integration in the region, to improve economic relations with the countries of the Asia-Pacific and to circumvent American-led attempts to impose upon China the status of an international pariah. Thus Beijing played an active role in diffusing and limiting the two outstanding regional conflicts of international significance: Cambodia and Korea. Its new enhanced role was recognised by Indonesia which restored diplomatic relations in 1990 (soon to be followed by Singapore) and then in 1992 by South Korea which Beijing had been assiduously cultivating as an economic partner since 1985. Economic ties have been deepened with neighbouring countries and adjoining provinces have been encouraged to engage economically with bordering states even at the risk of encouraging centrifugal tendencies within China.[35] The ASEAN countries have become important allies in resisting Western pressure for human rights.[36]

But there are limits to China's regional cooperation. Beijing has participated in a whole variety of multilateral organisations, but it has so far resisted attempts to circumscribe its autonomy. Thus even when it agreed within the APEC framework that the developing countries, ten years after the developed countries, would cut all tariffs by the year 2020, China made it clear that it would do so only voluntarily. Moreover, China has so far resisted all attempts to develop a multilateral solution to the competing territorial claims in the South China Sea or indeed to anything that smacks of a multilateral regime to manage the sea in terms of navigation, the environment, piracy, fisheries, etc. China has steadfastly proposed to deal with these issues on a bilateral basis only. Its professed intentions of putting sovereignty aside while developing economic resources jointly have yet to be realised. Meanwhile some Chinese unilateral actions have belied the relative benevolence implied by their formal posture that includes a readiness to settle outstanding disputes within the framework of international law. Vietnam and the Philippines have been victims of what has been called Chinese military 'creeping assertiveness', and Vietnam in particular experienced the sharp end of what might be called 'interdependence Chinese style'.[37] By granting exploration rights to an American company in a section of the South China

Sea that was contested with Vietnam, with the promise to come to its defence if necessary, Beijing cleverly involved a foreign company domiciled in the world's greatest power on its side in a territorial maritime dispute of great significance, thus greatly complicating the possible response open to Vietnam.

What gives these conflictual elements in Chinese regionalism a particularly sharp edge is the re-emergence of Chinese nationalism as a major political force within China at a time of relatively weak leadership that is consumed with the problems of political succession. In Allen Whiting's terms, the conditions in China exist for assertive rather than confident nationalism and a danger exists of the emergence of aggressive nationalism.[38] The Chinese use of military exercises to intimidate Taiwan may also be seen as a warning to the region and to the international community that Beijing will use force on this issue of sovereignty, even at the risk of disruptions to the region that could jeopardise its own economic well-being and political stability. In other words, no reliance can be put on rational calculations of self-interest to prevail when an issue deemed to be of such high national value confronts the weak leadership in Beijing. Such an atmosphere bodes ill for Hong Kong even though it is in the evident interest of Beijing to ensure a smooth transition of sovereignty for both economic and political reasons and to facilitate China's deeper economic integration in the region, especially when the consequences of a bad transition are taken into account.[39] In sum, this suggests that no reliance can be put on Chinese interdependence in itself as a guarantor of peaceable cooperative relations.

ENGAGEMENT AND CONTAINMENT

The question of the depth of Beijing's commitment to the processes of interdependence or the extent to which Beijing may be said to be constrained by interdependence is of great significance to China's neighbours. It is central to the strategy of dealing with China as a rising power by the ASEAN countries in particular. This strategy seeks to constrain the Chinese authorities from exercising dominance in East Asia, without regard for the interests and concerns of its smaller neighbours, by a process of engagement that incorporates elements of interdependence. The goal is to involve the Chinese central government and the multiplicity of regional and functional organisations and leading personalities in a series of economic exchanges and linkages that also involve institutionalised multilateral and bilateral meetings so as to forge habits of consultation and dialogue. The long-term aim is to produce a pattern of relations not dissimilar to the one that pervades ASEAN in which the political independence and security of separate governments is enhanced by mutual recognition of the linkages between regional and national instability. This has generated informal processes of consultation by which conflict has been avoided or diffused rather than fully resolved. By virtue of its size, the geopolitical extent of its regions, which lie within South, Central and Northeast as well as Southeast Asia, and its great power status, China could not be incorporated within an exclusively Southeast Asian format. Nevertheless, it was hoped that important dimensions of China could be enmeshed within the region to give the country a stake in regional stability and status quo. It was hoped that through participation in the numerous consultative bodies of the region, Chinese participants would become accustomed to that as a process for dealing with problems and would come to realise that the costs of challenging the status quo by military means were counter-productive.

But the Chinese have shown a readiness to use force in the pursuit of high-value issues concerning sovereignty, whether in terms of asserting national unity in the case of Taiwan, or in terms of substantiating claims over islands and maritime resources in the South China Sea disputed by others with which China enjoys deep economic exchanges considered vital for the continued rapid growth of the national economy. Even in the case of Hong Kong, where there is no question about the retrocession of sovereignty, the Chinese have displayed a degree of intolerance and a misunderstanding of the basic institutional framework and legal processes on which international business and finance rely that cannot but cast doubt on the effectiveness of the strategy of engagement. It may be argued that if the Chinese side has shown an incapacity to 'learn' on the Hong Kong issue, it bodes ill for those who argue that the political and cultural gap between mainland China and the outside world can be bridged.

The earlier analysis, however, did point out many instances where the Chinese have 'learned' and profited from mutual accommodations with international bodies and processes. Moreover, it noted that Chinese leaders recognise the importance of economic interdependence for the generation of rapid economic growth, social stability and, ultimately, the preservation of Communist Party rule. It can be further argued that from a longer historical perspective the trajectory of the complex transitions that China is experiencing necessarily involve a continuation of the movement from a continentalist to a maritime orientation. And it is the latter that is sympathetic to the demands and constraints of interdependence.[40]

Thus the question of how best to deal with a rising China may be best considered in terms of phases. If it can be argued that in the longer term the constraints of engagement are likely to be more effective, it would make little sense to weaken that trend in favour of a more confrontational one, especially as there is little evidence to show that neighbouring countries in Southeast Asia have the collective will and tenacity to carry out such a policy. Indeed so far they have shown the opposite.[41] The ARF was found to be irrelevant and the other ASEAN countries did not rally to the support of the Philippines when it was challenged by China over Mischief Reef in 1995. The following year, when Chinese forces carried out intimidatory exercises near the approaches to Taiwan's main ports, only Singapore and Japan among the East Asian states voiced open disapproval. Indonesia and Malaysia, for example, refrained in public from going beyond asserting that this was an internal Chinese matter.

The one power that has been prepared to confront the Chinese about their infringements of international norms and obligations is the United States. It has often done so alone when other regional state leaders profess their agreement in private while they publicly acquiesce in the Chinese infringement and hope to benefit commercially. A glaring example was the mute public response by all but one of the ASEAN states to the American despatch of two carrier battle groups to the vicinity of Taiwan when China's military actions were judged by Washington to be 'provocative and reckless'. But given the East Asian doubts about the American willingness in the long term to shoulder the burden of maintaining stability through the deployment of superior power in the region, there is a tendency to free-ride and appease China at the American expense. This, paradoxically, may have the effect of accelerating an American withdrawal which they all profess to wish to avoid.

The challenge therefore for those in Southeast Asia in particular who argue in favour of dealing with China through engagement and interdependence is to combine these with American power. Such cooperation would meet immediate concerns about Chinese aggressiveness, while preparing for the long term by deepening the processes of engagement. The element of free-riding could be addressed by continuing the acquisition of advanced weapons designed for defence and maritime security with the aim of raising the costs for any possible local small-scale challenges by China. In the short term such action is more likely to be respected by the realists in Beijing until such time as the process of engagement and interdependence take deeper root. But as historical experience has shown, those processes alone do not guarantee the avoidance of armed conflict.

NOTES

1 This chapter has been revised in the light of the discussions that took place at the conference in San Diego and the author would like to thank Professor Roderick MacFarquhar for his commentary on the original paper.
2 For a profoundly scholarly account of the salience of hard realism in traditional Chinese strategic culture see Alastair Iain Johnston, *Cultural Realism: Strategic Culture and Grand Strategy in Chinese History* (Princeton, NJ: Princeton University Press, 1995). He also claims, without arguing the point at length, that especially at times of crisis, policy-making in China has been imbued with hard realism as shown by its far greater readiness to use violence in disputes over military security questions such as territory as compared with other major powers (p. 256).
3 Robert O. Keohane and Joseph S. Nye, *Power and Interdependence: World Politics in Transition* (Boston, MA: Little, Brown & Co., 1977) p. 25. For a general analysis see chapters 1–3.
4 See *Ci Hai* (Shanghai, 1938) which cites a reference to *zili* as opposed to *tali* – i.e. 'self strength' as opposed to the strength of another – as Buddhist terms in the *Tang Shu*. The former refers to drawing on one's own spiritual strength as opposed to appealing to that of Buddha or a Bodhisattva. I am grateful to Michel Oksenberg for alerting me to the antiquity of the term.
5 Lucien W. Pye, 'Deng Xiaoping and China's Political Culture', *The China Quarterly* (No. 135, September 1993) p. 442.
6 Gordon White, *Riding the Tiger: The Politics of Economic Reform in Post-Mao China* (London: Macmillan, 1993).
7 For an analysis of the dynamics of the interdependence of security between the three major powers in the 1960s, see Gerald Segal, *The Great Power Triangle* (London: Macmillan, 1982).
8 See Michael Yahuda, 'The Significance of Tripolarity in China's Policy Toward the United States' in Robert S. Ross (ed.), *China, the United States and the Soviet Union: Tripolarity and Policy Making in the Cold War* (Armonk, NY: M.E. Sharpe, 1993) pp. 11–38.
9 *Peking Review*, Supplement to No. 15 (12 April 1974) p. IV.
10 Cited in Michael Yahuda, *Towards the End of Isolationism: China's Foreign Policy After Mao* (London: Macmillan, 1983) p. 150.
11 *Selected Works of Deng Xiaoping Vol III (1982–1992)* (Beijing: Foreign Languages Press, 1994) p. 201.
12 Ibid., pp. 96–7.
13 Michael Yahuda, *Hong Kong: China's Challenge* (London: Routledge, 1996) pp. 34–40.
14 Joseph Fewsmith, 'Neoconservatism and the End of the Dengist Era', *Asian Survey* (July 1995) pp. 635–51.
15 *Selected Works of Deng Xiaoping Vol III (1982–1992)* (Beijing: Foreign Languages Press, 1994) p. 143.
16 'Deng Xiaoping de Zhonggong suanming' ('Deng Xiaoping sees the future for the CCP'), *Zhengming*, Hong Kong (No. 151, 1 May 1990) p. 357.
17 Ibid., p. 359.
18 Wendy Frieman and Thomas Robinson, 'Costs and Benefits of Inter-

dependence: A Net Assessment' in The Joint Economic Commission of the United States Congress (ed.), *China's Economic Dilemmas in the 1990s: The Problems of Reforms, Modernization, and Interdependence* (Armonk, NY: M.E. Sharpe, 1992) pp. 718–40.

19 'Statistical Communique of the State Statistical Bureau of the People's Republic of China on the 1995 National Economic and Social Development (1 March 1996)', *Beijing Review* (7 April 1996) p. 22 and p. 26.

20 Alastair Iain Johnston, 'Learning Versus Adaptation: Explaining Change in China's Arms Control Policy in the 1980s and 1990s', *The China Journal* (No. 35, January 1996) pp. 27–62.

21 For an upbeat account of Chinese acquisition of such knowhow and of growing participation in cooperative international practices, see Harold K. Jacobson and Michel Oksenberg, *China's Participation in the IMF, the World Bank, and GATT: Toward a Global Economic Order* (Ann Arbor, MI: University of Michigan Press, 1990).

22 For an extensive and careful analysis, see Samuel S. Kim, 'China's International Organizational Behaviour' in Thomas W. Robinson and David Shambaugh (eds), *Chinese Foreign Policy: Theory and Practice* (Oxford: Clarendon Press, 1994).

23 Robert Kleinberg, *China's 'Opening' to the Outside World: The Experiment with Foreign Capitalism* (Boulder, CO: Westview Press, 1990), especially pp. 254–68.

24 Samuel S. Kim, *China In and Out of the Changing World Order* (Princeton, NJ: World Order Studies Program Occasional Paper No. 21, Princeton University Press, 1991) pp. 25–7.

25 Alastair Iain Johnston, 'Learning Versus Adaptation' (op. cit.).

26 On Japan see Allen S. Whiting, *China Eyes Japan* (Berkeley, CA: University of California Press, 1989) and on the United States see Michel Oksenberg, 'The China Problem', *Foreign Affairs* (Summer 1991) p. 12.

27 Allen S. Whiting, 'Chinese Nationalism and Foreign Policy After Deng', *The China Quarterly* (No. 142, June 1995) pp. 295–316. See also Allen S. Whiting, 'Assertive Nationalism in Chinese Foreign Nationalism', *Asian Survey* (June 1984) pp. 913–31; and Michel Oksenberg, 'China's Confident Nationalism', *Foreign Affairs* (Vol. 65, No. 3, 1987) pp. 501–23.

28 For details see Michael Yahuda, *Hong Kong: China's Challenge* (op. cit.) Chapter 3, 'The Troubled Negotiations'.

29 David Shambaugh, *Beautiful Imperialist: China Perceives America, 1972–1990* (Princeton, NJ: Princeton University Press, 1991) and Allen S. Whiting, *China Eyes Japan* (op. cit.).

30 David Shambaugh, 'Patterns of Interaction in Sino-American Relations' in Thomas Robinson and David Shambaugh (eds), *Chinese Foreign Policy: Theory and Practice* (Oxford: Clarendon Press, 1994) p. 215.

31 Kenneth Lieberthal and Michel Oksenberg, *Policy Making in China: Leaders, Structures, and Processes* (Princeton, NJ: Princeton University Press, 1988) and Kenneth Lieberthal, *Governing China: From Revolution Through Reform* (New York: W.W. Norton, 1995).

32 For accounts, see successive issues of *Strategic Survey* (London: Brasseys for IISS, years 1991–2 to the present).

33 For analyses of relations after Tiananmen, see John W. Garver, 'The Chinese

Communist Party and the Collapse of Soviet Communism', *The China Quarterly* (No. 133, March 1993) pp. 1–26; and Lowell Dittmer, 'China and Russia: New Beginnings' in Samuel S. Kim (ed.), *China and the World: Chinese Foreign Relations in the Post-Cold War Era* (Boulder, CO: Westview Press, 1994) pp. 94–112.

34 For the text of the joint statement, see *Beijing Review* (13–19 May 1996) pp. 6–8.

35 See the varied accounts in David S.G. Goodman and Gerald Segal (eds), *China Deconstructs: Politics, Trade and Regionalism* (London: Routledge, 1994).

36 Chen Jie, 'Human Rights: ASEAN's New Importance to China', *The Pacific Review* (Vol. 6, No. 3, 1993) pp. 227–37.

37 For the term 'creeping assertiveness', see Michael Leifer, 'Chinese Economic Reform and Security Policy: The South China Sea Connection', *Survival* (Vol. 37, No. 2, summer 1995) p. 51.

38 Allen S. Whiting, 'Chinese Nationalism and Foreign Policy After Deng' (op.cit.).

39 For a more detailed evaluation of the significance of the transition, see Michael Yahuda, *Hong Kong: China's Challenge* (op. cit.).

40 This would apply even if in the short term Deng Xiaoping was succeeded by a kind of neo-fascism, as suggested by Lucien W. Pye in his 'Review Essay: Politics in the Late Deng Era', *The China Quarterly* (No. 142, June 1995) p. 583; or if the anti-foreign nationalism were to take root, as suggested by Geremie R. Barme in his 'To Screw Foreigners is Patriotic: China's Avant-Garde Nationalists', *The China Journal* (No. 34, July 1995) pp. 209–38.

41 See Michael Leifer, 'Chinese Economic Reform and Security Policy', (op.cit.) and Tim Huxley, *Insecurity in the South China Sea* (London: Royal United Services Institute for Defence Studies, 1993).

3 How open is Chinese society?

David S.G. Goodman

It is often assumed that China's greater openness – both openness to the outside world and domestic freedom from political control – will lead not only to capitalism and democracy, but also to greater international interdependence. These may be rash assumptions, not least since it is misleading to apply nation-state perspectives to the operation of a continental system such as the People's Republic of China (PRC) and because there are different kinds of openness, whose inter-relationships are far from clear. The comparative analysis of Hainan, Zhejiang and Shanxi – three provinces that represent different aspects of China's recent regional development – suggests that external and domestic openness remain limited; and that in the provinces greater domestic openness is more likely to lead to increased external openness rather than vice versa. Moreover, though the impact of openness has been mixed it would seem that provincial conditions – and particularly the level of economic development – are the major determinants of the extent and nature of domestic, as well as external, openness.[1]

THE EXTENT OF OPENNESS

There can be little doubt that the PRC at the death of Deng Xiaoping will be considerably more open – both in the sense of openness to the outside world and in the sense of domestic freedom from control by government or the Chinese Communist Party (CCP) – than it was at the death of Mao Zedong in 1976. The reform era engineered by Deng Xiaoping since December 1978 has been explicitly predicated on openness in both those senses. Economic development based on integration with the international economy, technologically as well as for trade and production, deliberately followed the example of China's East Asian neighbours. Domestically, reform has brought the introduction of the market, the development of a consumer society, and a party-state prepared to surrender absolute control in return for economic growth and the continuation of its own political leadership.[2]

The results have included considerably less centralisation and government involvement in economic management, greater foreign involvement and influences in China, and increased social mobility. In 1994 the state sector of the economy accounted for only 34 per cent of the gross value of industrial output (GVIO), a long way ahead of the official (1990) estimates that looked forward to a situation in 2000 where the state sector would be directly responsible for only about 20 per cent of GDP.[3] In 1994 China's total foreign trade was worth 2,040 billion yuan *Renminbi* People's Currency (RMB) (US$237 billion) compared to 29 billion yuan RMB (US$14.8 billion) in 1976, and China had become the world's seventh largest exporter.[4] Realised foreign investment and loans had risen to US$43.2 billion by 1994[5] from very low levels of a few hundred million US dollars in 1976.[6]

In 1976 most of the few thousand visitors to China each year still travelled officially; by 1994 tourists and business visitors accounted for 43.7 million entries for the year, with tourism organised by a wide variety of providers as a US$7.3 billion a year industry.[7] Most remarkable, given the CCP's earlier emphasis on control of culture and communications, has been the expansion and popularisation of print and telecommunications media. In 1994, 103,836 books, 7,325 magazines and 1,015 newspapers were published, compared to 13,716 books, 476 magazines and 180 newspapers in 1975. Moreover, the thirty-five state publishing houses of 1975 have become the 513 commercialised publishing houses of 1994, which significantly are no longer required to obtain explicit political approval before publication.[8] During 1995 telephone and email provision grew dramatically: the number of telephones almost doubled from 18.3 million the previous year to 33.3 million; the number of email ports increased from some 3,000 at the start of the year to over 50,000 by the end.

While there has been change, it is the extent and consequences of this openness that are of greatest interest. China remains a Communist Party-state, at least to the extent of having a ruling Communist Party and a remnant infrastructure of state socialism, and even though the precise implications of that term may now be significantly different. At issue generally is the impact of openness, especially in economic development, on social attitudes and political institutions. In particular, there is a central concern in much of the literature on China's development in the 1990s as to the extent to which interaction with the rest of the world and greater domestic freedom may create pressures for capitalism and democracy. It is a concern shared by the CCP which – echoing earlier twentieth-century debates about the need to import 'Western forms' but to maintain 'Chinese essence' – has sought to welcome Western technology and economic advances but to restrict the social and political impact of openness. Predictably, the CCP held the Voice of America and the BBC World Service responsible for many of its difficulties in managing demonstrations in Tiananmen Square during May–June 1989 and for what it described as the 'Counter-revolutionary rebellion'.

However, 'openness' is not a single or a simple concept: the varieties of openness need to be clearly differentiated. In very broad terms it is possible to identify six relevant categories of openness that may lead to or result from China's domestic development or international interactions: domestic social, political and economic openness; as well as external social, political and economic openness. Though there is overlap between domestic and external openness, and the two are often equated, they are not identical – the last fifty years of world history have seen many examples of political rulers who, though committed to international economic integration (and even a high degree of social and political interaction at the level of inter-state relations) for their countries, still preferred the maintenance of narrow political dictatorships domestically. Similarly, social, political and economic spheres of activity generate different kinds of openness both domestically and externally. For example, domestically in the PRC during the last decade or more the freedom to organise economically separate from the party-state establishment has been far more readily granted than the freedom to organise politically. In terms of external relations, Christian missionary activity in China may have been related to international economic openness in the nineteenth and early twentieth centuries, and to even less subtle manifestations of international political openness – the spread of deliberately subversive ideas – in more recent times. However, neither its economic nor its political associations provide a complete explanation of the impact of Christian missionary activity.

The emphasis on the potential of openness to lead to capitalism and democracy is of course not a phenomenon confined to the observation of developments in China. Indeed, much of the debate on China's future – inside as well as outside the PRC – has been stimulated by events elsewhere, particularly the collapse of communism in the former Soviet Union and Eastern Europe, the end of the Cold War, and their accompanying literature.[9] For many, the economic rise of East and Southeast Asia – including its socialist, as well as more obviously capitalist, countries – during the 1980s and 1990s is seen as inherently a process of homogenisation leading to liberal politics: more rational, individualistic, democratic, secular and with concerns for human rights, the environment and the rule of law.[10] In short, there is the ready and comforting belief in the possibility that with economic modernisation, globalisation and openness, China may become 'more like us'.

There are of course other possibilities. Many commentators in China have argued for a stronger and more intrusive state, in contrast to the liberalisation of state–society relations that has accompanied reform.[11] Geremie Barme has recently drawn attention to the arguments for a 'closed' anti-foreigner nationalism – sometimes racially and obscenely extreme – that has resulted from openness and that for both structural as well as personal reasons may be commonly found in some sections of China's intelligentsia.[12] Though he does not place his analysis in an explicitly comparative historical context, there appear parallels with the rise of German and Japanese nationalism after the First World War. However, the comparison with apparent parallels – whether elsewhere in East and Southeast Asia, or historically – presents problems not least because there are significant differences between China on the one hand and all the most obvious examples on the other. Compared to the mid-century examples of Germany and Japan, China is not internationally isolated. Nor has China faced the social and economic difficulties that led to the collapse of communism in Eastern Europe and the former Soviet Union – openness in China is associated with rapid economic growth.

CONTINENTAL CHINA

Though China's social and political authoritarianism presents parallels with the countries of East and Southeast Asia, its size and scale are likely to prove a significant difference. China is massive in both land area and population, and still poorly integrated, with considerable internal communications problems. This is one but not the only reason that ensures provinces trade less with each other than they do with the international economy, and it is arguable that there is yet a single, unified Chinese market.[13] Thus although coal reserves in North China are theoretically adequate in size and quality to meet the whole country's requirements, there is investment in overseas coal mines, and South China imports coal from elsewhere in the world.

The PRC's weak economic integration is matched by a lack of social homogeneity. Although the 94 per cent of the population who are Han Chinese – that is, omitting consideration of the other, minority nationalities – all share the same dominant state idea of 'China', they nonetheless vary greatly in terms of language, belief systems, traditions and political culture.[14] Indeed, the unity of China under such conditions of heterogeneity is perhaps more remarkable than the often incorrectly imagined homogeneity of the Chinese. In consequence, a more accurate perspective might be to see the PRC as a more complex polity containing one or more South Koreas, Singapores, Hong Kongs, Taiwans, and indeed perhaps even a Germany and a Japan, rather than in direct comparison to any one. Despite the rhetoric now adhering to discussion of the nation-state that basically identifies every sovereign state as a nation-state, it is difficult to equate China with the original (European) concept of a nation-state based on a single, homogenous ethnic group.[15]

The consequences of China's size and scope are often not well understood. China's thirty provincial-level units[16] are each considerable social, economic and political systems in their own right. Most are at least the size and scale of a Western European country in population, land area and social complexity, though not always as big in land area as Tibet, or as large in population as Sichuan's 120 million. To regard them as simply component parts of a unitary nation-state – or even units of 'local government' (as is often misleadingly the case) – can obscure as much as it reveals. Most relevantly, the variety of conditions in China's provinces and the structure of the Chinese state makes it unlikely that openness could or would lead to democratisation or revolution 'from below', along the lines of the Eastern European experience of the late 1980s.

Cultural, economic and political conditions are not constant across China's provinces. As a result, degrees of openness in different parts of China, as well as in different areas of activity, all need to be disaggregated. There is likely to be an inherent variability to the ways in which each province's leaders will respond to these different kinds of openness, and to the impact that openness may have on social attitudes and political institutions.

One particularly telling example of provincial variability is suggested by the structural changes in the management and ownership of industrial production. Nationally, these have led to a significant decline in the state sector's share of production, and increases in the collective, private and foreign-funded sectors' shares of production – an apparently obvious measure of openness. However, the decline in the state sector's share of production is by no means a universal phenomenon, and in any case increases in the shares of production by the collective and foreign-funded sectors may not unreservedly indicate greater openness. The situation is considerably complex, not least because ownership categories are no longer as specific as once was the case under state socialism, and because proportions of both the collective sector and the foreign-funded sector have been derived from the reallocation or redesignation of state-sector resources. Indeed, the collective sector is probably best regarded as the local government sector of the economy.[17] Nonetheless, significant provincial variations are immediately apparent in the national statistics. In 1994, Heilongjiang's economy remained as dominated by its state sector as at any time since the establishment of the PRC, despite eighteen years of reform; Jiangsu had a very large collective sector, but almost no private sector, and only a very small foreign-funded sector; Guangdong's economy was dominated by its foreign-funded and collective sectors; and Guangxi had the largest private sector (as a proportion of provincial GVIO) even though industrial production remained dominated by the state sector.[18]

A successful move for democratisation from below in Beijing might succeed in nominally seizing national state power there, but it could not guarantee similar changes outside the capital, let alone that the writ of the new government would be accepted elsewhere. Some provinces would be likely to stand firmly behind the CCP, others might prefer yet further alternatives. The potential for compartmentalisation in China's politics has always been high, and similarly a revolution from below in one province would have difficulties in spreading its influence. It is one logical proposal to assume the collapse of central authority and the absence of reprisal, but it is quite another to assume that the collapse of central authority would result in or be met by the sudden emergence of another national organisation with a significant measure of popular legitimacy and support.

On one level the recognition of provincial differences represents little more than a warning to avoid over-generalisation about the impact of openness on social and political change. However, there is also an inherently provincial dimension to openness. Just as reform has entailed the increasing withdrawal of government from economic management and of the CCP from social direction, so it has also led to considerable decentralisation to the provincial level. The unity of the Chinese state may not have been necessarily brought into question, but the reform process has undoubtedly increased the relative importance of the provincial level of administration and politics.[19] An essential part of that process has been the assumption that each province will build on its comparative advantage, both externally and within China. Consequently, the nation-state may be a less appropriate comparative device for understanding China's development generally, and openness in particular, than the notion of a continental system of great extent and diversity in which each province is regarded as a single, though not completely autarchic, social, political and economic system.[20]

At this stage in the continuing transformation of the Chinese state the notion of Continental China is necessarily somewhat fluid. In particular there must be uncertainty about the changing roles of central government, but this is not the same as suggesting that its role will be minimal or non-existent: clearly even continental systems have central governments. A key question for the future concerns the roles that the PRC's central government may come to play both nationally and with respect to the constituent parts of the continental polity. It may, for example, be just one player amongst many, become the judge-arbiter for intra-continental debates or disputes, it may reserve certain powers for itself (most obviously defence, exchequer and currency control), and it may exercise a higher order of legislative, judicial or even political authority. Though the analysis presented here might benefit from consideration of central government alongside the examination of a number of provinces, uncertainty about its emerging role and difficulties about access to information (not least difficulties in operationalising a precise definition of the current boundaries of central government) render such an approach impractical at present.

Given those perspectives and constraints of both space and information, the following analysis considers the extent of openness, and the consequences for social and political change in three provinces: Hainan, Zhejiang and Shanxi. These three have been selected because they broadly represent different geopolitical stages in the development of China's 'open door policy'. Although Hainan became a province and Special Economic Zone (SEZ) only in 1988, it is located in South China, next to Guangdong, and is part of the first area in China to open externally. Zhejiang Province, in East China, has opened externally largely as a result of the second wave in the development of the 'open door policy' which coincided with the restructuring of neighbouring East Asian economies after 1987. Shanxi Province in North China lies outside those coastal areas most immediately able to build on their comparative advantage of access to the international economy through relative proximity: its development is expected to come through a 'trickle down' effect.

HAINAN[21]

As might be expected given its location, Hainan Province appears to be the most open part of China. A deliberate attempt has been made to build on Hainan's position as a tropical island in the South China Sea and to open the island wide to foreign economic influences, and location was a major stimulus to the granting of separate provincial status in 1988. The result has been significant foreign investment, loans and particularly trade, given the size of the provincial economy. While external social and political influences are less in evidence, at first sight Hainan seems to have achieved considerable domestic openness. Indeed, during the 1980s and 1990s Hainan has gained a reputation as an almost completely uncontrolled society: China's equivalent of the Wild West where 'anything goes', particularly socially. However, the extent and impact of openness are easily exaggerated. The structures of politics have changed little despite appearances to the contrary, and government still dominates society and the economy. Indeed, the creation of Hainan Province has proved a mixed blessing, making Hainan more susceptible to national politics and the direct influence of the central government than had previously been the case.

Openness – both externally and domestically – was an essential part of the design for Hainan Province and SEZ. Hainan's economy was to be based on the development of the island through foreign investment and trade, and presumably the establishment of an exporting base, though significantly from an early stage almost nothing was said about the nature of the manufacturing base planned for Hainan. Hainan was awarded preferential policy settings by Beijing, allowing it to offer attractive tax regimes and economic arrangements to investors. At the same time, in the late 1980s there was an explicit recognition by policy makers in both Guangzhou and Beijing that Hainan would also be domestically more open: an ideal testing ground for bold experiments in social and political reform. Hainan was more typical of the rest of China than the other SEZs, with a wider spread of social and economic conditions, a per capita GNP around the national average, and 80 per cent of its population engaged in agriculture. As a small economy, accounting for less than a half of national GNP, and physically separated from the mainland, there was a feeling that little harm would come to China as a whole if Hainan's experiments went wildly or violently wrong, and that in any case the results could be contained.[22]

Hainan's economy remains relatively small – US$3.84 billion in 1994.[23] However, growth has occurred largely through the policy of external economic openness advocated in two key State Council discussion documents of Hainan's development, first in 1980 and later in 1983.[24] By 1994 the ratio of provincial foreign trade to GDP in Hainan was 71.9 per cent, compared to a national figure of 45 per cent, and substantially behind only Beijing and Guangdong, with Shanghai just ahead in the national order.[25] Total realised foreign capital in 1994 was US$936.1 million, 24.4 per cent of the provincial GDP. This compared to a national average of 8.3

per cent of GDP, and Hainan's achievement was the highest proportion attained by any provincial-level unit, Guangdong included.[26] The results show in the ownership structure of the provincial economy where a significant share – 26.1 per cent in 1994 – of the gross value of industrial production is produced by the foreign-funded sector.[27] This compares with a national average of 13.6 per cent of GDP.

The planned from-the-top-down introduction of domestic openness is perhaps a more unusual and hence a more interesting feature of Hainan's development in the reform era. In 1986 and 1987 a working group within the Chinese Academy of Social Sciences started to draft an economic, social and political development plan for the future Hainan Province. The major proponent of social and political change was Liao Xun, who coined the phrase 'small government, big society' to characterise his desire to see government's withdrawal from many of its areas of activity under state socialism and its replacement by both a provincial government organised along new functional administrative lines, and by independent, autonomous, self-governing social groups.[28] There are obvious parallels between these ideas and those of civil society and it would be interesting to speculate on the extent to which Liao Xun's thinking was influenced by Western social and political theorists. Liao Xun himself was appointed to the new provincial government's Centre for Research on Social and Economic Change in 1988.

While the Hainan Provincial Government retains its commitment to a policy of 'small government, big society', the results have been somewhat muted in practice. Government retains a major role in economic management. In 1994 the state sector still produced about half of the gross value of provincial industrial production, when the national average was only a third.[29] Although Hainan has almost no collective sector, and so therefore local government economic influence is not great, nonetheless a large number of foreign-funded and joint venture enterprises involve cooperation and partnership with government agencies. Employment rates in the private and individual sectors of the economy would seem to suggest that this goal of openness has some purchase,[30] but the growth of social associations of self-government has remained limited to some 300 bodies, and is concentrated disproportionately in the provincial capital Haikou.[31]

The extent of Hainan's openness must also be assessed against the background of the social changes that have accompanied reform, and the more restrictive relationship with Beijing encountered by Hainan's leadership. Before the reform era, Hainan's politics were dominated by mainlanders who came to the island during the early 1950s. These included not only the island's leaders and cadre force, many of whom came from Guangdong, but also displaced and demobilised soldiers who were settled there and comprised a rural proletariat working on the extensive state farms.[32] Altogether, these more recently arrived groups accounted for about a quarter of the island's population. The native Hainanese, including Hainanese speakers (about two million people) and the Li nationality (a million people), who had themselves supported a largely independent Hainanese communist movement of considerable success from 1927 through to 1950, despite being in the majority, were increasingly excluded from a share in political power. Relations between these communities were poor, exacerbated by linguistic and cultural differences, and worsened after 1957 when almost all native cadres were dismissed in the wake of a failed locally derived attempt to establish a separate Hainan Province accompanied by instances of open rebellion.[33]

In communitarian terms the major result of the reform era has not been that political activity and influence have become more open or dispersed, but simply that there has been the replacement of one generation of incoming mainlanders by another. The 1980s and 1990s have seen a new wave of immigration of just under a million people from the mainland, though this time generally from further afield, with the migrants drawn more by the lure of the market than through administrative fiat. However, this generation of 'new mainlanders' hold on Hainan's politics is equally as closed as the predecessor generation of the 1950s. Of the twenty-nine individuals in the provincial leadership from 1988 to 1995, only nine (including three of the 1950s generation of mainlanders) had been in Hainan before 1988. Hainanese remain excluded from serving in senior positions on grounds that they speak inadequate Mandarin, and through the introduction of a particularly draconian law of 'locality avoidance' that prohibits senior cadres from the same locality serving together in any administrative unit.[34]

Hainan's communities have a relatively high degree of self-awareness and identity, reinforced by a distinct social and economic base. The 1950s mainlanders are to be found in governmental agencies, the state sector of the economy, and the state farms. The immigrants of the 1980s and 1990s are almost exclusively involved in the new industries and enterprises associated with reform and openness, and they live overwhelmingly in Haikou. Most native Hainanese remain as land-based peasants and few are involved in Hainan's recent industrialisation. Under these circumstances it is hard to escape the conclusion that the principles of 'small government, big society' may not be uniformly applicable across Hainan's communities.

Openness also does not characterise the relationship between Hainan's leadership and Beijing that has emerged in the reform era. There were four major leadership changes in the decade to 1995 and there have been major ambiguities in the relationship between Hainan's leaders and superior authorities on the mainland. Hainan's leaders have not been able to manage that relationship successfully, with events elsewhere in the Chinese political system having a disproportionate and deleterious effect, not least on the careers of the leaders themselves, within a relatively short period. Each resulted in resignation or dismissal in disgrace as well as organisational and policy discontinuities. Lei Yu, who was in charge in 1982–4, emphasised the idea of free trade and the advantages of a free flow of goods, capital, technology and personnel between Hainan and the outside world, but fell foul of Beijing's ideological nervousness when he exploited the preferential policies permitted to Hainan. Xu Shijie and Liang Xiang concentrated on a programme of marketisation and partial privatisation but were wrong-footed by their relationship with Zhao Ziyang and political problems in the wake of the events of 4 June 1989. Liu Jianfeng and Deng Hongxun were brought in to ensure Hainan's compliance in the wake of June 1989. However, they never settled and were unable to work together, bringing official counter-complaints against each other. They were replaced in 1993 by Ruan Chongwu who has brought a measure of political stability to Hainan and its relationship with Beijing.[35]

ZHEJIANG[36]

Zhejiang Province's experience is very different to that of Hainan, not least because it has not been a settler society and has long been at the centre of China's political and social development. Although the Zhejiang Provincial Government and CCP have been responsible for the policy settings for both external and domestic openness, there has been no further official attempt at a more proactive role to ensure openness, either economically or socially. The development of the non-government sectors of the economy, and indeed of all social organisation outside the influence of government, has been left largely to the market. Moreover, again unlike Hainan, Zhejiang's external openness has not been restricted to economic interactions, with a significant import of social influences, including those related to religion and life-style.

At the same time, like Hainan, Zhejiang's economic development had also been considerably restricted by the policies of the Mao-dominated era of China's politics. Although Zhejiang Province has an ideal climate for crop production and adequate rainfall, agricultural growth had long been constrained by the limited availability of additional cultivatable land. Industrial development suffered under a policy of regional self-sufficiency because Zhejiang lacks the necessary natural resources. As provincial leaders have not been slow to point out, Zhejiang has the lowest index of national resource provision of any provincial-level unit other than the metropolitan areas of Shanghai and Tianjin.[37] Moreover, local economic development was further constrained by policies that took little account of local conditions. Provincial leaders consistently advocated the development of large-scale heavy industry even though small-scale light industrial enterprises in the collective sector represented Zhejiang's comparative advantage and the most important source of its considerable remittances to central government.[38]

With reform and openness, the brakes on the development of Zhejiang's economy have been removed and the province has transformed its regular, average performance into one of the best in the whole country. In the 1990s Zhejiang's average annual growth rates in GDP have been about 19 per cent, and by 1994 its per capita GDP was on a par with the other powerhouses of the economic reform era – Guangdong, Liaoning and Jiangsu – and second only to the metropolitan areas of Shanghai, Beijing and Tianjin, at a level of about US$1,000.[39]

By 1994 Zhejiang had the fifth largest provincial economy after Guangdong, Jiangsu, Shandong and Sichuan, at some US$31 billion. However, the development of Zhejiang's economy has clearly not relied as extensively on foreign trade and investment as some other parts of China. In 1994 the ratio of provincial foreign trade to GDP in Zhejiang was only 29 per cent, compared to a national figure of 45 per cent, and substantially less than Guangdong or Hainan.[40] Total realised foreign investment in 1994 was US$1.16 billion, 3.75 per cent of the provincial GDP, compared to a national average of 8.3 per cent of GDP.[41]

The growth of the Zhejiang economy has involved external economic openness but it has been driven by the expansion of the collective and private sectors. By 1994 the collective sector produced just under 60 per cent of the gross value of provincial industrial production, and a further 18 per cent came from the private sector. The national averages were 41 per cent and 11 per cent respectively.[42] These figures are somewhat surprising given the relative proximity of Zhejiang to Japan and Taiwan, the coastal areas' tradition of sea travel, and perhaps more relevantly the origins of many mainlanders on Taiwan. Chiang Kai-shek was a Zhejiang native (from Ningbo) and the province was a considerable recruiting ground for the Nationalist Party and its forces at all levels. Of course there is foreign investment in Zhejiang and foreign trade with the province, but domestic investment from and trade with other parts of China have been the driving force for provincial economic development. This different pattern of deriving economic growth in the coastal provinces of East China – a similar phenomenon occurs in Jiangsu Province – from investment and trade interdependence with other parts of China, rather than predominantly from export-led growth, has even been characterised by some commentators as a second model of development for China.[43]

Nonetheless, Zhejiang's economic growth has been a function of openness, albeit domestic rather than external openness. Once the leadership of Zhejiang Province determined that government should withdraw from a high level of direct economic management and should encourage the development of the non-state sector, then it was possible for the local economy to build on its comparative advantages, both those that pre-dated 1949 and those that had emerged through the policies of the Mao-dominated years. Interestingly, there is evidence that the provincial leadership was more than a little conservative about these changes and had to be convinced not only by the central leadership but also by the actions of the peasants themselves. The latter ignored official policy and made reform in the villages, first by decollectivisation, and then by the establishment of town and village enterprises, subsequently the backbone of the collective sector in Zhejiang.[44]

Domestic economic openness is the most obvious feature of contemporary Zhejiang. The Wenzhou Economic Model – essentially one of private and individual enterprise development – was an early national exemplar for the reform era, and it was not coincidental that Zhejiang University was called on to write a report on the development of the private economy during the Eighth National Five Year Economic Plan.[45] The interrelationship between the individual, private and collective sectors is a particular developmental feature of the Zhejiang economy. As individuals and their enterprises grow in economic activity, they tend to merge with the local government economy, not only because they require political insurance but also because local government can offer access to land, labour and even capital. A particular feature of the development of the collective sector has been the transformation of suburban villages from largely rural, agriculture-based, socio-economic entities into suburban economic conglomerates usually based on light industrial production.[46]

However, Zhejiang has also experienced a degree of domestic socio-political openness. In early 1989, in a sign of a more open approach to government, the Zhejiang Provincial Government introduced the practice of holding press conferences, and the provincial press has regularly presented reports of contesting votes, opinions and comments that have occurred at sessions of the Provincial People's Congress.[47] The provincial leadership was able, as was also the case in some other provinces, to avoid confrontation with demonstrating students in May and June 1989 through a policy of open debate, and to some extent shared concern and sympathy.[48] More spectacularly, in January 1993 the Governor of Zhejiang was voted out of office and a new Governor elected by the delegates to the Provincial People's Congress, without the approval of the CCP at either provincial or central levels. Equally as remarkable was that the Provincial People's Congress decision was accepted by the central authorities. In addition, though it is a different kind of openness, there has also been the development of 'social organisations' in response to the socio-economic changes of the reform era. There is now a vast range of such social organisations that act to mobilise their members politically, to represent their interests to government and the state, and to look after welfare issues. Though these organisations are by no means completely independent of the state – either institutionally or associationally – they do represent the emergence of a new social space between state and society.[49]

Although Zhejiang's external economic openness has been somewhat limited, its external openness to other influences has been surprisingly developed. This is perhaps a function of a relatively well-educated population with a rapidly rising standard of living. Certainly, there seems to be a general openness of mind to new and different ideas, motivated no doubt to some extent by market forces, that is sometimes quite palpable. Many Zhejiang people have, for example, started to become interested in Guangdong, and the teaching of Cantonese in Zhejiang has itself become a mini-boom industry.

At the same time, Christianity (of various kinds) appears to have gained a new toe-hold in Zhejiang. Wenzhou, on the coast, isolated by mountains from the rest of the province, and a major centre of economic reform, particularly associated with the development of individual and private industry, built more than a thousand churches during the 1980s. Perhaps even more remarkably, the Wenzhou people themselves were conscious of Tawney's thesis about the relationship between Protestantism and the spirit of capitalism.[50] However, Christianity is by no means confined to Wenzhou, and throughout the province, particularly where the economy is growing more rapidly, it has become something of a fashionable activity for those who wish to identify with modernisation and Westernisation. In some ways this is similar to the development in the 1990s of restaurants offering tastes of the exotic, in surroundings if not in dishes. For example, 1993 saw the emergence of the 'English country house' (circa 1750) style of restaurant in Hangzhou which offered exclusivity in small dining rooms, with Palladian arches, statues of Graeco-Roman gods, oil paintings of the master and mistress of the house, and appropriate table settings.

SHANXI[51]

Shanxi, in inland North China, is almost self-evidently a less open province, both externally and domestically. The CCP has deep social roots: during the Sino-Japanese War of 1937–45 Shanxi was the site of the CCP's largest and most active base areas from which it led nationalist resistance and in the process established its claim to political legitimacy. As a consequence, many of the provincial population are still proud to identify themselves as '*tubalu* ' and the beneficiaries of CCP policies – peasants who received redistributed land (*tu*) under the aegis of the CCP forces at the time, the Eighth Route Army (*balu*), or later during land reform. Shanxi is coal-rich to an extent not found in many other parts of the world, and in consequence throughout the twentieth century the province has been developed as a mining and heavy industrial centre. With the establishment of the PRC this meant considerable state investment and the creation of a large and overwhelmingly dominant state sector. Moreover, Shanxi Province has long been seen as culturally distinct, not least by its own population. Its mountainous terrain has always isolated it somewhat from the rest of the country, let alone the world outside China; there is a strong sense of local identity with both native place and province;[52] and Shanxi people are proud of its traditions, regarding Shanxi as a major source area for Chinese culture.[53]

At the same time, Shanxi had not been completely isolated from external influences and interactions even well before 1949. Shanxi's local bankers used to travel out from the province all over China, providing rural credit. In the late nineteenth century Shanxi was a main centre of Christian missionary activity, and there are still towns and villages (especially in the Taiyuan basin) with many operational churches and adherents. The English missionary Timothy Richards, who was also involved with the Reform Movement, lived and worked in Shanxi. During the Boxer Rebellion, the Taiyuan Massacre (of foreign Christians) was an international *cause célèbre* that contributed to the pressure for an indemnity. In this case funds were provided that were later used to establish Shanxi University, modelled both physically and intellectually on someone's idea of an Oxford college, complete with crenellated roof-line.

Later, during the 1920s and 1930s, Shanxi was one of the most modernised and Westernised of China's provinces as a result of the policies introduced by its warlord, Yan Xishan. Shanxi established a modern education system, developed its industrial base and created excellent road and transport networks. In the reform era of the 1980s and 1990s Shanxi's economic openness, both externally and domestically, has been somewhat limited. However, Shanxi's earlier record may partly explain why the province's leadership has adopted a more proactive role in encouraging external interactions, and some of the more open aspects of its policies.

Shanxi's economy at US$9.9 billion in 1994 is currently one of the smallest of the regular provinces of the traditional core.[54] By 1994 the ratio of provincial foreign trade to GDP was 9 per cent, compared to a national figure of 45 per cent, and lower than every other provincial-level unit except Guizhou and Henan.[55] Total realised foreign capital in 1994 was US$52.6 million, 0.54 per cent of the provincial GDP, compared to a national average of 8.3 per cent of GDP.[56]

This lack of external economic openness is matched in the domestic economy where the state maintains its position of dominance. In Shanxi in 1994 the state sector still produced 43.7 per cent and the collective sector contributed 36.5 per cent of the gross value of provincial industrial production, compared to national averages of 34.1 per cent and 40.9 per cent respectively.[57] The state sector is particularly prominent in the coal industry, though far from every aspect of that industry is managed through government agencies. For example, with reform almost all coal transportation has been marketised, and the overwhelming majority is handled by private and individual entrepreneurs.[58]

On the other hand, very few of the new collective sector enterprises to have developed in Shanxi have emerged from private or individual sector initiatives, which have remained small-scale, even in the retail sector where they predominate. Local government has played a central role in the development of Shanxi's collective sector enterprises. Most have been created through the marketisation of activities previously part of the state sector or in the development of economic enterprises previously organised by cities, counties and townships. Since the beginning of 1994, there has also been an observable and increasing tendency for collective sector enterprises to be formed through cooperation with enterprises in other provinces seeking to invest in Shanxi.[59]

Shanxi's lack of external economic openness is not a matter of choice but really a function of its earlier economic development as a heavy industrial base which, as with other provinces where the state sector has a dominant role, creates a dependency relationship with Beijing. There have been and are advantages to that relationship; however, it can also bring frustration and for Shanxi there have been concerns over its integration into international transportation networks. Shanxi's economic strength is coal, but provincial development has been limited by the lack of access to markets within China and externally, for which it has had to depend on central government action. At the same time, whilst that transport access is not available, few external economic enterprises are going to want to invest in Shanxi's development, so that it becomes doubly difficult for the province to build on its comparative advantage. Taiyuan has had an international-class airport capable of accepting all types of aircraft, including the largest jets, only since the second half of 1995, and there are still no direct airline flights between Shanxi and the world outside China.

During the reform era, CCP membership has grown both in real terms and as a proportion of the population – reflecting the continued social centrality of the party-state. By the end of 1995 there were 1.6 million CCP members in Shanxi – 5.3 per cent of the 30 million total population. In contrast, during the mid-1950s Shanxi had approximately 3 per cent of its population in the CCP. Nationally, in 1995 CCP membership was approximately 4.5 per cent of the population.

Shanxi's leaders in the reform era have not resisted either domestic or external openness. Though more dependent on action from above, like Zhejiang, Shanxi has experienced the introduction of a degree of domestic socio-political openness. The first apparently competitive election of a governor for any province was held in Shanxi in 1983, and even though the process may be considered stage-managed, for its time and place the event was significant. In May 1989 the then provincial leadership successfully persuaded 400 students to cease their hunger strike, and avoided further confrontation, to a large extent through a sympathetic hearing and the exercise of repressive tolerance.[60]

In the 1990s the provincial leadership has developed a style of populist politics more familiar to the USA than to either CCP politics or traditional Chinese practice, with attention to frequent photo-opportunities, and the encouragement of sound and video 'bites' by accompanying journalists. The Provincial Party Secretary, more even than the Governor, makes sure he is visible wherever he goes and through the media. Moreover, policies are presented in similarly populist ways as 'roads for Shanxi' or 'the greening of Shanxi'. Indeed, attention to environmental concerns is one area in which Shanxi's politics have become decidedly more open. It may well be the case that Shanxi has more environmental problems than some other provincial-level units. Nonetheless, it remains an indicator of the commitment of its leaders to such issues that Shanxi should have substantially more environmental protection personnel as a proportion of its population than any other provincial-level unit, with the exception of Shanghai.[61]

Externally the provincial leadership has pursued an almost aggressive policy of internationalisation since 1987. The Provincial Government and

CCP Committee have established, and provided funding for, a Shanxi Provincial International Relations Association, whose function is to market Shanxi internationally and to bring the world to Shanxi. Various government agencies in Shanxi, including the Provincial Government and the Taiyuan and Datong City Governments, have established trading companies in Hong Kong to liaise with the rest of the world, and attempts are made to identify Shanxi natives living or posted abroad who might be prevailed upon for assistance in the provincial interest.

Shanxi is the only province that has its own educational endowment that funds students to study abroad. It was established in 1984, with an endowment from the Shanxi Provincial Government, at the suggestion of the former chairman of the provincial state education commission, who had just returned from serving with the national State Educational Commission in the USA, where he had seen such educational endowment funds in operation. Since that time some 100 postgraduate students a year from Shanxi have been supported in their studies in this way. The national scheme of sending students abroad frequently runs into political difficulties because of its low rate of returning students. Interestingly, and not least because of what it suggests about Shanxi's value system, the Shanxi scheme has fewer such problems and has a high proportion of students who return to their native province after graduation.

SOCIAL CHANGE AND POLITICAL CONSEQUENCES

The cases of Hainan, Zhejiang and Shanxi suggest that China's openness needs to be kept firmly in perspective. Although China has become much more open during the reform era, it would still be easy to exaggerate the extent of both external and domestic openness, both of which remain limited, not least to specific locations. Across much of the country openness has still had a minimal social impact, and to expect more far-reaching political consequences is at best premature. Moreover, except for Hainan, there is little suggestion of necessary contradictions between provincial conditions and culture, on the one hand, and openness and its consequences, on the other.

Of course, neither Hainan, Zhejiang nor Shanxi is representative of China as a whole on its own – exactly one reason for emphasising that China should be seen as a continental system rather than a nation-state. However, individual provinces may still be representative of certain kinds of provinces, or have certain common features with other provinces. At the same time, Hainan is probably one of a kind. It is the only genuinely new province introduced since 1952; an offshore island; and a settler society where the host communities are overwhelmingly Han Chinese. As a settler society often in a colonial relationship with Beijing, it clearly has some common features with Tibet and Xinjiang, but in Hainan the opposition to the status quo does not include a political movement for independence. Zhejiang has much in common with provinces like Jiangsu and Shandong, in terms of its social and economic development, external economic relations and domestic openness. Shanxi similarly has much in common with provinces in the interior that have had less opportunity for external economic integration – Shaanxi, Henan, Jiangxi – and where the dominance of heavy industry and the state sector places restrictions on openness in the shorter term – Jilin, Heilongjiang, Hubei.

The extent of external economic openness in the provinces is perhaps the most easily exaggerated. Although the gross national statistics for international economic integration are impressive, they mask considerable differences in geographical spread. The national average for foreign trade as a proportion of GDP is 45.3 per cent. However, only six provincial-level units exceed that average: Beijing (232.8 per cent), Guangdong (196.6 per cent), Shanghai (78.9 per cent), Hainan (71.9 per cent), Tianjin (66 per cent) and Fujian (62.3 per cent), and the figure for Beijing is presumably inflated through the inclusion of trade data for enterprises organised under central government agencies. For the remaining provinces, in all except one – Liaoning (34.1 per cent) – foreign trade as a proportion of GDP is less than 30 per cent.[62] In any case, of these provincial indices only those for Beijing and Guangdong are at the levels sustained by the East Asian NICs during their periods of expansion. The same six provincial-level units are the only ones where the proportion of realised foreign capital as a proportion of provincial GDP exceeds the national average.[63]

Counter-intuitively, the relationship between external economic openness and external social openness seems somewhat tenuous, but may be clarified by further research into the experience of other provinces. Though Hainan's economy is more externally open than that of either Zhejiang or Shanxi, there is comparatively little foreign tourism or other evidence of external social impact on the island. On the contrary, the social openness on Hainan is generated largely by visiting new rich from the mainland, many of whom regard Hainan as a safer and certainly more accessible exotic destination than travel abroad. In contrast, foreign visitors and ideas have had a more noticeable impact in Zhejiang, particularly in Hangzhou. Zhejiang has long been on many tourist routes through China; there has been not just the development of the hotel industry, but an associated infrastructure of tourism and the emergence of a sizeable and increasingly undifferentiated – as between Chinese and foreigners – leisure sector. Obviously it would seem that external social interaction depends heavily on communications and the ability to ensure the movement of people, particularly by air: Hainan and Shanxi both have inferior airport facilities compared to Zhejiang, and the latter is also easily accessible by land.

Similarly, though there seems to be a general assumption outside China that increased external openness will lead to greater domestic openness, it may well be more the case that in the provinces the domestic environment determines the extent of external openness. Shanxi's leaders appear to have sought external openness to some extent precisely because domestic openness has been limited by the structures of the provincial political economy. However, those same domestic limits have impeded the development of external openness. In Zhejiang, external economic openness, which is not negligible, has still certainly lagged behind domestic economic openness. Indeed, while Zhejiang's development has not been totally self-generated, that is a more reasonable explanation of its relatively greater domestic openness. Hainan's external economic openness and its greater domestic openness are both part of the provincial leadership's 'grand design' for a new and experimental province. However, the processes and benefits of openness are fully experienced by only about a fifth of the provincial population, and provincial politics definitely acts as a check on their further development.

The impact of openness has clearly been mixed. Observations about the importance of different provincial circumstances generally highlight their centrality in any analysis of social change. Indeed, it is difficult to escape the conclusion that social, economic and political environments have shaped the extent and nature of domestic as well as external openness in the provinces. In particular, in addition to transport and communication facilities, the overall level of economic development, the structure of the provincial economy, and the sense of identity and community would all seem to be important determinants of social change and openness.

The overall level of economic development, as measured for example by GDP per capita rather than aggregate size, would seem to be a more reliable indicator of openness than the actions and attitudes of provincial leaders. In Zhejiang, where GDP per capita is one of the highest in the country, and where generally openness is more advanced than elsewhere in China, its leadership has tended to be more conservative about change. In Shanxi, on the other hand, where GDP per capita is one of the lowest in the country, and where generally openness is less in evidence, the provincial leadership has more positively encouraged openness. This phenomenon is in itself a measure of the extent to which China has generally become more open. The PRC is no longer the CCP's playground to the extent that it was during the Mao-dominated era of Chinese politics.

Economic restructuring has been an essential hallmark of reform, and is by definition an indicator of openness since it entails a reduction in the economic profile of the state sector. However, taken together, the cases of Hainan, Zhejiang and Shanxi would seem to suggest that the growth of the private and foreign-funded sectors of the economy may not be as much a catalyst to further domestic openness as is sometimes assumed. Despite the extent of domestic openness in Zhejiang, it has no substantial private or foreign-funded sectors. Moreover, in Zhejiang the proportionate share of the private and foreign-funded sectors in the provincial economy is only slightly larger than is the case in Shanxi. On the contrary, the potential for further openness would seem to rest more with the strength of the collective sector. There are a number of explanations for this phenomenon. Most significantly, even restructuring that results largely in an increased role for the marketised collective sector represents a considerably greater openness compared to the status quo ante because of the consequences for the development of consumer society. Moreover, in rapidly transforming economies, control of resources may be considerably more important than ownership, and in this case control has largely passed to enterprise managers. It is also clear that the classification of specific enterprises as part of the collective or foreign-funded sectors may also be somewhat misleading. The collective sector is a broad category that includes not only restructured companies previously within the state sector, but also essentially private concerns wishing to expand. Similarly, as might be expected, the state sector is often involved in foreign-funded enterprises, not least as a joint venture partner.

The sense of identity and community in the provinces would also seem to be an important determinant of openness. Hainan and Shanxi present an extreme contrast. Despite economic factors and national policy settings that might otherwise seem to ensure openness, Hainan's openness has been limited considerably by its different communities in conflict over the definition of the provincial identity. Shanxi, on the other hand, where socio-economic conditions are less favourable to the encouragement of openness, has built on its strong sense of identity and political community to develop some elements of openness, albeit from above. In Zhejiang the sense of political community – formed to some extent in opposition to what were regarded as inappropriate national policies goals for Zhejiang during the Mao-dominated era – appears to have played a decisive role in forcing the pace of change, even in the face of resistance from senior provincial leaders.

NOTES

1 Susan Shirk *The Political Logic of Economic Reform in China* University of California Press, Berkeley, 1993, provides an excellent alternative interpretation.
2 See, for example: Gordon White *Riding the Tiger: The Politics of Economic Reform in Post-Mao China* Macmillan, London, 1993; Robert Benewick and Paul Wingrove *China in the 1990s* Macmillan, London, 1995; Lowell Dittmer *China under Reform* Westview, Boulder, Colorado, 1994; David S.G. Goodman and Beverley Hooper (eds) *China's Quiet Revolution* Longman, Melbourne, 1994; Harry Harding *China's Second Revolution* Allen & Unwin, Sydney, 1989.
3 *Zhongguo tongji nianjian 1995* [China Statistical Yearbook 1995] Zhongguo tongji chubanshe, Beijing, 1995, p. 377; PRC estimates for the year 2000 in *Wen Wei Po* 13 July 1992, p. 5.
4 *Zhongguo tongji nianjian 1995* op. cit. p. 537.
5 Ibid. p. 557.
6 There are no official comparative figures available for 1976. The annual average for realised foreign investment during 1979–82 was US$333 million. See, *inter alia* : Ding Yi 'Economic reform and opening to the outside world' in G. Toten and Zhou Shulian *China's Economic Reform: Administering the Introduction of the Market Mechanism* Westview, Boulder, Colorado, 1992, p. 246.
7 5.18 million foreign tourists and 38.4 million tourists from Hong Kong, Macau and Taiwan. *Zhongguo tongji nianjian 1995* op. cit. p. 560.
8 Ibid. pp. 644 and 647.
9 Of which perhaps the best known is F. Fukuyama *The End of History and the Last Man* Penguin, Harmondsworth, 1992.
10 For discussion of this general phenomenon as it applies to East and Southeast Asia, see Richard Robison and David S.G. Goodman 'The new rich in Asia: economic development, social status and political consciousness' in Richard Robison and David S.G. Goodman *The New Rich in Asia: Mobile-phones, McDonalds and Middle-class Revolution* Routledge, London, 1996, p. 2 ff.
11 Most spectacularly, Wang Shan *Disanzhi yanjing kan Zhongguo* [The Third Eye looks at China] Shanxi renmin chubanshe, 1994. Paradoxically, in the context of a discussion of openness, Wang Shan felt it necessary to dress his arguments as though they were those of a German and to present *The Third Eye looks at China* as a translation.
12 Geremie Barme 'To screw foreigners is patriotic: China's avant-garde nationalists' in *The China Journal* No. 34, July 1995, p. 209.
13 Anjali Kumar 'Economic reform and the internal division of labour in China: production, trade and marketing' in David S.G. Goodman and Gerald Segal *China Deconstructs: Politics, Trade and Regionalism* Routledge, London, 1994, p. 99.
14 See, for example: Leo J. Moser *The Chinese Mosaic: The Peoples and Provinces of China* Westview, Boulder, Colorado, 1985; and the papers presented to the Workshop on China's Provinces in Reform: Social and Political Change, Suzhou University, October 1995.
15 For an interesting discussion of this and other related points in other contexts

see: F.W. Riggs 'Ethnonationalism, industrialism, and the modern state' in *The Third World Quarterly* Vol. 15, No. 4, December 1994, p. 583.

16 Thirty-one if Taiwan is included. There are three municipalities (Shanghai, Tianjin and Beijing), five autonomous regions (Guangxi Zhuang, Tibet, Xinjiang Uighur, Inner Mongolia and Ningxia Hui) and twenty-two (or twenty-three) provinces.

17 Kevin Lee *Chinese Firms and the State in Transition: Property Rights and Agency Problems in the Reform Era* M.E. Sharpe, New York, 1991; Victor Nee 'Organizational dynamics of market transition: hybrid forms, property rights, and mixed economy in China' in *Administrative Science Quarterly* Vol. 37, No. 1; and David S.G. Goodman 'Collectives and connectives, capitalism and corporatism: structural change in China' in *The Journal of Communist Studies and Transition Politics* Vol. 11, No. 1, March 1995, p. 12.

18 The following table provides data on GVIO (Gross Value of Industrial Output) by ownership sector, by province, for selected provinces.

Table 3.1 Provincial GVIO by ownership system, 1994 (% of provincial GVIO)

Province	*State sector*	*Collective sector*	*Private sector*	*Foreign-funded sector*
All provinces	34.1	40.9	11.5	13.6
Highest percentage provinces in each category:				
Heilongjiang	69.3	17.4	6.2	7.2
Jiangsu	20.0	63.0	5.0	12.0
Guangxi	42.9	26.4	22.1	8.5
Guangdong	21.7	33.4	7.3	37.7
Provinces considered in detail later:				
Hainan	49.7	13.3	10.3	26.1
Zhejiang	16.1	56.4	17.7	9.9
Shanxi	43.7	36.5	17.3	2.5

Source : Derived from Table 12-6: *Zhongguo tongji nianjian 1995* op. cit. p. 379.

Here and generally national statistics from *Zhongguo tongji nianjian* have been used for comparative purposes. Each province has its own statistical compilations, frequently employing different methods of calculation. In any case it is not unusual for provincial and national statistics of apparently identical phenomena to be different.

19 Opinions differ on this impact of openness. Those who fear for the coherence of the Chinese state include: W.J.F. Jenner *The Tyranny of History* Allen Lane, London, 1992; and Maria Hsia Chang 'China's future: regionalism, federalism, or disintegration' in *Studies in Comparative Communism* Vol. 25 No. 3, September 1993, p. 211. Countervailing views may be found in *inter alia* David S.G. Goodman and Gerald Segal *China Deconstructs: Politics, Trade and Regionalism* op. cit.

20 David S.G. Goodman 'China in reform: the view from the provinces' in *China's Provinces in Reform: Class, Community and Political Culture* Routledge, London (forthcoming).

21 Research on Hainan was undertaken during 1993–5 with the assistance of Dr Feng Chongyi, the Hainan Provincial Government Centre for Research on Social and Economic Change, and the Hainan Provincial Association of Science and Technology, and with the support of the Clough Engineering Group, Western Australia and the Australia-Asia Linkages Program of the Department of Foreign Affairs and Trade, none of whom is responsible for any of the views or opinions expressed in the analysis presented here.

22 Feng Chongyi and David S.G. Goodman *China's Hainan Province: Economic Development and Investment Environment* University of Western Australia Press, Perth, 1995, p. 20 ff.

23 Calculated from *Zhongguo tongji nianjian 1995* op. cit. Table 2-11.

24 State Council, Document 202, 1980 'A Summary of the Forum on the Hainan Island Problem' authorised Hainan to 'copy the experience of Shenzhen and Zhuhai in its economic activities with the outside world'. In April 1983, the State Council and the Central Committee of the CCP jointly issued a further document – 'A Summary of the Forum on Speeding up the Development of Hainan Island' – to elaborate the 'quasi-special economic zone' policy adopted for Hainan, particularly preferential policies for importing foreign goods and attracting foreign investment. See Research Office of Hainan Party History *Xin Hainan jishi* [A Chronicle of New Hainan] Zhonggong dangshi chubanshe, 1993, p. 473.

25 Excluding the case of Tibet whose figures are skewed by disproportionately large amounts of external imports. Figures calculated from *Zhongguo tongji nianjian 1995* op. cit. p. 35 and p. 551. By comparison the figure for Guangdong was 197 per cent.

26 Figures calculated from *Zhongguo tongji nianjian 1995* op. cit. Table 16-15. By comparison the figure for Guangdong was 22.2 per cent.

27 Figures calculated from *Zhongguo tongji nianjian 1995* op. cit. Table 12-6.

28 Liao Xun's ideas may be found in Liao Xun *Xiaozhengfu, dashehui – Hainan xintizhi de lilun yu shijian* [Small Government, Big Society – the Theory and Practice of Hainan's New System] Sanhuan chubanshe, Changsha, 1991; and Liao Xun *Kaifeng de chengben* [The Consequences of Openness] Hainan chuban gongsi, 1993. Liao Xun's ideas are discussed in K.E. Brodsgaard 'State and society in Hainan: Liao Xun's ideas on "Little Government, Big Society"' in K.E. Brodsgaard and D. Strand (eds) *Reconstructing Twentieth Century China: State Control, Civic Society and National Identity* Oxford University Press (forthcoming).

29 Figures calculated from *Zhongguo tongji nianjian 1995* op. cit. Table 11-4.

30 Perhaps as much as one-fifth of the provincial workforce. *Hainan tongji nianjian 1993* [Statistical Yearbook of Hainan, 1993] p. 59.

31 Hainan sheng minzhengting shetuan dengji guanlichu (ed.) *Hainan sheng shehui tuanti* [Social Organisations in Hainan Province] Haikou, n.d.

32 Hainan's state farms are largely rubber plantations which have consistently produced about four-fifths of the PRC's rubber production.

33 Feng Chongyi and David S.G. Goodman 'Hainan: communal politics and the struggle for identity' in David S.G. Goodman (ed.) *China's Provinces in Reform: Class, Community and Political Culture* op. cit. pursues a communitarian analysis of Hainan's development.

34 Chen Jiang 'New move in Hainan: avoidance system for cadres' in *Ban Yue Tan* No. 15, 1989.
35 Feng Chongyi and David S.G. Goodman 'Hainan Province in reform: political dependence and economic interdependence' in P. Cheung and J.H. Chung (eds) *Provincial Strategies of Economic Reform in Post-Mao China: Leadership, Politics and Implementation* (forthcoming).
36 Research on Zhejiang was undertaken during 1991–4 with the assistance of Professor Yao Xianguo and Zhang Jian of the Department of Economics, Zhejiang University, and under the auspices of the Asia Research Centre, Murdoch University, none of whom is responsible for any of the views or opinions expressed in the analysis presented here.
37 *Zhejiang jingji nianjian 1988* [Zhejiang Economic Yearbook 1988] p. 417.
38 Keith Forster 'Zhejiang: plodder to galloper' paper presented to the Workshop on China's Provinces in Reform: Social and Political Change, Suzhou University, October 1995.
39 Figures calculated from *Zhongguo tongji nianjian 1995* op. cit. Table 2-11.
40 Figures calculated from ibid., Table 16-9. By way of comparison, in 1988 when the Australian government decided that the extent of its economic internationalisation was too low, Australia's foreign trade represented 34 per cent of its GDP.
41 Figures calculated from *Zhongguo tongji nianjian 1995* op. cit. Table 16-15.
42 Figures calculated from ibid., Table 12-6.
43 Wu Junhua 'Economic growth and regional developmental strategy in China' in *Japan Research Quarterly* Vol. 2, No. 3, summer 1993, p. 31.
44 Shang Jingcai *et al.* (eds) *Dangdai Zhongguo de Zhejiang* [*Contemporary China's Zhejiang*] Zhongguo shehui kexue chubanshe, Beijing, 1989, Vol. 1, p. 130 ff.
45 Zhou Wenqian and Zhang Jian *Guanyu woguo geti jingji de xianzhuang, wenti yu duice yanjiu* [*Research on the Present Conditions, Problems and Ways of Dealing with China's Individual Economy*] Zhejiang Daxue, Jingjixuexi, 1993.
46 David S.G. Goodman 'The People's Republic of China: the party-state, capitalist revolution and new entrepreneurs' in Richard Robison and David S.G. Goodman (ed.) *The New Rich in Asia: Mobile-phones, McDonalds and Middle-class Revolution* op. cit., p. 234.
47 See, for example: *Zhejiang ribao* [*Zhejiang Daily*] 23 March 1989 and 6 May 1989.
48 K. Forster 'Popular protest in Hangzhou, April–June 1989' in *The Australian Journal of Chinese Affairs* No. 23, January 1990, p. 97.
49 Gordon White 'Prospects for civil society: a case study of Xiaoshan City' in David S. G. Goodman and Beverley Hooper (eds) *China's Quiet Revolution: New Interactions between State and Society* op. cit., p. 194. Though not specifically on Zhejiang Province, see also Steven M. Goldstein 'China in transition: the political foundations of economic reform' in *The China Quarterly* No. 144, p. 1104.
50 On the Wenzhou experience, see: Ya-ling Liu 'The private economy and local politics in Wenzhou' in *The China Quarterly* No. 130, June 1992, p. 293; K. Parris 'Local initiative and national reform: the Wenzhou model of development' in *The China Quarterly* No. 134, June 1993, p. 242. 'Guanyu Wenzhou wenti diaocha de baogao' ['Report on an investigation into the

Wenzhou problem'] in *Guowuyuan yanjiushi songyuejian* [*State Council Research Unit Reference Matters*] No. 49, 12 February 1989.

51 Research on Shanxi started in 1987 and has been undertaken with the assistance of the Shanxi Association for International Cultural Relations and the History and Research Institute of Shanxi, Professor Tian Youru, Li Xueqian of Shanxi University, and Jiang Lirong of the North China Institute of Technology, and with the support of the Australia Research Council, none of whom is responsible for any of the views or opinions expressed in the analysis presented here.

52 Many Chinese, and particularly North Chinese, might make the same claim for other provinces. Two brief anecdotes may help support this assertion.

Shanxi's alternative classical descriptor is *Jin* – the name of a pre-Han dynasty that established itself in Shanxi during the Spring and Autumn period (770–476 BC). However, Shanxi is still also perhaps more frequently referred to even quite formally as *San Jin* in reference to the three states – in central, southeast and southwest Shanxi – that existed there during the Warring States period (475–221 BC).

Shanxi's cuisine is famous for its pasta, pancakes and vinegar, and includes very little rice. It is customary for travellers from Shanxi to take bottles of vinegar with them, in the completely justified belief that other vinegars are inferior.

53 *Raise the Red Lantern* was filmed at Qiaojiadayuan in Shanxi. *The East: anatomy of a great civilisation* and *The Peasants* – a couple of television series from the early 1990s dealing with the relevance of Chinese traditions to the present and the future – were both filmed in southwest Shanxi.

54 Calculated from *Zhongguo tongji nianjian 1995* op. cit. Table 2-11.

55 Figures calculated from ibid., p. 35 and p. 551. By comparison the figures were 8 per cent for Guizhou and 6 per cent for Henan.

56 Figures calculated from *Zhongguo tongji nianjian 1995* op. cit. Table 16-15. By comparison the figure for Guangdong was 22.2 per cent.

57 Figures calculated from ibid., Table 12-6.

58 *Shanxi nianjian 1993* , Shanxi renmin chubanshe, Taiyuan, 1995, p. 278.

59 *Shanxi tongji nianjian 1995* Zhongguo tongji chubanshe, Beijing, 1995, p. 471 and *Shanxi ribao* [*Shanxi Daily*] 19 September 1995, p. 3.

60 *Zhongguo gongchandang Shanxi lishi dashijishu* [*Events in the History of the Shanxi CCP*] Shanxi renmin chubanshe, Taiyuan, 1995, p. 296.

61 Calculated from data presented in Table 19-48 *Zhongguo tongji nianjian 1995* op. cit. p. 691 ff.

62 Calculated from data presented in Table 16-9, ibid., p. 551.

63 Calculated from data presented in Table 16-15, ibid., p. 557.

4 How much does the PLA make foreign policy?

Ellis Joffe

As China moves into the post-Deng era, its army is positioned as a pivotal player in the politics of transition. Accordingly, it has also acquired a new capacity to influence foreign affairs. Combined with an increased combat capability which the People's Liberation Army (PLA) has attained after several years of intensive military modernisation, this capacity is widely believed to be responsible for an apparently hard-line dimension that has been added to China's handling of sensitive issues, such as relations with Taiwan and the United States.

This dimension has been demonstrated dramatically in the course of the crisis over Taiwan that broke out in the spring of 1995. Triggered by what China deems to be accelerated moves by the Taiwan government to gain independent international recognition with American support, the crisis escalated as China applied military pressure – in the form of threats, military manoeuvres, missile tests off the Taiwan coast, and the leaks of PLA plans to attack Taiwan. The decision to resort to military intimidation was obviously taken with the active participation, if not on the initiative, of military leaders. In the view of some observers, the military have become the dominant factor in the making of China's foreign policy in the most sensitive areas.

Even so, little is known about their new role in foreign affairs. What accounts for their influence and how do the armed forces exert it? What is its thrust? Its intensity? What are the constraints on their influence? The answers to these questions are far from clear.

The Chinese are secretive about their armed forces in general, and about sensitive issues, such as the possible intervention of the military in foreign affairs, in particular. The result is an almost complete dearth of useful information from China. At the same time, the importance of the issue has generated numerous reports in the Hong Kong press about the intrusion of the military into the foreign arena. However, these reports often cannot be taken at face value because they derive from unnamed sources, they cannot be verified, they are sometimes unreasonable, and they appear in publications that do not have a record of credibility on these topics. Nonetheless, because of the information shortage, these reports have been widely used as sources for conclusions about the PLA's role in foreign affairs. Since such conclusions are necessarily tenuous, a critical side of Chinese foreign and security policy remains largely obscure.

This chapter attempts to throw some light on this shadowy side of China's foreign policy. Since direct information is unavailable, it will adopt a circuitous approach: inferences and generalisations based on background data, circumstantial evidence, logic-of-the-situation explanations. It will analyse the factors behind the military's influence on foreign policy and will examine the constraints on these factors. This will be undertaken in the light of the Taiwan crisis that erupted in the summer of 1995.

MILITARY INVOLVEMENT IN FOREIGN AFFAIRS

The increased importance of the PLA's foreign role has been the direct result of changes that are occurring on the Chinese political scene during the transition to the post-Deng era. This transition can be said to have begun in 1987, when the old revolutionary leaders formally retired from their top positions. It was held back by the Tiananmen crisis and its aftermath, when 'the elders' returned to the political arena and took a major part in decision-making. It continued after Deng's 1992 Southern Trip, which put an end to the political slack and accelerated the reforms; and it reached a high point in the Taiwan crisis of 1995, which has been handled by Deng's successor without any significant participation by the elders.

Before proceeding, it is necessary to ask a crucial and recurring question: in discussing the new role of the PLA in foreign policy-making, is it realistic to consider the armed forces as a unitary organisation? The answer is both no and yes. No, because the PLA contains factions that are the legacy of field army loyalties forged during the revolutionary period, or the result of recent groupings within PLA elites formed along departmental or service lines and connected to central party leaders. Both past and present ties are reinforced by norms of behaviour that emanate from Chinese political culture and emphasise personal bonds and patron–client relationships. These ties form a central axis around which party–army and intra-army relations revolve, and they go a long way towards illuminating bases of support and movement of personnel in the PLA.[1]

Despite this, in looking at the PLA's role in foreign affairs, it is justified to view it as a cohesive organisation. This is because, while factional manoeuvring takes place within the military elite, there is no indication that this elite has faced the political leadership as anything but a unified group. Factionalism has not seriously impaired the hierarchical functioning of the PLA high command or its control over the PLA. Furthermore, as the more senior soldiers die, the divisions rooted in the revolutionary period will fade away, whereas new ones have not hardened into similar patterns. These divisions will be noted if they have affected the PLA's external posture, but in general the military will be assumed to speak with one voice.

What, then, are the political changes that account for their much stronger voice?

Leadership politics

The starting premise of this chapter is that the PLA's increased foreign involvement has derived from its pivotal role in succession politics.[2] While other factors are also significant, their impact has been felt mainly because the PLA has attained this role. Therefore, to explain its increased involvement, it will help first to understand why the PLA has become politically prominent.

The chief reason pertains to the standing of Jiang Zemin as China's top ruler. Despite the enormous changes that have occurred since Mao's time, and the greater ones that are occurring at the end of Deng's time, China is still an authoritarian one-party regime, and in such a regime, politics are shaped first of all by the position of the top party leader. Jiang's position is very different from that of his predecessors, Mao and Deng. A brief look back will illuminate the differences and their implications.[3]

Mao's standing as China's supreme leader was unassailable due to his unique personal stature. This standing derived from a combination of several elements – Mao's brilliant revolutionary record, the successes of the communists under his direction during the initial period of rule, his political vision, and the connections that he had formed over the years. To these must be added Mao's ruthlessness and the fear that it inspired, his political skills and his charisma.

Although Mao was criticised, albeit rarely, by his top colleagues, such criticism was restrained – as in the case of Defence Minister Peng Dehuai in 1959 – or oblique – as in the case of Beijing Mayor Peng Zhen in the early 1960s. In any case, criticism of Mao was never intended to pave the way for replacing him; this was inconceivable due to the personal authority that underlay his despotic rule. Mao's grip on power, even when it was waning, was unshakeable, and remained so until his death.

Mao's position was unmatched, but Deng's was also underpinned by towering personal authority. Like Mao, he could draw on achievements as a revolutionary leader and on the networks of ties which that period had produced. Unlike Mao, he was more a practical politician than a dictator and his ruthlessness was tempered by collegiality. Above all, he formulated and implemented policies that were right for the time, and to which masses and leaders alike responded with unbounded enthusiasm. Deng's popularity soared as these policies bore fruit, and it reinforced his power.

Unlike Mao, Deng's political style tended towards consultation and consensus rather than coercion, towards coalition-building rather than rule by fiat. Deng was the great balancer between leadership groups. Members of these groups criticised his policies frequently and directly, but his critics never tried to challenge his dominant position. Although Deng paid much more attention to institutional procedures and boundaries than Mao, in the end he also stood above institutions. For all the differences between them, in this critical aspect Mao and Deng shared a vital characteristic: they were invulnerable and immovable.

Not so Jiang; he is both vulnerable and movable. His leadership qualities hardly inspire enthusiasm and he cannot draw on two essential sources of personal authority that Mao and Deng had: a revolutionary record of achievements and long-standing ties and loyalties. When this void is added to Jiang's unproven leadership abilities, the result is that his personal authority is shaky at best.

Consequently, in contrast to Mao and Deng, Jiang has to rely primarily on instruments of power other than personal authority. The first is his institutional position – or positions, since by 1992 Jiang had become General Secretary of the Chinese Communist Party, Chairman of the Military Affairs Commission and President of the People's Republic of China. The first two mean that he stands at the apex of the most powerful hierarchies in the Chinese political system, while the third adds lustre and international exposure. But for all their significance, institutional positions alone are no guarantee of Jiang's political longevity, since they can be taken away – as personal authority cannot. Therefore, they have to be undergirded by other sources of power.

One is support from leaders who head the vast bureaucratic groupings, each of which is in charge of a major sphere of governmental affairs, and which together make up the Chinese power structure.[4] Foremost among these groupings are the armed forces which are also the most problematic.

The reasons for the political prominence of the armed forces are obvious and need not be detailed. Until now, the military leadership has been a central force in Chinese politics due to the unique integrative relationship that had existed between party and army chiefs since the founding of the communist regime. Although this relationship is undergoing fundamental changes, the military will remain the indispensable backers of the post-revolutionary leadership. It is, therefore, essential for Jiang to ensure their support.

Such support came naturally to Mao and Deng because they were also supreme and active commanders of the PLA and were accepted as such without reservation by the military chiefs. In contrast, Jiang is not.[5] His command of the armed forces derives first of all from his chairmanship of the Military Affairs Commission, but he patently lacks the personal qualifications to hold this position. Even by his own admission, Jiang was not fit to assume the top post in the Chinese military. The reason was glaring: he had no military record, no military experience, no particular knowledge of military affairs, and no connections in the armed forces. He was put in the top PLA position only due to pressure exerted by Deng on military leaders, but as a result, their support for Jiang is conditional.

The first condition is that he perform adequately as national leader. Mao could cause the catastrophic Great Leap Forward, Deng could carry out the Tiananmen massacre, and both retained the backing of the military, but Jiang cannot afford to falter badly. He is not untouchable, and if his policies fail to ensure widespread support among powerholders throughout the political system or arouse dangerous resentment among the people, the military might back a more promising rival for the top post.

This is an essential but insufficient condition. A more specific one is that Jiang has to make special appeals to the military: by broadening their participation in policy-making; satisfying their sectoral interests; or even by giving in to their demands.[6] Whatever the case, the result is that the military are in an unprecedented position to strengthen their influence and to extend it to new areas. One such area is foreign affairs.

Institutional procedures

If the new political situation has propelled the military to greater prominence in foreign policy, changes in institutional procedures have facilitated the exercise of their influence. The most important change is in the direction of looser procedures. Under Mao, foreign policy decisions were a one-man show, including decisions that involved the military.

Although Deng was more disposed to consult with other leaders, he also made the final decisions, including those that involved the military.

Things are different under Jiang. For a start, it is safe to assume that the decision-making process under his chairmanship is more diffused among members of the Politburo and its seven-man Standing Committee, and final decisions are much less the sole prerogative of the top leader. This is especially true with regard to matters that involve the PLA or broader matters which military leaders want to influence[7] – something they would have rarely done under Mao or Deng.

Before such matters are considered in the Politburo, the position of the PLA is presumably formulated in the Military Affairs Commission, the supreme party organ for military affairs. Although Jiang is its chairman, he seems to be at a distinct disadvantage, for two reasons (or was until October 1995, when personnel shifts in the Military Affairs Commission put him in a stronger position). The first is that, though lacking any personal military authority, he presides over a gathering of China's foremost military leaders. The second is that the two vice-chairmen of this body, Liu Huaqing and Zhang Zhen, who were brought out of semi-retirement by Deng in 1992 to support Jiang and to smooth his way into the top military echelon in the face of suspicious commanders, both belong to the revolutionary generation and far outstrip Jiang in seniority and personal prestige in the PLA.

When military positions are brought before the Standing Committee, they supposedly already have the support of Jiang Zemin, in addition to Liu Huaqing, who is a member. Thus, on China's highest decision-making body the military has two representatives – three, if reports are true that Zhang Zhen also sits on it without being a Politburo member – and one of them is the paramount leader. This gives the military an inordinate advantage in the policy-making process, especially since in the transition period not only the paramount leader but all members of the leadership are unusually dependent on their military colleagues for support.

Another institutional channel for the PLA's participation in the foreign arena is the Foreign Affairs Small Leadership Group, which formulates policy proposals for the Politburo and oversees the operation of the foreign affairs establishment. Since the late 1980s, the PLA has had at least one representative on this body. Although the representative's task is apparently limited only to ensuring coordination with the PLA on issues that concern foreign affairs,[8] he may influence such decision-making in practice by communicating the views of the military – and also by keeping the military informed of decisions in the making.

The interest of the military in China's foreign affairs probably finds reinforcement from two directions that had been inconsequential during the Maoist period. One is the military-affiliated research organisations,[9] which grew in number and importance along with the military modernisation that began in the early years of the Deng era. The reason for their growth probably derives from the increasing complexity and diversity of the security issues facing China, combined with the apparently greater inclination of the new military leaders to rely on staff work and professional dialogue. Although the work of these organisations focuses mainly on problems that are of specific concern to the military, they evidently also deal with broad international topics that pertain to the future of the PLA, such as, for example, the global balance of forces or arms control. Their product – in the form of reports, analyses and briefings – is relayed to their employers, be it the Central Military Commission, the General Staff Department, the navy, or a wide range of other military organs. These activities, at the very least, heighten interest within the uppermost levels of the military in developments outside China and probably provide an additional push to their desire to influence these developments.

Another push has come from a very different direction – retired veteran military leaders.[10] The most senior have reportedly continued to exert influence after formal retirement by virtue of their personal stature and informal ties. They are said to have urged the military chiefs to take a firm stand on issues – most notably Taiwan – that involved China's national dignity. In addition to the handful of military elders, there is a large number of retired high-ranking officers who, though lacking the personal stature of the elders, undoubtedly have networks of connections in the PLA through which they may well try to influence their former colleagues, most likely on the same issues as the elders.

In sum, the political situation at the top of the policy-making structure during the transition, and the institutional procedures for making policy, are conducive to increased military intervention in foreign affairs. But why do the military want to intervene?

The military as champions of Chinese nationalism

The answer to this question is, first and foremost, because of the nationalistic imperative.[11] Its significance for the military derives from a combination of three factors.

The first is the centrality of militant nationalism in Chinese foreign policy. It stems from the widespread feeling among Chinese leaders in the last few years, whether genuine or contrived, that China is again subjected to encroachments on its independence, which are reminiscent of past imperialist humiliations, and which continue to obstruct the pursuit of its rightful place as a major power. The most blatant manifestation of this is what its leaders view as United States support for Taiwan's attempts to gain independent international recognition. This policy is completely unacceptable to the Chinese because they consider the Taiwan problem to be a symbol of their unfulfilled nationalistic aspirations. Furthermore, the disappearance of communism as an operative ideology has created a vacuum that has been filled by Chinese nationalism, to which new force has been added by the single-minded concentration on China's objectives, undiluted by any concern with a communist camp.

The second factor is the self-image of the military as chief protectors of these objectives. While they are shared by all Chinese leaders, these objectives are particularly potent in the armed forces because they are inseparable from the pride and patriotism that are universal hallmarks of the military profession. In the PLA, nationalism has an especially sharp, if not shrill, quality, because Chinese officers function in an intense nationalistic milieu and they are continuously inculcated with nationalistic values by the powerful political apparatus in the armed forces. It is hardly surprising, therefore, that Chinese officers see themselves as the main bulwark against violation of these values.

The third factor is Jiang Zemin's lack of revolutionary credentials. Under Mao or Deng the military would hardly venture to claim a special role in defence of nationalistic objectives. Although their nationalism was different – Mao was more Sinocentric and uncompromising – it was not in question. Jiang, however, still has to prove himself as the chief standard-bearer of Chinese nationalism. In the meantime, some elements in the military – in particular, it seems, younger officers and retired veterans – tend to view him with suspicion, and presumably consider it necessary for the military to step into the foreign arena to ensure that he does not compromise China's core principles. On territorial questions, of which Taiwan is by far the most important, nationalistic aspirations and the means for achieving them come together – a combination that invests the military with a central role.

The self-interest of the military

The nationalistic imperative is complemented by a materialistic one: the desire of the military for more money and prestige. A tough stand on Taiwan, with tensions high and the PLA prominent, is a sure-fire way of attaining both aims.

Their main aim is to get a greater share of national resource allocations in order to upgrade the armed forces, even though in recent years the military have gained two substantial achievements. One is a large increase in the official military budget, which has more than doubled since the turn of the decade. According to Western estimates, the real budget is at least two to three times greater than the official figure, due to off-budget expenditure and funds derived from the PLA's economic activities. The second is the acquisition of new weapons, especially from Russia: several squadrons of Russian advanced fighter aircraft, in-flight refuelling technology, several Russian troop transport aircraft, attack helicopters, surface-to-air missiles, several Russian Kilo-class submarines, three improved Chinese submarines, three guided-missile frigates, several missile patrol craft and two tank landing ships.[12]

However, the Chinese military claim that this is far from enough. The budgetary increases, they say, are eaten up by inflation and are spent mostly on salaries and maintenance. Training is suffering badly due to inadequate funding. There are no resources for large-scale weapons modernisation, and all they have been able to do is partially improve forces that had fallen into a state of backwardness.[13] The Taiwan crisis has turned the spotlight on the PLA and, although the military did not deliberately initiate it, they are likely to use it in support of budgetary claims.

They are also likely to use the crisis for prestige purposes. This is particularly important at a time when the PLA has to compete with the attractions of the market economy for qualified personnel. In addition, anything that helps wipe out the memory of the Tiananmen massacre is welcomed by the military. For these reasons, it is presumably in the interest of the PLA to keep the Taiwan issue at the top of China's foreign agenda – at a high level of tension.

A new international situation

A new factor propelling the military into the foreign policy arena appeared after the end of the Cold War and the collapse of the Soviet Union, which caused changes in China's global and regional role. In particular, these changes transformed the missions of the PLA and placed more complex responsibilities on its leaders.

During the Cold War, the overriding concern of Chinese leaders was with the perceived threat from the superpowers – the United States in the 1950s, both the United States and the Soviet Union in the 1960s, and the Soviet Union until the late 1970s. During this period, the sole mission of the PLA was to defend China against an invasion. This was to be accomplished by relying on the Maoist doctrine of 'people's war' – drawing the invading forces into China's vast interior, grinding them down by a protracted guerrilla war of attrition, and then driving them out with a full-scale counterattack. The essence of this strategy was that the war would be fought on China's territory, and its conventional armed forces were developed (or undeveloped) accordingly – as a massive, technologically backward, but highly indoctrinated force. Given the limited nature of the PLA's primary mission and its stark deficiencies in power projection capabilities, the connection between its leaders and foreign affairs was remote.

This relationship began to change in the mid-1980s when the Chinese acknowledged officially what had already been their operational belief for several years: that China no longer faced the threat of a major war. If war did break out in the future, they said, it would be limited and local. This momentous change signalled the virtual abandonment of Maoist doctrine – except in the unthinkable eventuality of a full-scale invasion of China – and a recognition that the PLA had to prepare for war outside its borders. For this a new force-building policy was formulated: the development of units that were more mobile, better equipped and better trained than the rest of the army. This policy was accelerated in the 1990s, with emphasis on the navy, the air force and rapid reaction forces.[14]

These concepts acquired broader and more direct relevance after the disintegration of the Soviet Union. The elimination of a threat that had constrained them for years, combined with a reduced US presence in the Pacific, presented the Chinese with fresh opportunities for pursuing a more vigorous foreign policy in their neighbourhood. This has increased the possibility, though still remote, that their armed forces may be called upon to act in support of China's foreign policy. In these circumstances, the military have a direct interest in influencing policy – since the PLA may have to bear its consequences.

External interests of the military

External interests, some of which are unique to the PLA, are likely to augment the desire of military leaders to put their stamp on foreign policy. The first has to do with arms sales. As is well known, China rose to prominence in the international arms market during the 1980s, primarily by selling to both sides in the Iran–Iraq war. The volume of sales was enormous – estimated at $21 billion for the years 1979–91.[15] Since then, arms sales have fallen drastically – for example, from $4.7 billion in 1987 to $100 million in 1992.[16] Nonetheless, arms sales are still important and the Chinese are aggressively searching for markets abroad.

Most companies selling weapons are affiliated with the military-industrial complex and not with the PLA. However, there are three PLA companies trading in weapons and equipment, including one of China's main arms merchants. Each of these companies is controlled by one of the PLA's three General Departments.[17] Even companies not tied to the PLA are widely managed by officials with PLA connections.

The link between arms sales and military intrusion into foreign affairs stems from the search for markets by the trading companies, which may lead them to intervene in policy decisions towards certain countries in order to promote arms deals. That they have the capacity to do this is indicated by the fact that many of their top officials – the so-called 'princelings' – belong to China's ruling families. Their independent behaviour reportedly generated tensions between them and foreign ministry officials, who tried to rein them in on the grounds that their arms deals were damaging to China's foreign relations.

A similar link possibly exists in relation to the economic activities of the PLA. These have spawned numerous companies, some of which have substantial operations abroad.[18] The PLA controllers or directors of these companies – also including 'princelings' – may intervene in China's foreign relations for the benefit of their operations.

A different foreign military interest lies in the PLA's relations with foreign military establishments. Given the backward state of the PLA, the Chinese are presumably interested in acquiring advanced technology and knowledge about every aspect of a modern army.[19]

These various factors leave little doubt that the PLA has moved to centre stage in foreign affairs during the period of transition. There is also little doubt that, with respect to the Taiwan crisis of 1995/6, this role has been cardinal and assertive. However, before any conclusions can be reached, it is essential to examine not only what makes the PLA run, but also what slows it down.

CONSTRAINTS ON THE MILITARY

Most of the forces drawing the PLA into foreign affairs are constrained to one extent or another by other factors. Although this is not a one-to-one relationship, the cumulative effect of these factors is substantial.

Workings of the political system

Despite Jiang's weak personal authority, he has great assets in his institutional posts. For all the importance of such authority, Chinese political culture still sets much store by these posts because it emphasises hierarchical compliance, and those at the top of the hierarchy command symbolic prestige, which is a major source of power. These posts also enable the supreme leaders to bolster their positions by installing supporters in key posts, as Jiang has indeed done in the party and the army.

Whatever his weaknesses, Jiang is hardly a political wimp. A leader does not survive for several years in the rough alleys of Chinese politics, even if backed by (an increasingly feeble) Deng, without substantial skills. One key reason for his survival is that, despite many difficulties, his policies have delivered the goods sufficiently to give him legitimacy. As long as he maintains this, the military can be expected to support him.

In the Chinese system the military are likely to exercise political influence as king-makers, not by taking over power directly. However, for the military to shift their allegiance from a leader in place, a rival would have to appear with sufficient grounds for challenging Jiang. Unless this happens, they will probably continue to back him. While such a challenge is possible, it is not probable as long as Jiang performs adequately. Without it, his dependence on the military is limited, and this also limits their influence in policy-making, including foreign affairs.

Limits on influence

PLA influence on Jiang and his colleagues will soon be further limited by a generational changeover. The present PLA commanders, Liu Huaqing and Zhang Zhen, overshadow Jiang Zemin in personal stature, and perhaps for this reason Jiang has reportedly tried – so far unsuccessfully – to ease them into retirement. Nonetheless, they will soon withdraw from active service and the revolutionary generation of leaders will finally pass from the scene. Their successors belong to the post-revolutionary generation of commanders and, like Jiang and his colleagues, they do not derive their standing from past exploits and connections. They will not be able to pull revolutionary rank on Jiang; in fact, they will owe their appointments to him.

The process of generational transition is already under way. In the autumn of 1955, Jiang carried out major changes in the PLA high command. Chi Haotian, the Minister of Defence, and Zhang Wannian, former Chief-of-Staff, were appointed vice-chairmen of the Military Affairs Commission, in addition to Liu and Zhang. Although Liu and Zhang remain senior, their influence has probably been diluted somewhat, especially since Chi was also appointed to the newly revived post of Secretary-General of the Commission, an important source of power since it enables him to direct the day-to-day work of the Commission. The new

Chief-of-Staff and Commission member, Fu Quanyou, a respected professional officer, is likewise a Jiang appointee.

The workings of the political system also raise doubts about the supposed pressure – primarily in the form of petitions – that the military have reportedly brought to bear on the leadership. First, a distinction has to be drawn between active and retired officers. It is possible that in discussions, war games and reports from military research institutes, officers have expressed militant views on the Taiwan issue. It is also possible that such views have filtered to the high command and have been incorporated into their positions. It is highly unlikely, however, that Jiang Zemin and top military leaders have been subjected to exhortations from the PLA urging them to take tougher measures on Taiwan, including military action.

As far as is known, this is not how the Chinese military works. The PLA is a hierarchical and disciplined organisation in which officers do not behave like cowboys. Whatever views they may have, they are not likely to petition the top leadership directly. Officers are not inclined to commit themselves on paper to positions that they might later regret.

Retired generals are a different matter. They may well have petitioned Jiang and the PLA leaders. These generals belong to the revolutionary generation, they tend to be ultra-nationalistic, and they view the civil war as incomplete until Taiwan is reunited with the mainland. They probably get together to discuss current affairs, reinforce each other's inclinations and sign joint petitions. After all, they have nothing to lose except their enforced inactivity.

Even so, their advice is not necessarily taken, for three reasons. First, officers who command forces tend to be more cautious about committing them to battle than those who do not. Second, officers who are moving into the top posts on the General Staff belong to the post-revolutionary, more professional generation and are likely to be more familiar with the intricacies of modern military operations. Third, despite the overall importance of nationalism, the commitment of these officers to repossessing Taiwan is probably less visceral and more calculating.

Consensus on Taiwan

China's bellicose posture in the Taiwan crisis of 1995/6 has been widely attributed to the predominant influence of the military. As shown in the previous section, there are indeed strong reasons for assuming that their role has been central. But have they goaded the political leaders to adopt aggressive positions against their will? This is unlikely. The desire to unite

Taiwan encapsulates the core aspirations of Chinese nationalism – to protect China's sovereignty and to ensure non-interference in its internal affairs. All Chinese leaders consider Taiwan an internal affair that is non-negotiable. Even if a leader thinks that compromise would benefit China, he could hardly advocate this in the transition period, when all leaders have to be assertive on nationalistic issues. Professional diplomats have reportedly tried to counsel restraint, but it is unlikely that senior leaders can do likewise, whatever their inner feelings, for fear of appearing weak or wavering. They all have to protect their Taiwan flank, even without military influence.

In this situation, military influence is not the critical factor. It may act as a reinforcement, but PLA chiefs are preaching to the converted and do not seem to be dragging an unwilling leadership towards a military confrontation.

Caution of the military

The assumption that the military is inherently cautious is based on two considerations: the past record of the Chinese military and their presumed present calculus. The record shows that Chinese forces have been sent into battle only when their leaders estimated the risks of escalation to be low and the expected gains from the operation to outweigh the possible political fall-out.

The only exception was China's entry into the Korean War, but at that time the Chinese perceived a threat to their national security that had to be met, whatever the risk, and even then it was Mao rather than the military who pushed for intervention. The 1954 and 1958 shelling of the offshore islands, for all the tensions that this raised, especially in 1958, never involved a serious risk of escalation, since China was in control and could de-escalate, as, in fact, it did. The 1962 invasion of India was designed as a swift and limited thrust that would be over before the United States could organise a response, even if it had wanted to. The first 1969 border clash with the Soviet Union was initiated by the Chinese without expecting a forceful and dangerous Soviet reaction, and when this came, they backed down. The 1979 invasion of Vietnam, also designed as a swift and limited operation, got bogged down because the Chinese overestimated their capabilities, but even so, without large-scale escalation by the Chinese, there was never any risk of Soviet military involvement.

The case of Taiwan in the mid-1990s is different because the ramifications of military action are uncertain from the start. This is due first of all to China's capabilities. The essence of expert opinion on the balance of forces in the Taiwan Strait is that China does not have the capability to overwhelm Taiwan's defences in a quick operation. If it brought all its assets to bear, China could probably conquer Taiwan in the end, but only after a long war that would destroy the island.[20]

The damage to China's global stature, regional relations and economic development would be incalculable. As for the military, an invasion would not only greatly hurt their sectoral interests – in arms sales, economic investments and contacts with foreign armies – but the PLA would bear the brunt of the blame for the invasion and would be treated as an international pariah. Its modernisation would be severely retarded.

China's military leaders are presumably aware of such considerations, and would have to take collective leave of their senses to advocate a massive invasion. The expectation that they are not likely to do this is strengthened by what is known of their personalities. The two top commanders, Liu Huaqing and Zhang Zhen, old veterans with long involvement in the development of the PLA, can be assumed to be fully familiar with the complexities of modern warfare and with the PLA's deficiencies. The same can be said, perhaps more emphatically, of the younger leaders who have moved into the Military Affairs Commission and the General Staff and will replace Liu and Zhang.

Short of a full-scale invasion, there are several limited military options the Chinese could adopt. The most frequently mentioned is a blockade of the island. Assuming it works, the purpose would be to cause economic difficulties, unsettle the population, and bring about the fall of the government that is making moves towards Taiwan's independence. However, what if a blockade does not work? Could the Chinese then back down or, having started on the military route, would they have to go a step further? Another option, which had apparently been leaked by the Chinese, is periodic firing of missiles at selected targets on Taiwan, presumably with the same purpose in mind. Assuming the Chinese can fire missiles with surgical accuracy, it is not at all clear whether this would turn the population against the government or solidify its support behind it. In the latter case, would the Chinese be able to turn back from further escalation?

Given the intensity of emotions surrounding the Taiwan issue and the high stakes in terms of national prestige, it must be clear to China's military chiefs that once they start substantial military operations against Taiwan, they will probably have passed the point of no return. This means that they will have to escalate the confrontation until the leadership can claim to have achieved its objective – which, at the very least, means terminating Taiwan's efforts to attain an independent international status. This is a compelling disincentive to taking any significant military action.

An equally compelling disincentive is uncertainty about the response of the United States. Although the Chinese have reportedly hinted that the United States is restrained by a nuclear balance of terror, this can only be pure bluster, and its military are surely much less sanguine. Given American willingness to go to war against Iraq, and its display of awesome high-tech power, which Chinese officers have studied carefully,[21] this must be a prime consideration.

IN CONCLUSION: THE MILITARY AND FOREIGN POLICY

In the Taiwan crisis of 1995/6, the Chinese resorted to a policy of brutal intimidation. They used a range of threats – from warnings of military action to well-publicised military preparations – to force the Taiwan government to comply with their demands. The essence of these demands was that Taiwan should desist from moves designed to obtain international recognition for the island as an independent entity. Because military force is central to this policy, the PLA was widely assumed to have been behind it, and even to prod the leadership towards launching military operations.

The real role of the PLA in China's high-level decision-making process remains unknown. However, the logic of the situation in the uncertain transition period – with a political leadership amenable to military influence and a military motivated to exercise influence – suggests that its role has been central. This logic also suggests that the PLA is likely, because of nationalism and self-interest, to support a policy that maintains tensions with Taiwan and gives it centre stage on this critical issue.

However, there is no concrete evidence that PLA leaders have pushed for military action, and logic does not point to this conclusion. Any military action carries the danger of escalation; its course cannot be foreseen, but its costs are likely to be enormous – to China, and to its armed forces in particular. If rationality prevails in the military, they will refrain from crossing the line between threats and action. But will rationality prevail? Not if intimidation and posturing acquire a dynamic of their own. If the Chinese back themselves into a corner, an exit from which will require an unacceptable national loss of face, they might well cross this line, regardless of the consequences. This might happen if Taiwan makes serious moves to secede from the mainland – a situation that China has threatened to forestall with military action. In that event, the force of militant nationalism might overcome logic and compel the Chinese to make good on the threat.

The crisis of 1995/6 did not escalate out of control. However, the underlying factors that set it off have not been removed. If anything, they have been strengthened by the democratic elections in Taiwan and the uncompromising hardline position of the Chinese leadership. Whether or not a new crisis breaks out will depend on the readiness of both sides to proceed with flexibility and restraint.

NOTES

1 Michael D. Swaine, *The Military and Political Succession in China* (Santa Monica, California: RAND, 1992).
2 Ellis Joffe, 'Party–Army Relations in China: Retrospect and Prospect', *The China Quarterly*, No. 110, June 1996, pp. 299–314.
3 Frederick C. Teiwes, 'The Paradoxical Post-Mao Transition: From Obeying the Leader to "Normal Politics"', *The China Journal*, No. 34, July 1995, pp. 56–94.
4 Kenneth Lieberthal, *Governing China: From Revolution Through Reform* (New York: W.W. Norton, 1995), pp. 194–208.
5 David Shambaugh, 'China's Commander-in-Chief: Jiang Zemin and the PLA', Paper prepared for the Sixth Annual American Enterprise Institute Conference on the People's Liberation Army, 9–11 June 1995, Coolfont, Virginia.
6 Ibid.
7 Private information from Michael Swaine.
8 Ibid.
9 Ibid. Also David L. Shambaugh, 'China's National Security Research Bureaucracy', *The China Quarterly*, No. 110, June 1987, pp. 276–304.
10 Private information from Michael Swaine.
11 Michael D. Swaine, *China: Domestic Change and Foreign Policy* (Santa Monica, California: RAND, National Defense Research Institute, 1995), pp. 31–4; David Shambaugh, 'The Insecurity of Security: The PLA's Evolving Doctrine and Threat Perceptions Towards 2000', *Journal of Northeast Asian Studies*, Vol. 13, No. 1, spring 1994, pp. 4–10.
12 Bates Gill and Taeho Kim, *China's Arms Acquisitions from Abroad: A Quest for 'Superb and Secret Weapons'* (SIPRI Research Report No. 11, Oxford University Press: 1995); Roxane D.V. Sismanidis, 'The Paradoxes of Asian Security', *The China Business Review*, November–December 1995, p. 12; *International Herald Tribune*, 8 February.
13 *Sino-American Relations: Mutual Responsibilities in the Post-Cold War Era* (A Report on a Project of the National Committee on U.S.–China Relations, Inc., 1994).
14 Paul H.B. Godwin, 'From Continent to Periphery: PLA Doctrine, Strategy and Capabilities Towards 2000', *The China Quarterly*, No. 146, June 1996, pp. 464–487.
15 Yitzhak Shichor, 'Military to Civilian Conversion in China: From the 1980s to 1995', Working Paper No. 142, Peace Research Center, Research School of Pacific Studies, The Australian National University, Canberra, December 1993, p. 23.
16 Harry Harding, 'A Chinese Colossus?', *Journal of Strategic Studies*, Vol. 18, No. 3, September 1995, p. 115.
17 Ellis Joffe, 'The PLA and the Chinese Economy: The Effect of Involvement', *Survival*, summer 1995, p. 33.

18 Ibid. See also Maria Christina Valdecanas, 'From Machine Guns to Motorcycles', *The China Business Review*, November–December 1995, pp. 14–18.
19 *Sino-American Relations*, pp. 19–23.
20 See Paul H.B. Godwin, 'Force Projection and China's National Military Strategy', and Chong-Pin Lin, 'The Power Projection Capabilities of the People's Liberation Army', both papers prepared for the Sixth Annual PLA Conference, Coolfont, Virginia, 9–11 June 1995, sponsored by the American Enterprise Institute; *Newsweek*, 19 February 1996.
21 You Ji, 'High-Tech Shift for China's Military', *Asian Defense Journal*, September 1995, pp. 4–10.

5 A blue water navy

Does it matter?

You Ji

The Chinese intentions for their armed forces are hard to judge. If we employ a long-term view, it is clear that we are witnessing a strong military and navy in the making. In the short term, China has to overcome a long and painful transition. Obsolete weaponry needs to be decommissioned but replacements are hard to come by. The armed forces often appear to be threatening, so as to disguise the reality of their lack of readiness – witness the 1996 Taiwan crisis. But when Chinese threats stimulate an American response, the PLA high command feel even more insecure.[1] The show of US naval power in March 1996 may have convinced the Chinese navy that it is in a long-term struggle with the United States. Thus understanding Chinese naval policies is crucial to obtaining a better sense of how China intends to behave as it grows strong.

A NEW NATIONAL DEFENCE STRATEGY

The PLA is in the midst of a fundamental change to a post-Deng military strategy known as 'high-tech national defence strategy' (*gaojishu guofang zhanlie*).[2] This strategy was the outcome of a lengthy debate among PLA commanders in the 1980s responding to the revolutionary effect of high-tech development on military science. The collapse of the USSR, worsening Sino-Western relations, and the Gulf War also stimulated the PLA to re-position itself in the era of multipolarity. Towards the end of 1992, the party's Central Military Commission (CMC) finally reached a consensus on the guiding principle for China's military modernisation in the 1990s and beyond, which was summarised by Admiral Liu Huaqing's call 'to fight a modern war under high-tech conditions'. General Zhang Zhen, the second most important official in the PLA's high command, called on the PLA to achieve 'five breakthroughs' in its military thinking, tactics, training, R & D and force structure.[3]

The adoption of this new strategy is significant in a number of ways. Politically, it is used as a banner to unify the faction-ridden PLA under the new CMC leadership established in October 1992.[4] In a way this was similar to what Liu did to the navy in the early 1980s when he successfully united it under the blue water strategy. This consensus on the PLA's future direction of development has served as a new rallying point to boost the PLA's corporate spirit and interest, thus contributing to a high level of unity among the PLA's top brass.[5]

Militarily, the new strategy has enhanced the PLA's search for professionalism. Now the PLA has recognised that fighting wars under high-tech conditions requires superior hardware, sound tactics and suitable force structure. With this knowledge the PLA has speeded up its efforts to build a qualitative military by initiating another round of force restructuring. The army is supposed to be trimmed by 700,000 men. At the same time, the specialised services continue to enjoy greater priority for expansion. Enormous efforts have been made to strengthen the second strike nuclear deterrence, to create offensive air power and to develop a blue water navy.[6]

What is the relationship between Deng Xiaoping's doctrine of fighting a people's war under modern conditions[7] and the post-Deng strategy of fighting a future war under high-tech conditions? The latter has clearly evolved from the former. Both envisage active defence in order to limit the enemy's invasion. Both prefer advanced military hardware and set out to build a standing army of quality. Both emphasise combined military operations and the decisive role of the air force and navy.

Yet they also differ in several important respects.[8] Firstly, the post-Deng strategy calls for linking active defence and forward defence, which means that forces may sometimes be deployed beyond the country's land borders. This is a departure from Deng's active defence which was confined basically to territorial defence. Forward defence is the key to the new strategy, as it recognises that high-tech weapons allow the enemy to strike from a long distance. This forces the PLA to enlarge its defence depth. According to PLA war planners, the air defence, for instance, should not be restricted within Chinese borders but should be stretched even beyond the enemy's first-line air bases.[9] Moreover, one form of forward defence is power projection in areas subject to overlapping territorial disputes. This entails permanent stationing of PLA units in, and regular military exercises around, these areas. In some extreme cases, this even entails a demonstration of brinkmanship.

Secondly, the new strategy emphasises the offensive nature of a high-tech war. Technological innovation has increasingly blurred the boundaries between offensive and defensive armoury. It is the offensive side that can catch the first initiative of the war and has the best chance of success.[10] This is especially crucial for a weak military in a high-tech war: pre-emptive offensive operations are sometimes indispensable to neutralise an imminent threat.[11]

Thirdly, the high-tech focus aims at defence against major powers, reflecting China's new perception of potential threat in the era of multipolarity. This is a revision of Deng's thinking on war, because Deng dismissed the possibility of a war with major powers occurring in the near future. As a result, for a time the PLA concentrated on regional limited wars along its periphery. However, events since 1989 may have convinced the PLA that its most likely adversary is the United States. Focusing on small neighbouring states would not entail a comprehensive modernisation programme for the military of a big country like China. Even a regional limited war may involve major powers: they are seen to be behind every regional crisis. With the free fall of Sino-US relations, a worst-case scenario has been considered: an air or missile surgical attack on PLA facilities without a real invasion.[12] Dominated by such a perception, the PLA re-set its war preparation. One particular effort has been to introduce more high-tech hardware for the modernisation of the PLA Navy (PLAN) and Air Force (PLAAF).[13]

A FORWARD-LOOKING NAVY

The PLA's new direction of development will accelerate its navy's search of blue water power. In fact it was those naval war planners under Liu Huaqing and researchers of the PLA National Defence University under Zhang Zhen who masterminded the post-Deng strategic shift. They have been quite successful in making PLA strategy forward looking. The navy's blue water power is a crucial component of such a forward-looking endeavour. It consists of a set of blue water power pursuits, including a comprehensive blue water hardware project, a blue water campaign theory and a blue water training programme. In essence, forward looking and forward presence are two key features of China's maritime strategy. As far as the first is concerned, it has two layers of meaning. The first is about an understanding of the law of future warfare dominated by high-tech weaponry. The second is more political, aimed at identifying the adversaries in the next decade so as to formulate concrete defence counter-measures.

The PLAN has recently initiated a discussion about how to meet the challenge of the new century. The significance of this discussion can be construed as an attempt to embrace the new ideas of the information age that have driven the naval development of the major powers. Traditionally, the navy, like other services of the PLA, was characterised as slow in transforming its mind-set once a particular war doctrine had been adopted.[14] Since 1992 the PLA has demonstrated an extraordinarily ideology-free absorption of the latest Western military thinking. In fact, the navy has spearheaded this learning campaign. As a result, the navy has become more open to advanced naval concepts and more future oriented in designing its objectives. For the Chinese naval commanders, to learn new ideas of naval warfare is crucial in their efforts to bridge the gap with advanced navies.[15] The following is what they have learned from their Western colleagues.

A land-air-sea-space doctrine

The Chinese naval planners foresee that sea warfare in the next century will be multi-dimensional. Long-range land- and space-based weapons will be available to attack targets at sea directly, as will be sea-based weaponry against targets on land. Without the space-based C3I system, it is difficult to achieve victory in even tactical battles. On the other hand, the technological breakthroughs will allow surface combatants further to expand manoeuvrability and submarines to submerge in deeper waters. The division between defence and offence will gradually become meaningless. So the PLAN is studying a land-air-sea-space doctrine as a guide for it to develop in the new century.[16]

Beyond-vision warfare

During the twenty-first century nuclear technology will become mature, enlarging the size of major platforms for fire delivery. They will move faster for rapid response. Consequently, traditional maritime warfare will be revolutionised so that long-range and beyond-vision battles will be the main form of engagement. The trend is that sea warfare will be short in duration, small in scale but high in intensity. Particularly threatening is the enhanced lethal power of the first strike.

Cruelty of the 'soft kill'

High-tech weaponry will soon dominate sea battles. The general application of 'soft kill' makes a huge difference in contemporary warfare, as micro-electronics accord a high level of artificial intelligence to weapons systems. At the same time, the sophisticated Stealth material will be widely used in naval vessels. Precision-guided missiles will automatically seek their own targets. Thus discovery of the target amounts to its destruction. Similar to the control of air and sea, control of electronic warfare will play a decisive role. Major actions will increasingly become programmed and digitalised. It is likely that one navy may be destroyed even before the real engagement, as its C3I system can be quickly paralysed. So the future weapons systems must be conceived against the characteristics of the information age.

Crack force structure

In the twenty-first century the high-tech nature of naval warfare will dictate major alterations of the structure of a navy. Surprise actions and rapid response will require substantial streamlining of the command system and the movement of land-based headquarters to major surface combatants. New components, such as naval space command and electronic warfare units, will acquire a key place in the navy, while many traditional branches are to be either de-emphasised or abolished. The structure as a whole will be leaner but the demand for human quality will be higher.[17]

In sum, towards the end of this century, the Chinese navy has positioned itself to face the challenge of the next century. Looking forward is imperative in order to absorb new ideas and technologies. It propels the navy to keep up with the advanced navies in the world. As one PLA general pointed out:

> In the future battles will be directed by information warfare. We cannot allow the PLA to be left behind in the industrial age that still dominates our strategy, tactics, equipment and mind-set. From now on we must recognise the new trend spearheaded by the information technology and use it as a mover for the PLA's modernisation.[18]

At the political level, a forward-looking PLAN is assessing who would be its most likely opponents in the next two decades. Influenced by the traditional security dilemma that one's gain is another's loss, the navy is more prone to a worst-case scenario: the order of battle. The PLA is now increasingly sensitive to the growing naval power of the countries with which it may have long-term security problems. The fast growth of the Japanese navy, for example, has been seen as a major potential threat to the PLAN. Moreover, there has been an unprecedented naval build-up in the Asia-Pacific. This partly reflects the region's new attitudes towards self-reliance due to an anticipated power vacuum, real or imagined. With numerous unresolved flashpoints, a naval arms race seems to be unfolding. In facing a mounting security challenge China sees history repeat itself in the new century: the naval race of the major powers in the last century helped trigger world wars.[19]

The downward spiral of Sino-US relations has already sparked a few incidences of military friction, such as the stalking of a PLA nuclear submarine by the United States in the Yellow Sea in October 1994.[20] To the PLAN, the show of force by the US navy in the waters close to the Taiwan Strait has clearly indicated the beginning of an Asian Cold War. Defence Secretary Perry's remark 'we have the best damned navy' has convinced the Chinese navy where its main challenge lies.[21] The events of March 1996 seemed to support a 1987 projection by Admiral Zhang Xusen, former naval chief of staff, that in the next fifteen years or more, a major war involving the PLAN may become unavoidable.[22]

Therefore, a forward-looking navy at the political level means a navy that is convinced of the inevitability of war in the long run and adopts a series of counter-measures to cater for such a reality.[23] For the PLAN officers this reality is seen in the irreconcilable conflicts between China and Taiwan over the issue of independence, it is reflected in the non-negotiable nature of the dispute over the Spratly Islands, and it is reflected in the lingering Cold War mentality between ideological foes. Above all, the war reality is perceived as the outcome of a clash of civilisations based on a clash of economic interests and value systems rooted in 'US neo-interventionism' (in the new PLA terminology).[24]

Accordingly the perceived threat will be translated into war preparations. A war may never break out but, for the PLA, the prospect of it will never go away. Between peace and war there will be a continued test of force. Sometimes it may just mean loud voices; at other times it may mean a kind of brinkmanship that is now a mission of the PLAN's forward-looking war game. The navy as such is subject to a nation's political and security impulse. According to Admiral Zhang, a future war in the China Seas will most likely erupt for political and diplomatic purposes. Such a war will not be fought according to the laws of military science. In fact, it may be initiated in defiance of them. For instance, victory in a sea battle may be easily attainable but the navy may have to stop promptly when the state believes that a cease-fire is likely to achieve more diplomatic benefits (e.g. in the Spratly scenario). Conversely, the state may order the navy to fight a war that in military terms should have never been waged as there is little chance of winning it. The navy may have to do an impossible job at whatever price (e.g. in the Taiwan scenario).[25]

A FORWARD-DEPLOYED NAVY

If the concept of a forward-looking navy provides a strategic guideline, then the efforts to deploy the PLAN's forward presence constitute practical steps to achieve blue water power in the next century. After Admiral Liu Huaqing assumed office as navy commander-in-chief (1982–8), he required the navy to attain four basic capabilities in its preparation for war:

1 Capability of securing sea control in the major battle directions in sea lane of communications in China's offshore waters.
2 Capability of blockading major (SLOCs) effectively and within a required space of time, in the waters in connection with China's maritime territories.
3 Capability of initiating major sea battles in waters adjacent to China's maritime territories.
4 Capability of waging reliable nuclear retaliatory strikes.

Aggregating the four fundamental missions, the navy was instructed to acquire capabilities of rapid response, independent offensive campaigns, and long-range power projection.[26] These were later materialised in Liu's active maritime defence strategy.[27] The key to this strategy was to fight in and beyond China's maritime territories, which by Chinese interpretation embraces a large proportion of the North and South China Seas, covering waters adjacent to Vladivostok in the north and to the Strait of Malacca in the south, and continues to the first island chain of the West Pacific in the east. Over time the navy's sea control will be deployed beyond the second chain of islands, incorporating seas around Japan, the Liuqiu (Ryukyu) Islands and the Philippines.[28]

Therefore, long distance is the first crucial feature of a forward-deployed navy, emphasising defence in depth which in turn offers space for fleet manoeuvrability. As reasoned by Admiral Zhang, compared with the army, the navy has no rear-line. The 12 nautical mile maritime territorial line is so thin that it cannot shield the country effectively. Defence in depth is a matter for the navy's survival, not to mention its strategic missions. So the PLAN should extend its defence forward as best it can, disregarding the limit of the territorial waters. Only when this is achieved can the defence for the country's coastal cities and the navy's rear-bases be relieved from the enemy's direct attack.[29]

The second feature of naval forward defence is that the navy has to be employed as an independent force, assuming both strategic and tactical missions.[30] Politically, the navy as an independent force acts as a big power's foreign policy tool. Vice Admiral Cheng Ming, deputy commander-in-chief of the navy, set this out in clear terms in 1991:

> Compared with the army and air force which cannot go beyond the national borders, an international navy can project its presence far away from home. It can even appear at the sea close to the coastal lines of its potential opponents. This constitutes a high level of deterrence. Such a function of projecting power has made a navy a most active strategic force in peace time, a pillar for foreign policy initiatives and an embodiment of a country's will and power.[31]

Militarily, the navy as an independent force projects forward defence in the areas subject to sovereignty disputes. Very often this forward deployment is carried out without the support of other services, such as in actions of sea control or denial, blockade of SLOCs and nuclear second strikes.

Related to this is the third feature of a forward-deployed navy, namely its offensive nature. In this sense the navy sees itself as a service fundamentally for attack purposes. Without fixed defence lines and depth at sea, only through offensive actions can naval fleets survive a high-tech war. It is almost impossible for a defence-motivated navy to fulfil its strategic missions.[32] According to a report by the PLAN Military Research Institute, towards the end of this century, the navy's action will be most likely offensive campaigns on a limited scale, such as attacking the enemy's fleets, blockading its islands, ports and naval bases, disrupting its SLOCs and making landings on islands. The actions will take place in a direction radiating beyond China's maritime territories.[33]

One crucial component for an offensive navy is its determination to launch pre-emptive campaigns. According to a former naval chief of staff, the PLAN should wage pre-emptive actions when it regards the situation to be critical: foreign navies intruding into China's territorial waters, seriously violating China's maritime interests and threatening China's national security.[34] The intensified China/Taiwan conflict and the 'brazen show of force' by the US navy close to the Taiwan Strait may meet these criteria. The recent events may have forced the PLAN to adjust its war preparation. The navy now has to simulate actions on a larger scale than previously, involving troop levels at fleet and above. A military confrontation seems to have become inevitable in the navy's contingency plans, and any such action has to be a PLA initiative of a massive proportion, at least as far as troop mobilisation is concerned. For instance, the PLA has made serious efforts to study how to cope with aircraft carrier battle groups.[35]

One major endeavour of the PLAN's forward presence has been its southward movement into the South China Sea. The long distance (1,500 km) from the mainland justifies the acquisition of larger surface combatants, long-range aircraft and aerial refuelling technology, sufficient logistical supply capability and forward naval bases.[36] So far, no other case can substitute for the Spratlys as a stimulus for the navy to conduct forward operations. Inevitably, the campaigners for a blue water navy regard the capability of reaching the Spratlys as a key parameter in safeguarding China's national interest.[37] The need to overcome this distance forced the navy to learn how to cope with difficult tasks in the high seas.

The permanent nature of the PLAN's forward deployment in the Spratlys can be observed from two angles. The first is the creation of a new headquarters in the area: the Spratly Maritime Surveillance Command. The uniqueness of the Command lies in its extraordinarily high rank (divisional) for a fairly small force of a few hundred soldiers. Indeed the Command is composed of four commodores. Apparently, this high-level authority allows the Command to oversee Spratly affairs from not only a military but also a political and a diplomatic perspective. In addition, the Command is formally incorporated into the navy's South Sea Fleet, meaning that China sees its missions in the South China Sea as long lasting.

Secondly, the navy has launched several military projects in the South China Sea. A Paracel Command was created at the regimental level in Yongxing Island (Woody). In this largest island in the Paracels there are deployments of marine (tank) units, AA batteries and high-speed missile and patrol boats. There is also a command, control and communication information (C3I) centre capable of processing satellite-transferred information.[38] A runway for fixed-wing aircraft has relatively reduced the burden of air coverage for a Spratly operation from the PLAN's nearest Yulin Base by several hundred kilometres, and quickened the navy's rapid response for a Spratly incident.

Nevertheless, the navy's forward deployment in the Spratlys has visible weaknesses that prevent it from taking drastic actions. The number of soldiers that can be stationed in the nine islets is far smaller than that of other claimants. The long distance from China poses a formidable barrier impeding the PLAN's contingency plans. For instance, its main surface combatants are vulnerable to land-based air assault by other claimants from nearby. In contrast, China's land-based medium-range bombers cannot sustain an operation in the area due to their small numbers and short stay in the region (only a few minutes). The same can be said about China's submarines whose technological deficiencies restrict their activities in the Spratlys, where the shallow waters and complex seabed features raise the question of whether they would survive during a protracted sea battle. But, most importantly, it is the political constraints on China that have forced the PLAN to limit its ambition to maintain a small presence.

A naval *presence* in military terms, which in turn creates a form of *fait accompli* in legal terms, is vital for China for two reasons. It would enhance China's position in the West Pacific both economically and strategically. But the most urgent reason for China to have a foothold there stemmed from its concern that without a presence in the Spratlys it would be either excluded or marginalised. So in a sense the PLA's move against Mischief Reef in 1994 was similar to the *Play Go* tactics: laying a piece in the area to be contested later. For PLA strategists, China's presence at the moment is useful only in terms of 'point control'. Yet it should achieve 'section control' in the long run.[39] Mischief Reef serves as a new presence in the southeast Spratlys. This may or may not be removed in the future, depending on China's perception of its usefulness, but it has given China a better bargaining position in negotiations.

The PLAN's quest for high-tech power is ambitious. To this end, according to Vice Admiral Cheng Ming, deputy commander-in-chief, the development of new generations of major surface combatants, larger submarines and long-range aircraft will be the priority in the years to come.[40] The navy's fleets of major surface combatants and submarines are now in the midst of a generational change. Since the late 1980s, a number of new class guided missile destroyers and guided missile frigates have entered service.[41] The navy continues to place development of its submarine fleet as a top priority. At the tactical level it believes that its submarines can help achieve a degree of a combat edge over its neighbours, which do not possess sophisticated anti-submarine warfare (ASW) capabilities. At the strategic level, its nuclear submarines will assume the role of China's most reliable second strike deterrent. So the plan to modernise submarines has a dual focus: inventing new models of conventional submarines and expanding the nuclear submarine fleet. For the former, the new designs that have been put on trial since 1990 have larger displacement and are quieter than the existing classes. For the latter, the number of 09 Units will reach over a dozen early next century, as nuclear submarines are to comprise a higher proportion of the major warships.[42] Meanwhile, to overcome the transitional shortage of advanced conventional submarines, the navy has purchased Russian Kilo-class as a 'quick fix'.

These new destroyers, frigates and submarines are meant to fulfil three missions of force restructuring for the twenty-first century:

1 Forming battle groups through concentrating major surface combatants. These groups will be used as rapid response units and specifically trained for blue water missions.

2 Specialisation. Specialised warships should be designed out of the existing classes of destroyers and frigates in order to enhance the group's anti-air and anti-submarine capabilities. They cater for different tasks required by deep ocean combat missions, and potentially for the formation of aircraft carrier groups.
3 Numbers of ocean-going combatants. The navy is to equip its three fleets with sufficient numbers of major combatants. The objective is to allow each fleet to conduct independent warfare at certain levels so as to avoid trading off strength in key strategic directions. Numbers also make up for the insufficient weapons.[43]

For the PLAN, its forward deployment has to redress a number of legacies left by the era when it confined its activities to the inshore waters. As pointed out by Zhang Xusen, due to its stress on defensive missions in the past, the navy had constructed few forward bases, especially airports and navigation facilities in islands away from the mainland. Preparations for action in deep seas, such as information about marine meteorology, magnetic field intensity and nautical charts for the likely battle areas, were largely neglected.[44] These have been the primary targets for naval restructuring efforts in the last few years. Indeed, the navy has adopted an even longer view forward. The observation stations in Burma may service this objective. China's heavy investment in South Pacific islands may also pave the way for its naval port calls in the future when needed.

TOWARDS THE NEW CENTURY: A DANGEROUS TRANSITION

A forward-looking and deployed navy must base its grand strategy on sufficient weapons systems, otherwise it is just a 'paper tiger'. So to introduce as much high-tech hardware as possible will remain a top priority for the PLAN well into the new century. However, real breakthroughs can be expected only when China's general technological level is qualitatively upgraded. And the progress here depends not only on China's economic growth providing more financial inputs, but also on availability of foreign technology and China's ability to absorb it. It is worth noting that the Chinese are quite slow in mastering the technologies already purchased, be they Western or Russian.[45]

At the hardware level, most Chinese major surface combatants suffer from a low level of sophistication. With their technologies dating back to the 1950s, they are of little value in extended operations in deep seas.[46] For instance, the *Luda* class DDG and *Jianghu* class FF were first designed to engage the enemy at a short distance with their big guns. They lack SAM systems and are vulnerable to the F-16s that are being added to the high-tech inventory of some Asian countries. In general the navy's poor ASW and electronic counter measure (ECM) capabilities and its less than effective fire and navigation control systems do not make it a blue water navy.[47]

The navy's air force represents the weakest link in the navy's long-term plan to become a blue water power. A large number of J-6s, the bulk of the NAF, are being de-commissioned.[48] The supposed replacement, J-8II, is not up to standard for high-tech warfare. At the moment only a small number of SH-5 and H-6 are capable of oceanic aviation. The design of both was based on the Soviet prototype of the 1950s. Since the 1980s, China has implemented a programme of retrofitting its aircraft with Western technology, as a transitional measure before its new generation of planes becomes deployable.[49] However, the Western technology and obsolescent Soviet design seem to be incompatible. So far not a single retrofitting plan has yielded results that meet the PLA's expectation for a narrowed gap with the third-generation aircraft of the West.

The slow upgrading of naval hardware has seriously limited the navy's search for blue water power. While the bulk of its weaponry has reached the end of its service life, the replacement is hard to come by. The new classes of *Zhenjiang* destroyer and *Jiangwei* frigates have now entered series production but they are not regarded as a substitute for *Luda* and *Jiangdong* classes. At best they are transitional designs to fill the immediate gap. Both are the embodiment of Western technologies. But their major weapons systems are China-made with outdated technology. For instance, the short range of the Rada/fire control system cannot provide effective target acquisition for C-801 SS missiles. This was seen as a major defect when the navy simulated a sea battle.[50] The electronic warfare systems are vulnerable to a level of 'soft kill'. Air and missile defence systems are primitive and no match for modern sea-skimming anti-ship missiles equipped with counter-measures capabilities.[51]

On the other hand, these ships cannot be the desired replacement for existing systems precisely because they are the embodiment of foreign technologies. The PLA is most reluctant to submit the control of its fleet modernisation to foreign hands. Therefore it is one thing to purchase foreign technology and hardware as a measure of 'quick fix' but it is quite another as a long-term development strategy. As a result, the PLAN's modernisation has encountered an insurmountable obstacle in its transition: it can neither rely on foreign transfers nor produce its own hardware quickly. As a result, there has been only minimal quantitative expansion in the PLAN since 1989. Even though another *Zhenjiang* destroyer and two new Han class SSN may enter service soon, the levelling off of the naval build-up will continue for some time.[52] Some progress may be temporarily attained through the purchase of Russian ships. Again, this cannot offer the PLAN a solid base for modernisation. China's vigorous economic growth may quicken technological improvement and eventually boost its military power. Yet this will not happen in the near future.

However, the fluid international relations in the post-Cold War Asia-Pacific may not leave too much time for the PLA to wait comfortably: the Taiwan crisis looms larger and the Spratly dispute may escalate. This presents a security dilemma for the Chinese leadership. Should they go ahead with a major build-up based on the current technology available to the PLA, or continue to bet on a breathing period of time during which they may concentrate on economic and technological development before they have to accelerate military modernisation. In the years leading up to the Soviet collapse, the Chinese leadership resolved this dilemma by reaching a consensus that there was no immediate security threat to China. So it formulated a guiding principle for its weapons programmes, which can be characterised as a middle of the road course between a strategy of steady generational upgrading and a strategy of generational leap. This has been spelled out by the CMC as 'concentrated research on key items, selected production for "fist" units, coordinated retrofitting of some current equipment and co-existence of both old and new weapons'.[53] Without an imminent threat, the Japanese way of incremental military build-up seems to fit the Chinese design: it will not hurt the economy and in duc time the military will become powerful with augmented inputs.

The PLAN claims that each year it injects some high-tech weapons into service but on the whole it relies on its existing equipment. It would have afforded the time through which quantitative change leads to qualitative change, had it needed to plan for only small-scale actions such as those similar to its clash with Vietnam in 1988. But the principle of selective introduction of high-tech hardware will not work in the confrontation with Taiwan. Any action there can quickly escalate into major proportions. And Taiwan will soon surpass China in its accumulated inventory of high-tech weapons. Under the circumstances, China will have to make enough inferior weapons to compensate for the technological gap. This dilemma reveals the worsening of a dangerous transitional vacuum for the PLA. It seems that history may repeat itself in the last years of the twentieth century. In the late 1960s, when China was forced to the brink of war with the USSR, it had to produce large quantities of tanks and anti-tank weapons for immediate use. Yet they never fitted into modern warfare and constituted a huge waste of human and material resources.

DOES A BLUE WATER NAVY MATTER?

Given the current backward equipment of the PLAN, for a fairly long time to come the Chinese navy's blue water dream will probably remain a dream. It seems that it is too early to ask the question of whether a blue water navy matters: the PLAN has a long way to go first. And in any case China is at a wider crossroads. China's domestic socio-political and economic changes may not even give the PLA the time to fulfil its cherished goals.

On the other hand, thinking strategically about China may mean thinking about it in a different way. China's rising nationalism may still drive the national search for a powerful navy. The Chinese new military strategy has increased the onus on the navy to explore new defence frontiers. What is the nature of PLA ambition for a blue water navy? Firstly, it transcends military significance. Naval power is closely linked to promoting national interest. Different countries identify their national interest in different terms. China's slow naval build-up before Liu Huaqing reflected its slow recognition of the importance of sea vs. continental territory, and this reflected fundamentally a value judgement. China's current oceanic initiative indicates that it views its maritime pursuit as a key component of its overall national interest: maritime territorial integrity, economic potentials, control of SLOCs, and so on.

Such a change has brought about a fundamental change in China's value judgement. In recent years the government and the PLA have sponsored a campaign to promote a sense of ocean among the civilians. The country is now portrayed as both a continental power and a Pacific power. Against the traditional view of 'yellow culture', which glorified China's heart-land history, China's scholars are now keen to introduce a concept of 'blue culture' (ocean culture) to the population. Yellow culture is seen as synonymous with 'closed-doorism': it is inward looking, autarkic and rural-based. In contrast, blue culture stimulates outward expansion and industry and is trade-oriented. Above all, it is a spirit of enterprise. China's present-day backwardness is blamed partly on the Ming Dynasty's sea concealment policy in the fourteenth century. This was a practice adopted by the Yonglo Emperor whereby domestic ships could not travel overseas and foreign ships could not enter Chinese waters. It rendered useless the adventurous blue water voyage of Zheng He who sailed to Africa before Columbus set his sails and with much larger fleets. The message is clear: if China had developed a sense of ocean 600 years ago, it would have long been a superpower; and if China still sticks to its yellow earth, it will never acquire its rightful place in the world.[54]

The education campaign has been instrumental in the revival of a sea power mentality (*haiyang yishi*) in China. This is in part driven by China's increased involvement in world trade. More fundamentally, it is a key feature of China's defence culture, built upon the nation's historic desire to become economically wealthy and militarily powerful. Now this sea power mentality has been channelled to feed national patriotism and is interwoven with popular irredentist sentiments. When the state is pressured externally, these sentiments can be easily aroused, as the people are constantly reminded of China's humiliating modern history.[55] For instance, when some citizens suggested that everyone in the country donate a few *yuan* to the navy for the construction of an aircraft carrier, the proposal was warmly received from a people still struggling to move out of a subsistence economy.[56] In a way the navy now functions as the linkage between the populous sea power mentality and rising nationalism. This defence culture is thus at odds with a general trend of global interdependence, which means not only increased trade flows but also discounts the Victorian value of sovereignty.[57]

As far as the PLAN is concerned, the sea power mentality helps change its traditional view of its role in the national defence. Mahan's sea power theory is no longer seen as equivalent to 'gun boat' imperialism but as a guide to understanding sea warfare in the modern world.[58] Among other things, this new recognition of naval power in the pursuit of the national interest laid the groundwork for the navy to demand more governmental attention, national resources and popular support. Now the navy is represented in the top party and military leadership, as its former boss Admiral Liu is the de facto commander-in-chief of China's armed forces. The navy's share of the PLA's overall budget has grown in proportion to about 33 per cent.[59] Similarly, its manpower strength has risen from 8 per cent to 11 per cent of the PLA's total in contrast to the reduction of the army from 81 per cent to 75 per cent.[60]

It seems clear that the navy will, in due time, be more forward deployed, offensively postured and superpower focused. Undoubtedly this will exert a major impact on the military balance in Asia and the Pacific in the next century. Indeed, in a recent article in the *People's Daily*, US domination and the rise of Japan were said to represent the major world trends in the twentieth century. Reading between the lines, one can sense the author's confidence that the rise of China would do the same in the twenty-first century.[61] This ambition is there.

NOTES

1 Events such as the US navy's stalking a Chinese nuclear submarine in the Yellow Sea in 1994 and US naval exercises close to Taiwan in March 1996 have alerted the Chinese leadership. Such things did not occur even with the Soviet Union at the height of the Cold War; and the navy believes that as it launches more blue water activities in the future, it becomes inevitable that such encounters will increase.

2 The CMC has not yet coined an official terminology for this new strategy. However, this is due largely to its prudence to avoid undue political repercussions that may be caused by openly discarding Deng Xiaoping's doctrine of people's war under modern conditions at a sensitive time. See General Wu Guoqing, 'Duidangdai zuozhan lilun fazhan qiushi de tantao' (On the developmental trends of the theory of modern warfare), *Zhongguojun-shikexue* (China Military Science), No. 2, 1994, pp. 43–51.

3 Liang Minglun, 'The Basic Traits of Combined Operations under the Condition of Hi-tech Wars', *Journal of the PLA National Defence University*, No. 1, 1993, p. 42. For a more detailed analysis of the new strategy, see You Ji, 'In Quest for a Hi-Tech Military Power: The PLA's Modernization in the 1990s', in Stuart Harris and Gary Klintworth (eds), *China as a Great Power in the Asia-Pacific: Myths, Realities and Challenges*, New York: St Martin's Press, 1995, pp. 231–57.

4 This leadership is centred on Liu Huaqing and Zhang Zhen, the last two active serving long-marchers. However, in the Fifth Plenum of the fourteenth Central Committee held in October 1995, General Zhang Wannian and General Chi Haotian were promoted to deputy chairmen of the CMC. They are now in a position to succeed Liu and Zhang and will lead the PLA towards the new century.

5 For more on this point, see You Ji, 'Jiang Zemin: in Quest for the Post-Deng Supremacy', in Maurice Brosseau, Suzanne Pepper and Tsang Shu-ki (eds), *China Review 1996*, Hong Kong: The Chinese University of Hong Kong Press, 1996, pp. 1–27.

6 Liu Zuoxin, 'Kongzhong jingong zhanyi liliang goucheng he zhanyi zhihui chutan' (Initial research on the force structure and command for offensive air campaigns), *The Journal of the PLA National Defence University*, No. 10, 1995, p. 40.

7 Deng's doctrine was actually the brain-child of Su Yu, the former chief of general staff, who was the first senior PLA general to argue against Mao's costly people's war strategy. He proposed to deploy heavy troops in major battle directions to stop the Soviet invasion. PLA historians agree that the most forceful impetus for the change was his speech at the PLA Academy of Military Science on 11 January 1979, entitled 'Exploration of several questions concerning the strategy and tactics during the initial phase of a war against aggression'. In the second half of the 1980s when the Soviet threat subsided, Deng's doctrine lost its target and triggered another round of debate. In the transitional period, the PLA shifted the defence priority to preparation for limited regional wars.

8 He Wenlong, 'On the Counter-Measures to Win a High-tech Regional War', *Journal of the National Defence University,* No. 1, 1993, p. 63.

9 Guo Yongjun, 'Fangkong zuozhan ying shuli quanquyu zhengti fangkong de sixian' (Air defence should be guided by the theory of area and integrated defence), *Junshi xueshu* (Military Science), No. 11, 1995, pp. 47–9.
10 Zhou Yingcai, 'Think of the Phenomenon of Limited War that Cannot Be Limited', *Journal of the PLA National Defence University*, No. 1, 1995, pp. 24–8.
11 Ouyang Wei, 'Guanyu jundui bushu wenti' (On the question of troop deployment), *Journal of the PLA National Defence University*, No. 6, 1995, p. 20.
12 Zhu Yingcai, 'Guanyu gaojishu yiubu zhanzhen bujiubu xianxiang de sikao' (On the phenomenon of unlimited war in a high-tech limited war), *The Journal of PLA National Defence University*, No. 1, 1995, p. 26.
13 Yao Zhenyu, 'Wojun wuqi zhuangbei xiandaihua de kexue sixiang' (The scientific guidance for our army's weapons program), *The Journal of the PLA National Defence University*, No. 7–8, 1993, p. 2.
14 One vivid example was the navy's in-shore naval strategy formulated in the 1950s. This strategy was a combination of the Soviet 'small battle' theory and Mao Zedong's people's war principle. It remained unchanged for the next three decades.
15 Wan Pufeng, 'Meeting the Challenge of Information War', *China Military Science*, No. 1, 1995, p. 15.
16 Li Jie, *Gaojishu yu xiandai haijun* (High-tech and modern navy), Beijing: PLA Academy of Military Science Press, 1994.
17 This section is an analysis of an official report by a research group of the PLAN headed by Commodore Shen Zhongchang. The report is entitled 'Discussion of Sea Warfare of the 21st Century', published in *China Military Science*, No. 1, 1995, pp. 28–33.
18 Wan Pufeng, op. cit. p. 15.
19 Wang Yunlan, 'Zhoubian guojia haijun lilang de fazhan ji duiwoguo de yingxiang' (The naval development of our periphery countries and its impact), *Junshi xueshu* (Military Science), No. 10, 1995, pp. 7–10.
20 For a good analysis of worsening Sino-US relations, see Harry Harding, 'Asia Policy to the Brink', *Foreign Policy*, fall 1994, pp. 57–74.
21 *Reuters*, 20 March 1996.
22 Zhang Yusan, 'Shilun weilai haishang zhanyi de zhidao sixiang' (On the guiding principle of our campaign tactics in the future wars), in the PLA National Defence University (ed.), *Tongxiang shengli de tansou* (Exploring the ways towards victory), Beijing: PLA Publishing House, 1987, p. 984.
23 Wang Zhenxi, 'Continued Shock of the Post-Cold War and Uncertainties in the Adjustment Process', *China Military Science*, No. 1, spring 1994, p. 89.
24 Ibid. p. 90.
25 Zhang Yusan, op. cit. pp. 975–6 and 984.
26 Ibid. p. 984.
27 For more on this, see You Ji, 'In Search of Blue Water Power: the PLA Navy's Maritime Strategy in the 1990s', *The Pacific Review*, Vol. 4, No. 2, 1991, pp. 137–49.
28 The second island chain lies a few hundred nautical miles east of the first island chain and more than 1,000 nautical miles away from continental China. See Lu Rucun and others (eds), *The Contemporary Chinese Navy*, Beijing: Zhongguo shehui kexue chupanshe, 1987, p. 477.
29 Zhang Yusan, op. cit. p. 979.

30 Li Dexin *et al.*, 'A Balanced Development is the Key Task for the Navy in the New Era', in Academy of Military Science (ed.), *The Standing Army in the New Era*, Beijing, Academy of Military Science Press, 1990, p. 221.
31 *Jianchuan zhishi* (Naval and Merchant Ships), No. 11, 1991, p. 2.
32 Pi Guoyong, 'Xinshiqi haijun zhanlie zhongde gongshi fangyu' (The offensive defence in the navy's strategy in the new era), *Haijun zazhi* (The Navy), No. 8, 1995, p. 8.
33 Yan Youqian, Zhang Dexin and Lei Huajian, 'Haishan zhanyi fazhan jiqi duiwojun zhanyi de yingxian' (The development trend in campaigns at sea and its impact on the PLAN campaign actions), *Tongxiang shengli de tansou*, p. 1000.
34 Zhang Yusan, op. cit. p. 977.
35 Zhang Yuliang, 'Gaojishu tiaojianxia kangdenglu fangkong zuo tantao' (The study of anti-air attack in landing offensive campaigns), *The Journal of the PLA National Defence University*, No. 11, 1994, p. 25.
36 Wang Ziqiang, 'The Key Questions Concerning the Naval Development in the New Era', *Thinking of the PLA's Modernization*, 1988, pp. 375–89.
37 Cheng Shoukang, 'Our Country Must Have an Offshore Defence Navy', *Thinking of the PLA's Modernization*, 1988, pp. 390–2.
38 Andrew Mack and Desmond Ball, 'The Military Build-up in Asia-Pacific', *The Pacific Review*, Vol. 5, No. 3, 1992, p. 200.
39 Pan Shiying, *Xiandai zhanlie sikao* (Thinking on contemporary strategy), Beijing: Shijiezhishi chubanshe, 1993, p. 265.
40 *Jianchuan zhishi,* No. 8, 1991, p. 2.
41 For more on this, see You Ji. 'A Test Case for China's Defence and Foreign Policy', *Contemporary Southeast Asia*, Vol. 16, No. 4, March 1995, pp. 375–403.
42 Li Dexin *et al.*, op. cit. p. 227.
43 In the clashes with Vietnam in 1974, the navy had to dispatch ships hurriedly from its East and North Fleets to the South, weakening the strength in these key areas. After the South Sea Fleet had been reinforced in the 1980s, it was able to plan the incident in the Spratlys with great ease in 1988.
44 Zhang Yusan, op. cit. p. 980.
45 Bates Gill, 'Determinants and Directions for Chinese Weapons Imports', *The Pacific Review*, Vol. 8, No. 2, 1995, pp. 359–82.
46 George Galdorrisi, 'China's PLAN', *Proceedings*, March 1989, p. 103.
47 G. Jacobs, 'Chinese Navy Destroyer Dalian', *Navy International*, No. 9–10, 1992, p. 264.
48 It has been proposed that the number of J-6s should be halved over a short period of time. The money saved should fund the R & D of the new generation of attack aircraft. See Zhang Cangzhi, 'On Transforming our Air Force from Defensive Oriented to a Combination of Defensive and Offensive Oriented', *The Standing Army in the New Era*, Beijing; The Military Science Academy Press, 1990, p. 245.
49 Wang Yamin, 'Several Questions Concerning the Modernization of Weapons', in The PLA University of National Defence (ed.), *Thinking of the PLA's Modernization*, pp. 187–95.
50 Fu Renren, 'Beyond Vision Attack under the Guidance of Rada Reconnaissance Ship', *The Navy*, No. 8, 1995, p. 18.

51 Bates Gill, op. cit. p. 378.

52 See Greg Austin, 'The Meaning of Military Modernization for Asia-Pacific Security', in Hung-maw (ed.), *Asian-Pacific Collective Security in the Post-Cold War Era*, M. E. Sharpe, 1997.

53 General Zheng Wenhan, 'Speech at the Conference on the Army-Building, Academy of Military Science (ed.), *Xinshiqi changbeijun jianshe yanjiu*, Beijing, The Military Science Academy Press, 1990, p. 10.

54 See, for instance, Su Dushi, 'Lunwoguo haifang sixian de yanbian yu fazhan' (On the evolution of China's seaward defence theory), *China Military Science*, No. 3, 1993, pp. 54–62.

55 It is difficult to measure how much appeal Chen Xitong, the former mayor of Beijing, made to the population when he addressed the crowds emotionally in Beijing Airport after returning from a failed mission for the Olympic bid. I personally experienced a highly charged nationalistic audience in Beijing University, in November 1992, when Professor Xiao Weiyun 'explained' why Mr Patten put forward his plan for political reform in Hong Kong.

56 The navy has received numerous donations from retired workers, primary school pupils and university teachers. *Zhongguo gongshang shibao* (The Chinese industrial and commercial times), 11 November 1992.

57 Gerald Segal, 'The Challenges to Chinese Foreign Policy', paper presented at the workshop Change in Northeast Asia – International Implications for the 1990s, Australian National University, February 1990, p. 6.

58 Su Dushi, 'Lemeng de haishang zhanlie' (The maritime strategy of Lyman), *China Military Science*, No. 2, 1994, p. 156.

59 Wang Shichang, 'Zhengshi haiyang, tiaozhan julang' (Confronting the high seas and challenging the big waves), *Tiaozhan: Yanhai fazhan yu guofang jianshe* (The coastal development and defence modernisation), Beijing: Guangming ribao chubanshe, 1989, p. 186.

60 Zhang Yihong, 'China Heads toward Blue Waters', *International Defence Review*, No. 11, 1993, p. 879.

61 Ai Feng, 'Queding kuashiji fazhan zhanlie' (Mapping out the strategy for the new century), *People's Daily* (overseas edition), 4 March 1996.

6 Does China have an arms control policy?

François Godement

There are many criteria according to which one may judge any particular country's proclivity for arms control. The first criterion to be considered might be self-restraint in arms development or acquisition of arms. In the Chinese case, this has arguably been its most important contribution to arms control. Military modernisation in China has often taken a back seat to other goals. But to judge a degree of self-restraint, one must evaluate a country's defence needs, its perceptions of threats and even its economic or technological potential to acquire weapons. Judgments on these issues concerning China differ widely.

Spiralling arms races, such as the one that dominated the Cold War, or regional strategic confrontations, such as the Indo-Pakistan stand-off, also complicate the issue because they dilute responsibility between the participants in the arms race. But China is a different case. It is a developing country that has never been part of a mutual arms race process such as the US–USSR Cold War confrontation. The only exception to this situation may be the relationship with Taiwan, where it would seem that steps taken by Taiwan to upgrade its air force have resulted in similar gestures by China.

Historically, China has been a weak country in conflict with the world's leading armed powers – whether they be the Soviet Union or the United States. But the special position of the weak leads also to ambiguous results in the field of disarmament policy. One could sum up this ambiguity by saying that any developing country, or in fact any country that is not at the forward edge of the arms race, can have a poor man's approach to disarmament. It can tailor its disarmament strategy and declarations to revolve only around the need for the other, more developed countries to disarm, or at any rate to disarm first. Its declarative disarmament policy may revolve around the peace-time version of the celebrated phrase 'Que messieurs les Anglais commencent' (Let the British shoot first): this is a traditional fixture of disarmament diplomacy from the underdog's point of view. Thus the second most important criterion by which to judge Chinese arms control policy is whether China's posture entails consequences only for other states. Is it designed to save China itself from restraint or disarmament, or does it have a bearing on China's actual defence policies?

A third criterion for judging Chinese arms control policy is the manner in which it approaches the disarmament process and negotiations. Does China lead the way by making proposals of substance, or does it react to declared policies and norms set by others? Theoretically, a less favoured country from the defence point of view has a clear edge in making normative proposals for disarmament, and can in fact hope to define the field of disarmament with these proposals. This is not equivalent to the poor man's approach described above, since it involves preliminary self-restraint, for whatever cause. Japan, with its call for a UN register for conventional arms transfer (Japan's Constitution forbidding it to sell weapons) and its non-nuclear policies, is a case in point. For reasons concerned with conflict avoidance, or because of genuine internal political objectives, a country can also generate international disarmament. Such have been New Zealand's push for the South Pacific nuclear-free zone and its fight against nuclear armament in general, or Sweden and other Nordic European countries' pitch for policies of neutrality. The Carter administration's hint of unilateral reduction in many categories of forward-deployed forces, and Gorbachev's very real withdrawal of the Soviet armed forces from several theatres, are also examples of nearly unilateral commitment to disarmament.

Most approaches to arms control fall into an intermediate category, however, where tough bargaining, compliance with agreements, and verification are the order of the day. It is particularly difficult to measure the degree of 'good faith' in these processes when they are linked to a strategic equilibrium, since every side has to be concerned with the maintenance of its edge, or of parity. 'Linkage' may occur in the negotiating process, as each side hunts for concessions in sometimes very different areas. As we all know, successful disarmament has been based not so much on the switch from mutual deterrence to mutual trust, but on the notion that mutual deterrence might be preserved at lower levels of armaments, irrespective of trust. To achieve this lower level of deterrence, however, a good deal of trust must be invested in mutual knowledge and verification, leading to the new growth industry of 'confidence-building measures', as in the European theatre.

It is in this last field that arms control studies would seem most difficult to apply to China. For in spite of tremendous efforts by China's military planners since the 1950s, the level of armaments deployed in Asia and around maritime China has simply not ensured anything resembling a 'level playing field' for arms control negotiations. Whether this maritime build-up was intended solely for China, is another question. But the messy reality has remained a major problem for arms control of any sort. China has not been a party to any bilateral or multilateral security arrangement in the Asia-Pacific, except the old Sino-Soviet Treaty. It has always had at the core of its foreign policy and security strategies the notion that the world is based on competition and confrontation with the United States (and sometimes also the former Soviet Union). Yet China has had to live with what can be called forward deployment by these large powers right to the edge of its borders, until 1989 in the Soviet case, until today in the other direction. This is the basic inequality that policy statements intended for the general public tend to reiterate, as they did in March 1996 when two US aircraft carriers emphasised the resolve to defend Taiwan, and after US Secretary of Defense William Perry reminded China that the US was 'the premium power in the Western Pacific'. Leaving aside the question of whether these policies towards Taiwan are sensible, one must admit that in such an atmosphere, attitudes to arms control cannot be expected to be similar. In every area except that of conventional or guerrilla defence, China is clearly vastly inferior to its 'premium' opponent. As a result, and in all fairness to China, the third criterion for gauging China's adhesion to arms control policies cannot be its enthusiasm in promoting forces reductions. Nor should it be judged on the basis of its compliance with international agreements of which it is not a leading partner, and sometimes not even associated with the decision. The irony here is that China, although a permanent member of the Security Council and a legitimate nuclear power, is in many ways more a member of the larger 'have-not' club.

With these three sets of criteria in mind, we can now turn to a detailed assessment of China's record and its current intentions.

SELF-RESTRAINT

Although defence and strategies towards the outside world have been at the centre of China's leaders' preoccupation, defence industries and weapons production have taken varying degrees of priority. To make matters even more complex, it is important to note that every time China has embarked on a fundamental, long-term revision of its defence posture, it has started by cutting its defence spending (as a share of the State budget). In other words, some of these variations in priority have been a choice between short-term defence results and long-term weapons acquisition. Under Mao Zedong's leadership, and in fact also after him, China has shown an uncanny ability to defer the fulfilment of immediate defence needs in order to make possible a greater build-up at a later stage.

In Mao's speech on The Ten Great Relationships of April 1956, he put forward a new defence model based on the two extremes of people's war and the building up of the scientific apparatus necessary to acquire a nuclear force. For every subsequent year until the 1979 offensive against Vietnam, the share of defence spending in the central State budget declined. The actual size of the military establishment (always much larger than the budget indicated) and its acquisition of modern technology would be the focus of debate and struggle between the radicals and the moderates of the Maoist leadership. While radicals, including Marshal Lin Biao, had no preference for modern weapons and conceived the armed forces solely as a continental-based instrument to be used in internal power struggles, moderates, headed by Prime Minister Zhou Enlai, sought to exempt the armed forces (if not its individual leaders) from the worst of the Cultural Revolution, and in practice expanded considerably the economic base of the defence industries. This was evident in the early 1960s when the Third Front project of national defence industries was built in Central China, and again during the Cultural Revolution when the PLA acquired more state enterprises from other industrial sectors in order to shield them from radical activism.

Mao led the long-term effort to build a nuclear force and made it possible with cuts in the short term of the conventional military budget. However, Mao consistently took defensive views about this nuclear development, stressing a 'no first use' philosophy that was indeed wise, considering the difference in scale with China's adversaries. He also refrained from engaging the PLA directly in many confrontations, but above all in the Vietnam War in January 1965. Although radical in speech, Mao knew how to retreat, for example over the Taiwan Strait in 1958, and how to turn flashpoints into long-term, low-level irritants. Such was the case with border conflicts with India and the Soviet Union.

Despite these military activities, it is unquestionable that China's priority was both on independence and the furtherance of a radical, highly volatile foreign policy. Actual defence preparedness sank to very low levels. Today's China is still recovering from this era, where the level of conventional defence technologies, if not their numbers, remained of pre-1960 vintage. Apart from the acquisition of a limited nuclear deterrence capability, China's defence strategy before 1976 showed an incredible neglect of arms requirements. The neglect is all the more striking if one contrasts it with the magnitude and diversity of defence needs that Mao's radical ideology could require, if reality was to have matched rhetoric.

It goes without saying that it would have been unexpected for a regime that saw the idea of demographic planning as an imperialist trick to defeat poor nations to accept the philosophy of arms control. The first portents of serious arms control in the Cold War between the United States and the Soviet Union, and in particular the first summit meeting between President Eisenhower and Chairman Khrushchev announced in July 1958, were fundamental causes for China's break with the Soviet Union and for its decision to take a world-wide revolutionary stance for the next two decades. Both Mao and Deng Xiaoping predicted a world war between the two superpowers. Neither sought in the least to prevent it from taking place. The reasons for China's restraint in arms development over this period lie, like China's actual behaviour, in the leaders' acute realisation of their fundamental military weakness, of the futility of efforts to change that situation (except through the nuclear weapons programme) and in their total lack of trust in any external alliance. But their modest military strength went hand in hand with dire predictions about contemporary geopolitical trends.

Deng Xiaoping, who was the leader of the moderate wing in the leadership, did away very quickly with the contradiction between radical ideology and expertise, which had hampered the military establishment in every field except nuclear development. But he did not abandon Mao's basic philosophy of international conflict, with its emphasis on strategic struggle and tactical flexibility. Deng, for example, would be the leader who would insist as early as 1984 on the deployment of PLA troops in Hong Kong after 1997, while Maoist-vintage military leaders themselves had suggested publicly that there would be no troops. Deng was an ardent advocate of 'teaching a lesson' to Vietnam in January 1979. There is also every reason to believe, given his personal proximity to Admiral Liu Huaqing, who had headed China's navy throughout the 1980s before becoming PLA chief of staff, that Deng Xiaoping has been directly behind the navy's long-term push into the South China Sea. Deng emphasized again in the early 1980s the priority of force modernisation, although ironically with the same consequences as Mao: budget rises were lower than overall GDP growth from 1980 to 1989. From 1985 there was a major cut in troop strength in order to facilitate professionalisation and arms acquisition. Budget trends have again sharply moved upwards since 1989, although the yearly increases since that date are usually ascribed by official Chinese literature to monetary inflation. In 1995, China's official military budget had reached $7.5 billion, or a sixth of Japan's official budget.

It is clear that this figure does not represent the total amount of Chinese military spending. The omission of pensions and related social costs, of military-run industries, of arms sales, of much of the nuclear and ballistic research and development, of military police, and even more broadly of the economic base of the military establishment, as well as the extreme undervaluation of manpower costs, can lead to an odd estimate of China's real defence budget. These estimates also ignore a fundamental aspect of today's PLA: defence is only one of its collective or individual businesses and 'PLA Inc.' makes it very hard to calculate what part of the PLA is order of battle and where budgets flow.

China under Deng Xiaoping chose between different areas of force modernisation, clearly favouring the 'Second artillery corps' (e.g. land-based nuclear missiles). The navy came second, the air force third, leaving behind ground forces modernisation except for a few crack troops. One result is that China clearly lacks the coordinated resources between different types of forces that is necessary for power projection. It has an incipient blue water navy but no air force to protect it, except to some extent close by China's shores. It does not have landing crafts of the type that would be necessary to transport ground troops ashore to Taiwan in the event of an invasion. And Deng Xiaoping stuck close to Mao's philosophy by deciding to have a few of every category of strategic weaponry, rather than a larger quantity of select weapons.

This attitude of 'sampling' permeates almost every sector of modern weapon development or acquisition, and all the while China's conventional weapons industry of Soviet vintage cranked out its products by the thousands. Thus, only one nuclear submarine has been really deployed, while the second submarine seems to be perpetually in waiting. China has a very limited number of Dong-Feng 5 A intercontinental missiles, with liquid fuel characteristics that preclude any quick response. There are thought to be comparatively few DF-21 mid-range solid fuel missiles. In fact, during China's military exercises off the coast of Taiwan from August 1995 to March 1996, the PLA launched only one DF-21 missile, and then followed with much less sophisticated M-9 models. China's purchase of Sukhoi-27 planes has also been parsimonious, with a first batch of less than thirty planes. The second order implies a production transfer to China and is therefore both of a different nature and most likely a decision aimed at achieving more long-term results.

Even in the nuclear weapon area, China is the smallest of the five declared nuclear powers, and has consistently tested far less than any other: its average of one to two tests per year, or forty-three tests since 1964, represent only 2 per cent of the world's known tests. By comparable standards, this level of testing would be considered just adequate to ensure continued reliability of existing nuclear weapons, and not enough to develop new ones. At a figure in the range of 375–450 warheads, with up to a third of them not deployed, China's nuclear force is comparable to the British, and somewhat under the level of the French armament, even more so if one considers sophistication and delivery capacity.

These disappointing results, however, have to be seen in the context of China's protracted drive towards the acquisition of a modern nuclear force.[1] As the author of a recent and seminal study concludes after listing all the power projection capabilities that China would need to pose a credible threat towards Taiwan and the South China Sea, 'the PLA has none of these capabilities on a large scale but hopes to acquire them'.[2] When one considers the intensity of the effort and the constant push for the most modern technologies, one realises that the temporary failures or mixed results have to be put in a much longer-range perspective. Solid fuel, multiple warheads, neutron bombs, mobile deployment, launch on warning, delivery vehicles of all kinds, permanent deployment at sea, are all sought, if they are not yet achieved. Although China can claim, in many areas, the status of a nuclear underdog that is being pushed by other, more advanced, nuclear powers to stop its slow progression, it is also clear that China is committed to acquire, in due course, every facet of the most modern nuclear force. Restrictions in numbers and types do not appear to result from doctrinal choice or self-restraint, but merely from temporary choices and material limitations. Changes in strategic concepts, such as the shift from minimal to limited deterrence, are most likely a consequence of improved capabilities, and not vice versa.[3]

From the point of view of arms control, China's past and present defence posture and weapon development policy present the worst possible combination. Defence policies have gyrated wildly, leading to a strong aversion in the PLA establishment to any change imposed from outside, and sanctifying in retrospect the elite scientists and engineers who managed to keep nuclear and ballistic development under way in spite of ideological struggle. In some ways the radical wing of China's leadership was much more amenable to practical compromises. Budget trends are no great portent of actual strategy. When the budget has gone down, it has generally meant that more effort was put into long-term technological goals at the expense of conventional spending. When it has gone up, as is the case since 1989, this coincides with a diversified spawning of new weapons that enter service at the best possible rate. A government that has a clear long-term military ambition, yet knows how far it is from achieving any kind of parity in a shorter time frame, is likely to be most hostile not only to actual force reductions on its own part, but also to any potential limitation that might constrain it in the future.

One consequence, as we shall see, is that China has not taken the lead, or even any active steps, to prevent new categories of weapons from being developed elsewhere. This included in the mid-1980s the SDI-type systems which carry with them the potential for making obsolete China's nuclear arsenal. In the SDI case, China's apprehension was balanced by its satisfaction at seeing the Soviet Union potentially put on the defensive by President Reagan's programme. It has always greeted these developments as unavoidable and as to be expected from the world's superpower(s). Implicitly, it has always decided to bite the bullet and wait until it could go ahead with its own development. Statements of support usually come after, rather than before, the conclusion of a treaty, such as the ABM Treaty. Today China holds this treaty in higher regard than when it was signed, since it may prevent the United States (and Taiwan or Japan, by extension) from acquiring a shield against Chinese missiles. In part this attitude may stem at least as much from China's strategic situation as from the confrontational strategic thinking of its leaders since 1949.[4] But it is also the direct consequence of the realist, zero-sum thinking that goes on in Beijing.

DISARMAMENT: POSTURES AND MOTIVATIONS

China's attitude to disarmament has moved through three stages. The first was a stage of denial (when Mao claimed that nuclear weapons were a 'paper tiger' while acquiring them) until 1964. The second was a stage of contradiction between an all-out disarmament policy targeted at other nuclear powers while China accepted no limitation. The third stage, since 1979, has been more subtle. Now its defence doctrine has outgrown the initial declaratory stage of 'no first use' that took care of all questions, and has instead entered a phase where the deterrent value of nuclear weapons implies more gradual, but also earlier, use of nuclear weapons, and is meshed with conventional defence. In this sense, China's defence posture today is less propagandistic, and therefore less reassuring to outside public opinion. It is also more realistic, and closely mimics, for instance, the French arguments about deterrence from a weak position and from uncertainty. It also has features of the Pentagon's concepts of limited or tactical nuclear engagement.

In this third historical stage, China has begun to accept practical restrictions on weapon development, if not arms control *per se*. These new moves, however (and for the time being leaving aside the question of whether they were dictated by necessity or decided freely), have not made China revise its basic framework. While China's earlier disarmament posture was out of sync mainly with its own developments, they now also conflict with China's own moves towards limitations in certain categories of armaments. The compromise between these two attitudes, however, is that China moves last rather than first in the direction of disarmament.

China's stance in favour of global and general disarmament was a consequence of its refusal, in 1963, to join the partial ban on nuclear testing. From that moment onwards, China would see partial disarmament steps as a tool in the hands of the world's superpowers, with a particular emphasis in the early 1970s on the relative strengthening of the Soviet Union. Instead, China argued for a total stoppage of nuclear tests and the complete prohibition of nuclear weapons, a position it stuck to until the late 1970s. Within the framework of the UN disarmament conference, it qualified this absolute stand in 1982, by spelling out a more precise framework for world disarmament that implied stages of reduction for nuclear forces, and not simply instant elimination. Major nuclear powers were asked to go first and make 50 per cent cuts. Concurrent demands such as a pledge of no first use, no targeting of non-nuclear states or denuclearized areas, conventional forces reduction, a total freeze on nuclear weapon development and a total test ban, made it unlikely that China's conditions would be met. China's sole concession was to open up the theoretical possibility of its own disarmament, but this did not apply at all to the present or foreseeable circumstances. When the international climate would begin to shift radically in 1986, and the two superpowers agreed unexpectedly to a 50 per cent reduction in nuclear armament, China stopped quantifying the amount of reduction it thought to be satisfactory. In 1988–91, China would spell out a requirement for other nuclear powers to reduce the size of their arsenal to its own present status, before initiating its own phase of nuclear disarmament. It is this type of 'adaptation' that leads some to consider that 'China's stand on nuclear disarmament has been an ever-shifting, contradictory, self-serving, inconsistent and unprincipled one'.[5]

This is clearly not an attitude very conducive to arms control. Nevertheless, China could, in many areas, lean both on the similar attitudes taken by aspiring nuclear powers such as India, who decried the global disarmament talks as a ploy to preserve exclusivity on the part of established powers, and also on the general disarmament philosophy of France, which shared with China a junior nuclear power status *and* an ambition to keep its options for modernisation open. France was even less innovative than China in its proposals for 'innocuous' disarmament steps.

Whereas China decided to join regional denuclearisation treaties (South America in 1974, Antarctic in 1983, South Pacific in 1989), which certainly did not harm its own nuclear prospects, France could not, because of its testing site in Mururoa, even consider this move. France could not subscribe either to 'neutral' spaces in Northern Europe or to demilitarised corridor concepts in Central Europe, since its defence posture relied on keeping conflicts away from French territory itself. China, on the other hand, as a founding member of the Non-Aligned Movement, felt absolutely no qualms in approving moves to neutrality in Asia. One cannot help but feel that China's diplomats and growing community of specialists in arms control may have thrown their hands up in despair, from time to time, as their French colleagues did in the 1980s, because a closed military establishment and a dogmatic rigidity precluded any innovative proposal.

A more fundamental qualification, however, is that China did start a process of accepting arms control and limitations in various areas.[6]

Some developments outlined in Table 6.1 are striking. First, some arms control developments have stemmed from China's own strategic needs and do not necessarily reflect a change of position from the Maoist era. These are the nuclear-free zone concepts and the no first use pledge, and they are perhaps the most striking aspect of China's arms control posture, since it was already there in 1964, and figures today prominently in China's approach to a comprehensive test ban. However, what in the past would have been deemed to be an evasive strategy now acquires new weight, as nuclear-free zones are expanding, including among them countries that are allied to the West's nuclear powers, and the extension of the Non-Proliferation Treaty has been accompanied by assurances to non-nuclear nations given by nuclear states (China, and others, reject them as not equivalent to a no first use pledge). Second, China's participation in international fora where cooperative security or arms control is an issue does not necessarily mean a significant shift in position. China joined UN committees for reasons of status long before it articulated a real disarmament policy, and one can presume it has joined ARF for reasons that have little to do with its arms control posture. In the words of a senior diplomat who has dealt extensively with China, 'the fox does not necessarily enter the hen coop to make peace'. The ASEAN Regional Forum was set up largely as an incentive to multilateral security discussions with China. China entered as a founding member largely because it did not include Taiwan, and refused for the next two years to envisage even the theoretical possibility of a multilateral dialogue on the South China Sea disputes.

Table 6.1 China's arms control record

Year	*Formal accession*	*Unilateral commitment*	*Ongoing participation*
1952	Geneva 1925 Convention		
1964		No first use	
1974	Latin America NWFZ		
1980			UN First Committee Conference on disarmament
1982	Inhumane weapons		
1983	Antarctic Treaty Outer space Treaty		
1984	Biological weapons		
1985			CTB talks in Geneva
1986	Limited Test Ban Treaty		
1989	Border CBMs with USSR South Pacific NWFZ		
1991	Seabed Treaty		
1992	Non-Proliferation Treaty		
1993	UN Conventional Arms Register Chemical weapons		
1994			ARF regional security dialogue
1994	MTCR pledge		
1995	Extension of NPT		
1996	Restrictions on anti-personnel landmines ARF CBMs		

That attitude holds as well for track-two discussions. The foundation of the Council for Security Cooperation in the Asia-Pacific in 1994 was also seen as a means to engage China, this time on an informal and private basis, in talks on security in the region. Its original charter provided for membership of 'territories' as well as national committees. But China has held off joining until it is completely assured that this does not imply any participation by a Taiwanese committee, even though this is a non-governmental forum.

A recent study of China's involvement in multilateral institutions concludes that China 'is at a crossroads' on this matter.[7] One can wonder if it is not likely to remain indefinitely at this crossroads, preventing dialogue on sensitive issues when it is a member, or refusing to join when it does not want to be faced with undesirable dialogue. Over time, however, there is a record of China turning passive or negative participation into more constructive moves.[8]

It is also not really clear that the growth of China's small community of 'arms controllers',[9] and other experts who have published about these issues,[10] has really produced a shift in China's policy. From the chronological evidence, there is a possibility that it is China's political shift towards acceptance of arms control perspectives that has resulted in the growth of this group, not the other way around. There is also a possibility that different categories of Chinese, decision-makers and experts, may have different explanations and reasons for going into the same type of arms control agreement, as seems to be the case for signing the NPT. Learning may be a footnote to adapting, as befits an authoritarian society ruled from above. It is particularly striking that China's long and tortured political history, where scientists, engineers and administrators of advanced arms projects were at the edge of the repression going on against intellectuals and experts, has never produced an arms control dissident, neither a Sakharov nor of course a Herbert York. Throughout the two recent explorations of China's arms control community cited above, there appears no discernible trend away from the concept of self-help (or, in the Chinese tradition, self-reliance or self-strengthening).

Have China's stands on arms control since the early 1980s produced real constraints on its own defence? This is certainly not the case for its approval of strategic arms treaties between the two superpowers, from the ABM to Start I and II (at present thresholds) to the INF treaty. In so far as participation in the five-power strategic nuclear arms control process is concerned, there is almost a counter-proof, since China was forthcoming in the first phase, when no envisaged cut applied to it, but receded from active participation when a range of new cuts obviously called for some similar gestures on the part of junior nuclear powers.

China's record on outlawed weapons – biological, chemical and inhumane warfare – is more consistently positive, but that also stems from a historical consideration rather than from a recent policy shift: Chinese positions remind the outsider that China was the victim of biological warfare during the Second World War, and this was the first convention that it signed. The argument that it prepares nonetheless for conflicts involving these biological or chemical weapons is not to be held against China, since that is also the case, directly or through indirect possibilities, of advanced military powers. China's recent participation in a new convention restricting (rather than outlawing) the use of anti-personnel landmines may be one of the most positive signs, as it has itself practised this type of warfare as a matter of routine in the people's war era, and has furnished these weapons in large quantities to allies and clients. China's participation in the conventional arms transfer register since 1993 is also a positive development, but a minute one, since this is in no way a restriction of these arms transfers. Furthermore, the date when the register was established happened to coincide with a steep decline in China's sales of conventional weapons, for reasons beyond its will.

The real decisions that have implied sacrifices, either actual or potential, for China lie in three related decisions:

1 the joint statement with the United States in 1994 promising to abide by the Missile Transfer Control Regime provisions that it had shunned previously under pretexts of missile range definition;
2 the approval of the Non-Proliferation Treaty extension in 1995, since China has been the target of inquiries and sanctions related to nuclear technology transfer;
3 and, much more importantly of course, its present participation in negotiations towards a comprehensive nuclear test ban.

We shall treat the first two items in this list as good cases for studying China's motivation. The third, being an on-going story, deserves separate consideration.

The MTCR case is an instance of other powers cooperating to gang up on China. The MTCR had been set up by the other four nuclear powers (or permanent members of the Security Council), excluding China. It drew up a regime that was specifically targeted at China, which was criticised at the time for its CSS-2 sales to Saudi Arabia, and its rumoured sale of M-11 missiles to Pakistan and Syria. China saw through the ploy and succeeded in having the United States rescind sanctions in the high-technology area before agreeing to join the MTCR. China later underlined that its pledge was by no means irreversible, and it hinged on other countries refraining from imposing sanctions on China for whatever political motivation. 'Conditional engagement', a new key concept that is now competing with 'constructive engagement' in the United States, may have been thought of first by China under the form of conditional compliance with rules of any club of which it is not a member. China's attitude to the new 'clubs' being created in Southeast Asia (ARF, CSCAP and ultimately ASEAN) may be a variation on this theme: 'we'll join if we don't need to comply' or 'we'll comply locally if you don't interfere with our behaviour elsewhere'.

As to the NPT extension, it is probably one of the first instances where China, as evidenced by its expert literature, saw the advantage of siding with the established members of a club rather than helping to challenge it.[11] When China joined the NPT in 1991, however, it was as much because it was the only remaining holdout among nuclear states, and because it wanted to escape its pariah status following the 1989 events. The risk of a chain-reaction in Northeast Asia that could come from North Korea becoming a nuclear power has, however, reinforced China's stake in the NPT. Chinese negotiators were outwardly indifferent to a twenty-five year or indefinite extension, but rallied to the second position when it looked like carrying the day. The NPT in no way constrained China's ability to develop its nuclear weapons, except by a general pledge of self-restraint that France also signed in 1995, but saw as compatible with the resumption of its last nuclear testing campaign.

In the MTCR regime, which heavily constrained China, conditional compliance with outside pressure rather than voluntary participation in a cooperative area of international security was the key factor. In the NPT, we have possibly the first case of voluntary participation resting on an analysis of global security that does not, however, conflict with China's security needs. Different authors place different stress on such issues as China's cultural and historical grudges against the West and on the sociological importance of the learning process in arms control. There is also a growing trend to view long-term economic development of China as a favourable trend but nobody suggests that China has in any way moved from the world of realist self-help to reliance on cooperative security arrangements and international guarantees.[12]

This takes us back to a basic argument. For a very long time, China's inferior technological and military situation will prevent it from viewing arms control as a symmetrical and fair process. There may develop debates among China's elite about the absolute or relative values of international norms, but it is highly unlikely that these debates will prevail over the tough bargaining and 'us or them' philosophy that is also a key basis for the legitimacy of China's leadership.

THE TEST BAN TREATY AND BEYOND

The intended purpose of a CTB has always been to constrain the technological arms race. As a CTB looms in the near future, the French and Chinese are beginning to feel this constraint, and are complaining that their programs are left far behind those of the USA. They feel a CTB is somehow unfair. It freezes them into second-rate status, leaving the USA (and Russia) with extensive knowledge and a rich database. To catch up – if only a little bit – is part of their rationale for testing during a moratorium by the other powers, and in the face of global opposition. Some of these same feelings are also simmering in India.[13]

Seen from a French perspective, the above judgment makes plain that the CTB poses a major problem for China. It is in fact too optimistic about China's situation. Although France does not have nearly so many warhead designs and types as the United States, the level of reliability and sophistication reached is much greater than China's. A second difficulty from China's point of view is that the testing moratorium decided by other nuclear countries, the zero option agreed in practice by the three Western nuclear powers in September 1995 (and subsequently accepted by Russia), effectively repeat the Chinese experience of the MTCR regime. The four major powers came to an agreement among themselves and then challenged China to accept what appeared to be, at least for a while, a nearly finished deal.

Given these basic difficulties, China's attitude has been encouraging. As the 'deadline' for the completion of the CTBT loomed in June 1996, China did eventually capitulate and accept a zero-level CTBT, while still disagreeing on other issues (such as intrusive verification) where there was not yet full agreement among the main players. China had, of course, repeatedly committed itself to a successful conclusion in 1996 for the CTBT and the delay in reaching the agreement cannot be blamed unambiguously on China.[14] China had also agreed in 1994 to participate in fissile material production cutoff talks, perhaps helped by the fact that it has an abundant supply of fissile material for weapons.

It appears that China is now conscious of the relative cost/benefit ratio of two possible attitudes: delaying the treaty ensures the continued upgrading of its nuclear force, but also allows others (such as India) to catch up, and may contribute to proliferation in Northeast Asia. Ensuring that it enters into force, on the other hand, helps China maintain its status as the only nuclear power in Asia. Although Chinese positions on no first use and negative security assurances link these issues with the extinction of nuclear weapons, Chinese experts are clearly not at the forefront of technical proposals towards this last goal. It is possible that China, rather than sticking with its Third World attitude, has now chosen to go with the Second World – e.g. countries such as France, Great Britain and Russia which see the political value of the CTBT from the point of view of their own status, apart from its effect to restrict the nuclear arms race.

The jury is still out on China's readiness for a CTBT but the points covered above suggest that China may be hedging in order, perhaps, to gain some time, or multiplying the number of objections in order to cover its real preoccupations, which have to do with upgrading its nuclear force. China is slowly conceding ground, however, and not contributing in any way in forming a united front with other states that happen to be Asian, such as India and Pakistan. It may not have escaped China's attention that the world's most advanced nuclear power has the means, through advanced simulation and previous data collection, to keep moving forward in nuclear explosion technologies without resorting to tests, while China, in spite of its supply of high-energy physicists and even with the transfer of some simulation data, cannot achieve the same results.

In the final analysis, the CTBT process is an example of many of the positive and negative features of the broader Chinese attitude to arms control. China's policy has moved in parallel with two other factors: its own acquisition of a respectable arms development establishment and of a minimal but burgeoning deterrence capability. China's adherence, since the mid-1970s, to disarmament treaties and provisions that did not tie it down directly suggests that its political leaders have always been sensitive to the political value of appearing to favour disarmament processes. China did not need a specialized community of arms controllers to be made aware of this. Moves into areas where China itself may be bound one day by its own commitments have been the object of bargaining, a process where it is difficult to distinguish the respective roles of outside pressure on China and China's own playing of the linkage game. China's increasing compliance in areas such as proliferation and arms transfer (for instance over the MTCR regime) has also given it additional leverage in its international relations. It may be this process, rather than a deep-seated cultural change which would make it 'more like the West', that will entice China to make the most significant move to date in disarmament, and one that puts a heavy cap on its own arms development – signing the CTBT. This trend, were it to be confirmed, would allay suspicions that China is 'a very slow learner or duplicitous'.[15]

NOTES

1 These efforts have been documented in great detail by John Wilson Lewis and Xue Litai in their two books, *China builds the bomb*, 1988 and *China's strategic seapower* 1994, Stanford University Press, Stanford.

2 James Shinn, 'Conditional engagement with China', in James Shinn (ed.), *Weaving the net, conditional engagement with China*, 1996, Council on Foreign Relations, New York, p. 17.

3 See Alastair Iain Johnston, 'China's new "old thinking": the concept of limited deterrence', *International Security*, Vol. 20, No. 3 (winter 1995–6). Johnston, however, writing from a theoretical rather than chronological perspective, emphasizes the conceptual distinction but does not identify a factual cause for this shift.

4 See J.C. Hopkins and W. Hu, *Strategic views from the second tier, the nuclear weapon policies of France, Britain and China*, 1995, Transaction Books, New Brunswick.

5 J. Mohan Malik, 'China's unprincipled stand on nuclear disarmament', *Pacific Research*, Vol. 7, No. 4, November 1994, p. 6.

6 This takes as a conceptual, if not factual, basis table 1 (China's arms control record), p. 37 of Alastair Iain Johnston, 'Learning vs. adaptation: explaining change in Chinese arms control policy in the 1980s and 1990s', *The China Journal*, No. 35, January 1996, to which we have added a chronology and a few other events. We have not followed Johnston when he includes PLA forces reductions in 1985–7 as a 'unilateral commitment', because we believe it was one of China's sharpest self-strengthening moves in the military area. We have also deleted the 'statement of support' category as the items covered (Start I and II, INF agreement, ASAT Ban, Space Arms Control and Five-power NFU) either did not constrain China directly, or were approved only rhetorically, while China did not move its own policies in reflection of this approval.

7 Paul M. Evans, 'The new multilateralism in the Asia-Pacific and the conditional engagement of China', in James Shinn, 1996 op. cit., p. 264.

8 As is well recorded by Alastair Iain Johnston's track record of China's votes in the UN First Committee and Conference on Disarmament since 1980, Johnston 1996 op. cit., pp. 38–9.

9 Banning N. Garrett and Bonnie S. Glaser, 'Chinese perspectives on nuclear arms control', Vol. 20, No. 3 (winter 1995/6), p. 46, quoting a Chinese interview.

10 Alastair Iain Johnston, 1996 op. cit., pp. 39–42.

11 The two recent articles quoted in the above notes cite these experts' views at great length.

12 Paul Evans, 1996 op. cit., p. 262, cites the ingrained habit of China's tributary relations with the outside world.

13 Robert S. Norris, op. cit., p. 51.

14 Sha Zukang (China's ambassador to the CD), 'China and the NPT', *Disarmament*, Vol. 18, No. 1, 1995, pp. 18–23.

15 Gerald Segal, 'Tying China into the international system', *Survival*, Vol. 37, No. 2, p. 69.

7 Economic growth and trade dependency in China[1]

Christopher Findlay and Andrew Watson

The underlying perspective adopted in this chapter rejects the view that China's rapid economic growth represents a 'threat' to the rest of the world, or that China is a recalcitrant, realpolitik power that has 'adapted' its outward behaviour but has not 'learned' a new way of thinking.[2] Our analysis demonstrates that China's interaction with the world economy has created a level of trade interdependency that has transformed both China's international role and the way in which the rest of the world relates to China. This has not only demonstrated to China the benefits of its new trading regime but has also stimulated growth and change in the Asian region and in the world at large. What is more, China's participation in a broad range of international economic agencies has underlined the extent to which it has become a member of the world economic community, even though problems remain in the management of that relationship.

China's economy is one of the largest in the world, and instability in its trading relationships could pose major problems for international markets. By the same token, countries that feel challenged by China's growth need to consider the benefits to be obtained from building a more stable trading relationship and from using that relationship to advance their own economies, rather than adopting a defensive posture. Many Asian economies have reacted to China's emergence as a major centre of labour intensive manufacturing by positive structural change of their own. Seen from that perspective, China has become one of the engines of growth of the Asia-Pacific region. In our view, therefore, the issues facing both the world and China are not how to 'contain' China, but how to manage the consequences of China's emergence as a major trading nation and how to ensure that trade interdependency evolves smoothly and beneficially.

One of the most profound features of China's reform period has been the extent to which the country has joined the world economy.[3] Since 1978 the underlying focus of China's development strategy has moved from import substitution to active engagement in foreign trade as an engine of growth. As a result, its trading position has changed substantially. In 1978, it was ranked thirty-second in world trade.[4] By 1995, its two-way trade was worth US$280.9 billion, and it was eleventh in the list of the world's top trading countries.[5] Over the same period, its share of world trade had risen from 0.8 per cent to 2.9 per cent,[6] and there was a significant change in the structure of its exports. Before the reforms, some 54 per cent of China's exports were typically primary products, and imports were strongly biased towards producer goods.[7] By 1995, while imports still had a major producer goods content, they included a diverse range of consumer goods, and some 86 per cent of exports were manufactured products.[8]

These changes in the volume and structure of trade were accompanied by equally significant changes in the domestic organisation of foreign trade, the management of foreign currency and the degree of openness to foreign direct investment. Foreign trade management has been largely decentralised to allow more direct trading links by local administrations and by trading enterprises. The controls over foreign exchange have been steadily reduced, and, by 1994, the planned exchange rate was abandoned in favour of a managed float. In addition, a set of policies ranging from the establishment of special economic zones to tax incentives have been adopted to attract foreign investment. By 1995, therefore, China had become one of the major destinations for international investment flows.

All of these developments tended to reinforce the changes taking place in China's trade. They meant that trade began to influence the structure of domestic production and consumption, that border prices began to affect domestic choices and that foreign investment promoted the growth of export manufacturing to make use of China's abundant labour. As a result, China's experience during the 1980s and 1990s tended to support the argument that openness to trade is a mechanism for achieving more rapid and efficient growth and better distribution of domestic resources.[9] China's increasing participation in the world economy has become an important factor in promoting both growth and economic restructuring. The linkage between trade and domestic reform is thus an essential element in China's economic success and in the effectiveness of gradualism in reform.

The transformation of China's international position has inevitably also increased the level of China's reliance on the rest of the world as a source of raw materials, as a source of capital and as a market for products. While China has large resources of energy and raw materials, the quality, distribution and structure of those resources do not match the structure of demand, and the amount per capita is low. In particular, the shortage of arable land and the large population means that China has no competitive advantage in agricultural production.[10] Agriculture is declining as a proportion of the economy, and the competing demands for food and for agricultural raw materials place great pressures on supply. Furthermore, the huge size of the Chinese population and the expectations of demand growth as incomes rise mean that there will be rising imports for some raw materials. Though the current level of dependency should not be overstated and there are still many impediments in the way in which trade is organised and managed, the growth in imports of both raw materials and food has already been substantial.

The net effect of this process is to raise strategic questions about the extent to which China might become dependent on the rest of the world to sustain its current growth trajectory. Given its modern history and the legacy of the plan system's bias towards autarkic growth, it is not surprising to find a continuing sense of suspicion about the motives of the rest of the world and the dangers of becoming too dependent.[11] The rejection of China's bid to enter the WTO, the annual difficulty of the MFN approval by the US Congress, and the trend during 1995 and 1996 to define a 'China threat', have given weight to China's strategic concerns. Nevertheless, China's commitment to its policy of interaction with the world economy remains strong.[12]

The following analysis will address these issues by examining the relationship between growth, structural economic change and trade. We argue that concerns about resource dependency cannot be separated from those about export market access. Our focus, however, is China's trade in resources and raw materials and the implications of that for ideas of 'dependency' and 'interdependency'. Two key examples – grains and energy – will be used to illustrate the nature of China's trade and its implications for the world.[13] The conclusion will return to the discussion of the strategic issues involved.

GROWTH, STRUCTURAL CHANGE AND TRADE

Trade growth and openness – how open?

Since the reforms, China's trade has consistently grown faster than output. The average rate of growth of exports between 1978 and 1993 was 14 per cent, compared to 9 per cent for real GDP. Trade growth, it appears, has been an important contributor to overall economic growth.

There is, however, considerable uncertainty over the measurement of China's openness to trade. A common measure of the degree of openness is the ratio of imports plus exports to gross national product. Both sides of this equation are, however, open to interpretation and debate. As Lardy has pointed out, in China's case the calculations of the ratio are difficult since the conversion of the domestic data into US dollar terms is problematic.[14] In general, official exchange rates tend to understate the purchasing power of the domestic currency and thus to overstate the degree of openness expressed by the ratio. Using the official data, Lardy shows a ratio of over 26 per cent in 1989,[15] and according to the official *Statistical Yearbook 1995*, the ratio had risen to around 45 per cent in 1994.[16] This high ratio suggests a strikingly large degree of openness to trade, especially given the huge size of the Chinese economy. Lardy, however, challenges this assessment and cites competing analyses of China's GNP based on purchasing power parity which indicate a substantially lower ratio of around 10 per cent in 1988. Lardy subsequently updated this method to 1990 and finds a trade to GNP ratio in that year of a little over 9 per cent (using an estimate of real per capita income of about US$1,100 in 1990).[17] The Asia Pacific Economics Group has also done similar calculations to produce an estimate of real per capita income in 1994 of US$1,543 and an exports to GDP ratio in that year of 6.6 per cent, implying a trade ratio of over 13 per cent.[18] In other words, when the figures are adjusted, China begins to look like many other large countries, a little more open than India and a little less than the USA. The economy as a whole is thus not so dependent on trade as might appear on the surface.

Structure of trade – specialisation and concentration

This growth in trade has also been accompanied by major changes in its structure. Tables 7.1 and 7.2 provide data on the composition of China's trade since the reforms.[19] Overall, China has developed some of the typical characteristics of the pattern found in other East Asian economies in earlier phases of growth. It has a reliance on labour-intensive exports and a tendency to be restrictive in its imports.

Table 7.1 illustrates the dramatic changes in the composition of trade. Since the reforms, there has been a large fall in the shares of agricultural and minerals intensive products: in 1980, these two categories accounted for over half of China's exports but by 1994, their share had fallen to 15 per cent. The share of minerals intensive products in exports fell faster than that of agricultural products. In their place were larger volumes of manufactured products, especially labour intensive products. The most important export items are clothing, toys and footwear.

China's exports therefore became highly concentrated within a particular product group, at least in the period up to the mid-1980s. It is

Table 7.1 Composition of exports

Year	Agricultural intensive products %	Capital intensive products %	Labour intensive products %	Minerals intensive products %
1980	25.4	15.1	29.1	26.3
1981	24.6	15.9	31.4	27.6
1982	23.0	15.7	32.0	28.8
1983	23.6	15.4	35.1	25.4
1984	22.6	13.7	37.3	25.7
1985	21.7	12.9	35.5	28.8
1986	22.7	16.0	44.3	15.7
1987	19.3	18.3	47.6	13.6
1988	18.2	22.4	46.6	11.8
1989	15.3	25.1	49.4	9.4
1990	12.4	26.8	50.8	9.4
1991	11.8	27.0	53.1	7.7
1992	10.8	27.2	55.4	5.9
1993	9.5	28.9	56.3	4.8
1994	9.8	31.1	53.7	4.9

Source: UN Trade data, the International Economic Data Bank, the Australian National University

interesting, however, that since then the share in exports of products classified as capital intensive has also increased rapidly. This suggests that the transition out of labour intensive products has already begun, and some analyses suggest that this has started much sooner than in other East Asian economies.[20] This could reflect the observation that 'China is not an integrated economy. Rather it is a set of provincial and regional economies with widely differing resource endowments and comparative advantages and separated by high resistances to trade and factor flows'.[21] The change in the aggregate trade pattern may thus be driven by adjustments in some coastal provinces rather than by the national economy as a whole.

The main changes in the composition of imports have been the fall in the share of agricultural products and the rise in the share of capital intensive products. The latter now account for about two-thirds of total imports. The share of resource sector (agriculture and minerals) products in imports has about halved.

In 1980, China was a net importer of agricultural products and capital intensive products. By 1994, it was back to being a net importer of agricultural products (after a period of net exports, a consequence of the productivity growth associated with the rural reforms), was still a net importer of capital intensive products and had become a net importer of minerals intensive products.[22]

Table 7.2 Composition of imports

Year	*Agricultural intensive products* %	*Capital intensive products* %	*Labour intensive products* %	*Minerals intensive products* %
1980	32.6	51.0	7.8	4.0
1981	35.0	50.2	11.0	2.5
1982	36.1	46.3	11.7	4.8
1983	25.3	57.4	9.5	6.7
1984	17.5	65.7	10.3	5.5
1985	10.8	73.3	9.7	5.1
1986	11.3	71.8	10.3	5.3
1987	15.7	66.9	12.2	3.8
1988	18.3	65.9	10.8	3.5
1989	16.5	63.2	13.1	5.3
1990	16.2	60.7	16.0	5.1
1991	14.7	62.1	15.7	7.5
1992	12.0	64.4	14.4	8.6
1993	8.8	70.1	12.1	7.4
1994	12.3	65.7	13.8	6.4

Source: UN Trade data, the International Economic Data Bank, the Australian National University

Zhang Xiaoguang's assessment of these changes in trade structure is that China has moved much closer to its comparative advantage.[23] The reform has therefore led to a better allocation of resources. Zhang argues, however, that the pattern of export trade has shown a much greater change than the pattern of import trade. He considers that this may be because exporting firms have had relatively greater management autonomy and because foreign investors have played an important role in exports. Ultimately, therefore, he believes that the influence of trade on the patterns of domestic production has been 'limited', despite the fact that trade has grown faster than output. Important barriers to imports remain, and China continues to protect domestic industries and raw material producers with substantial import tariffs, quotas and licences.

In the early 1990s, China's tariff rates were relatively high among APEC members at 37.5 per cent: only Thailand had a similar average rate, with most other APEC members having average tariff rates of less than 20 per cent. The frequency with which China used non-tariff barriers on merchandise trade was also relatively high in that period.[24] These reported tariff rates may, however, overstate the effective rates because of the extent of tariff exemptions. Furthermore, the lack of consistency and transparency in the administration of trade policy is sometimes argued to be more important than the border barriers.[25]

Nevertheless, the adoption of the first Foreign Trade Law in July 1994[26] and the announcement by Jiang Zemin at the Osaka APEC meeting in November 1995 that China would reduce tariffs on a wide range of commodities[27] are indications of the interest in achieving a greater degree of openness. A fall in the tariff rates will also reduce the range of uncertainty associated with the administration of trade policy.

Foreign investment – China's experience unprecedented

Within this growth of trade, an important feature has been the role of foreign invested enterprises. From 1993, China became the second largest recipient of foreign direct investment in the world. It is the single largest developing country host. The stock of foreign investment rose from less than US$1 billion in 1979 to nearly US$96 billion in 1994.[28]

Lardy cites evidence to show that by 1994, foreign funded enterprises accounted for nearly 30 per cent of China's export value.[29] Moreover, most of these exports consisted of products assembled from imported parts and components, and made up nearly half of the value of manufactured goods exports. This clearly shows that the role of foreign investment in changing the structure of China's imports and exports has been very significant. It also underlines the extent to which imports of raw materials and parts contribute to the growth of exports. The significance of this foreign invested sector means that there may be more gains in efficiency to be made as domestic manufacturing comes to play a bigger role in trade.

The importance of this issue was recognised by Zhao Ziyang's coastal strategy put forward in 1988, which aimed to ease controls over the imports of raw materials used for export processing in the coastal regions.[30] The goal was to ease the constraints on export industries caused by the then controls on foreign exchange and domestic raw materials supplies. As Lardy points out, however, the policy was never fully developed.[31]

Dependency or interdependency?

In economic terms, there are two main forces for a protectionist trade policy in China: one is the motivation for protecting particular sectors of the economy from import competition, and the other is a concern about reliance on world markets. The second motivation is our focus in this chapter. It arises from the perception within China of the size of the Chinese economy in world markets and the impacts of China's decisions on world prices. There is the possibility that, in the case of a large country, rapid trade growth will shift the terms of trade against it (by lowering its export prices and raising its import prices). The large country, especially one that is the recipient of a large capital inflow that also drives export growth, could then lose from the terms of trade changes (although still gain overall from the growth in trade).

There is a question, however, of whether these price changes will be sustained in the long term. There may be a short-run price response, but that is expected to lead to longer-run adjustments, through such things as the disappearance from world markets of competing exporters or the emergence of new sources of supply of imports. Part of the concern about 'dependency' is therefore the fear that these longer-run adjustments may not occur. As we illustrate in the discussion below of particular sectoral issues, there is not a lot of evidence to support this perception of how world markets work. The other part of the concern about dependency is that even if there are long-run adjustments to changes in relative prices, there will still be some adjustment required within China, or at least there will be some uncertainty about the extent and timing of the long-run responses. Both involve costs from the Chinese perspective. It is to avoid those costs that Chinese policy makers may prefer to limit the degree of openness of the Chinese economy.

The perception of those costs depends, however, on the responsiveness of the rest of the world to China's trade reform and growth. The key issue in that case is one of 'interdependency' and not 'dependency'. China's choices are not independent of those taken in the rest of the world. According to this argument, rather than concerns about terms of trade changes or reliance on particular sources of supply of raw materials, the response of the rest of the world is the more important dilemma facing a 'big' country. Seen from this perspective, the economic choices are thus also open to strategic considerations of the political pressures that can be brought to bear by outside forces, should dependency become too great. Nevertheless, this is also a two-sided issue. Fluctuations and instability in China's trading behaviour can have powerful negative effects on trading partners, especially those who have a big stake in trade with China.[32]

Shares in world trade

Table 7.3 shows China's shares in world imports by product group. China's shares in total world imports are less than 3 per cent. Its share in world imports of minerals intensive products are about half that. These small numbers for import shares seem unlikely to be the basis of serious concerns about dependency in the way that the term was defined above.

Table 7.3 China's shares in world imports

Year	*Agricultural intensive products* %	*Capital intensive products* %	*Labour intensive products* %	*Minerals intensive products* %	*Total* %
1980	1.8	1.1	0.8	0.1	0.9
1981	1.8	1.0	1.1	0.1	0.8
1982	1.9	0.8	1.0	0.1	0.8
1983	1.5	1.2	0.9	0.2	0.9
1984	1.3	1.7	1.3	0.3	1.2
1985	1.3	2.8	1.8	0.4	1.9
1986	1.2	2.1	1.4	0.5	1.6
1987	1.6	1.8	1.5	0.4	1.5
1988	2.1	2.0	1.6	0.4	1.7
1989	1.8	1.8	1.7	0.5	1.6
1990	1.6	1.5	1.7	0.4	1.3
1991	1.8	1.8	2.0	0.8	1.7
1992	1.8	2.3	2.2	1.3	2.0
1993	1.8	3.4	2.5	1.5	2.8
1994	2.5	3.1	2.9	1.4	2.7

Source: UN Trade data, the International Economic Data Bank, the Australian National University

However, these aggregate data may hide significant issues for particular products which we examine in more detail below.

The more important issue, on the face of it, lies on the export side. Table 7.4 shows China's share of world exports in the same product groups. China's share of world exports of labour intensive products has risen from 3 per cent to 18 per cent. Lardy notes, however, that despite the rising shares of China in some export markets, the prices it received for its exports actually rose between 1980 and 1992.[33]

Pomfret[34] points out that a combination of rapid export growth and the absence of falling prices received for exports could be due to a high elasticity of demand for China's exports, a shift in the demand for exports of those types or the upgrading of exports which kept Chinese products competitive. Pomfret argues that the main contributor, given the composition of China's exports, has been the first of these. He goes on to note that the growth in exports occurred despite the application of tariff and non-tariff barriers to China's exports, such as the Multi-Fibre Arrangement (MFA). He concludes that 'there is little evidence from the past that the aggregate growth in the value of China's manufactured exports has been substantially impeded by protectionism'.[35] Another point is that China's emergence into world markets was also facilitated by

Table 7.4 China's shares in world exports

Year	*Agricultural intensive products* %	*Capital intensive products* %	*Labour intensive products* %	*Minerals intensive products* %	*Total* %
1980	1.5	0.3	3.0	0.8	0.9
1981	1.7	0.4	3.7	1.0	1.1
1982	1.8	0.4	3.8	1.2	1.2
1983	1.9	0.4	4.2	1.2	1.2
1984	2.0	0.4	4.9	1.4	1.4
1985	2.3	0.4	5.2	1.9	1.6
1986	2.5	0.5	6.1	1.6	1.6
1987	2.4	0.6	7.0	1.6	1.8
1988	2.6	0.8	8.1	1.8	2.1
1989	2.6	1.1	9.7	1.5	2.4
1990	2.4	1.2	10.3	1.6	2.6
1991	2.8	1.5	12.8	1.7	3.2
1992	2.9	1.7	14.5	1.6	3.6
1993	3.0	2.1	17.1	1.5	4.2
1994	3.4	2.4	17.9	1.8	4.5

Source: UN Trade data, the International Economic Data Bank, the Australian National University

adjustment by other suppliers to its export markets, particularly the NIEs and Japan. Their exit from the market was related to China's entry.

There is, however, the question of what might have been. Could China's labour intensive exports have been even greater? China, for example, might then have taken longer to switch to capital intensive products. Assessments of the MFA indicate that China will gain substantially, and that its export growth could have been even greater, if the MFA had been removed.[36] The strong growth of exports in spite of the current restrictions, therefore, should not be taken to imply that the restrictions are not significant. Furthermore, those restrictions may also feed into the Chinese perception of the lack of benefit from relying on the world market and therefore limit the extent to which production in the economy shifts towards China's comparative advantage.

SECTORAL ISSUES

With this background on the patterns of development in China's trade and openness established, we now turn to a series of sectoral issues.

Grains[37]

The low level of arable land per capita is the source of China's lack of competitive advantage in agricultural products. It has led to substantial concern within China over food and raw material supplies. The pressure of population on land also presents important environmental challenges.[38] While the official figure of around 100 million hectares for the total amount of arable land is probably an underestimate by as much as 40 per cent,[39] the potential to increase farming land is limited. Furthermore, since the mid-1980s there has been a substantial loss of land to urban development and to non-agricultural production, and this accelerated during the real estate boom of 1992–4.[40] The need to preserve arable land has thus become a major concern for the government, and in recent years major efforts have been made to ensure a minimum grain sown area.[41] The under-reporting of arable land area does mean that actual yields are likely to be lower than official calculations, and that there is some potential to continue to increase output. The realisation of that potential, however, requires further technological investment, and it conflicts with the economic incentives to shift resources out of agriculture towards other sectors.

When this basic situation is related to rapid economic growth which raises incomes and demand, the pressures facing agricultural resources are intensified. During the 1980s, China began to import substantial amounts of grains, fibres, sugar, timber and other agricultural raw materials. Official intervention in domestic production to try to maintain high levels of self-sufficiency was also associated with subsidies to producers and substantial opportunity costs for the resources used. By the mid-1990s, there was growing evidence that some domestic prices for grain were already above world market levels,[42] and border prices began to represent a measure of the costs of self-sufficiency policies. The pressure of demand thus presented significant challenges for the supply of agricultural raw materials.

The deep-seated commitment to self-sufficiency after 1949 and fears of food instability led to considerable caution on the part of the government in its management of change in the grain sector after 1978. As a result, grain has been among the last of the agricultural commodities to be considered for full liberalisation. This wariness was most clearly demonstrated by the stalling of grain system reforms in the mid-1980s. It was not until the economic growth and structural changes of the 1980s had become consolidated that grain market reform began to move ahead again after 1992, and even then the fluctuations in market supplies and the rise in prices have led to a further phase of uncertainty.

Table 7.5 China's role in the world wheat trade

Year	*World wheat prod'n (million tonnes)*	*Wheat prod'n in China (million tonnes)*	*World trade in wheat (million tonnes)*	*China's wheat imports (million tonnes)*	*Apparent wheat consumption in China (million tonnes)*	*China's share of world wheat trade %*	*China's imports as a share of world output %*	*The ratio of imports to wheat cons'n in China %*
1987–8	505	85.8	107	15.4	101.2	14.4	3.7	15.2
1988–9	500	85.4	98	15.9	101.3	16.2	3.8	15.7
1989–90	537	90.8	95	12.9	103.7	13.6	2.9	12.4
1990–1	592	98.2	92	9.4	107.6	10.2	1.9	8.7
1991–2	543	96.0	108	15.9	111.9	14.7	3.6	14.2
1992–3	561	100.5	105	6.7	107.2	6.4	1.5	6.3
1993–4	558	106.4	93	4.5	110.9	4.8	1.0	4.1
1994–5	527	102.0	95	10.2	112.2	10.7	2.4	9.1

Source: Australian Bureau of Agricultural and Resource Economics, *Australian Commodity Statistics 1995* (Canberra: ABARE, 1995)

During the 1980s, there was an increase in the role and volume of grain trade, although the trading position remained deeply influenced by the self-sufficiency goal. In many years China was a net exporter, but it is necessary to disaggregate the trade by different grains in order to get a full picture of developments. During the 1980s, China was a consistent wheat importer and, apart from 1989, a consistent rice exporter. The two-way trade in rice reflected the differences in the quality of domestic production and of imports, and also regional differences in availability. The growth in imports of Thai rice, for example, was in response to a consumer shift towards better quality. Maize shifted to a net export position from 1984, and soybean from a couple of years earlier.

Details of China's position in the world wheat trade are reported in Table 7.5. The import share of consumption has fluctuated since the late 1980s from a high of nearly 16 per cent to a low of just over 4 per cent. Some of the origins in output and trade are discussed below. This discussion illustrates the important impacts on China's trade of shifts in domestic policy. China's share of the world wheat trade has moved in a similar pattern. Its share of world output (net of its own production) has, however, never exceeded 4 per cent in this period.

Table 7.6 reports China's role in the world rice trade. The rice market is relatively 'thin', with only a small trade volume relative to output. China's position has, however, swung from net exporter to net importer in 1993–4, when it also accounted for a large share of world trade. Nevertheless, the importance of its trade in world output (net of its own output) is insignificant, and the role of imports in domestic consumption is also very small.

After the grain market crisis of late 1993, the Chinese government acted to reduce the level of maize and rice exports. It was reported by the China Newsagency on 1 December 1994 that China would immediately cease all rice and maize exports as a means of stabilising domestic prices.[43] Recent trends therefore indicate that the constraints on trade remain important and that trade policy is still subject to the key goals of stability and maximising self-sufficiency.

A number of policy factors shaped these developments in the grain trade. In the early 1980s, the growth in food grain imports was influenced by the deliberate policy of reducing the quota burdens on the peasants. As domestic production grew under the stimulus of the rural reform policies, however, the need for imports declined, and the large harvest of 1984 was taken as a sign that China's long-term shortage in grain supplies had eased. As a result the unified purchase and sales system was abandoned. The impact of this reform and the subsequent changes in marketing and

Table 7.6 China's role in the world rice trade

Year	*World rice prod'n (million tonnes)*	*Rice prod'n in China (million tonnes)*	*World trade in rice (million tonnes)*	*China's rice imports (million tonnes)*	*China's rice exports (million tonnes)*	*Apparent rice cons'n in China (million tonnes)*	*China's (net import) share of world rice trade %*	*China's (net) imports as a share of world output %*	*The ratio of imports to rice cons'n in China %*
1988–9	330	126.8	12	0.06	0.33	126.555	−2.3	−0.1	−0.2
1989–90	343	135.1	12	0.07	0.69	134.455	−5.2	−0.3	−0.5
1990–1	351	142.0	15	0.09	0.93	141.135	−5.6	−0.4	−0.6
1991–2	349	137.9	16	0.11	1.37	136.59	−7.9	−0.6	−0.9
1992–3	352	139.7	16	0.7	1.52	138.83	−5.1	−0.4	−0.6
1993–4	353	133.3	20	2.0	0.1	135.175	9.5	0.9	1.4
1994–5	360	131.9	n.a.	n.a.	n.a.	n.a.	n.a.	n.a.	n.a.

All data in milled terms.
Source: Australian Bureau of Agricultural and Resource Economics, *Australian Commodity Statistics 1995* (Canberra: ABARE, 1995)

pricing, however, soon undermined this optimistic picture.[44] The shift of resources to non-agricultural production and the diversification of production within agriculture led to a stagnation and fluctuation in grain output. The situation thus reflected the underlying resource endowment and economic relationships. The returns to investment in agriculture were limited, and the opportunity costs of the resources used were high. Market forces were encouraging a shift to other types of production. Imports began to rise, and the political pressures to sustain a high degree of self-sufficiency once again came to the fore.

During the late 1980s and early 1990s, the Chinese government therefore adopted a series of policies to restore controls in domestic grain production. These included enforcing contract quotas more rigidly and providing producers with incentives to produce and sell to the state. The greater stability in domestic production that ensued was associated with a high cost of food subsidies in the state budget. The period also saw growing exports of maize and rice. These exports reflected the lack of infrastructure to transport grain between regions in China and the changes in the international market caused by the US pressures to open up the Japanese grain market to imports. Maize and rice exports from northeast China thus became very attractive to the local governments.

Against this background of a more relaxed supply situation and renewed growth in total output, a second round of major reforms to the grain system was attempted after 1992. The remaining levels of state intervention in grain marketing were reduced, and the system was opened to the free market. The ensuing market crisis of late 1993 cut this experiment short. A decline in rice output set off panic buying in major cities and the markets were not able to respond.[45] Although the underlying target of market reform remained in place, the government was forced to reintroduce a series of measures to stabilise production and market supplies. In addition, as noted above, an end to rice and maize exports was declared.

This cycle has led some observers to speculate that China is beginning to follow the path of agricultural development experienced in other Asian economies as growth occurs, and it may be on the brink of shifting from taxing agriculture in order to promote industrial growth towards protecting agriculture through trade controls and subsidies.[46]

The other major development during the 1980s was the increase in domestic grain consumption and the changes in its composition. After many years of grain rationing, the growth in production during the 1980s led to a rise in consumption levels. By the mid-1980s, per capita grain availability was in the region of 400 kg. At the same time, the growth in urban incomes during the 1980s and the changes in the structure of food consumption meant that grain and oil costs had declined to be a smaller proportion of consumer budgets, falling from 24.25 per cent of urban living expenses in 1964 to 8.36 per cent in 1989.[47] Consumers began to shift from grains towards better quality foods and greater variety. Direct consumption of grain fell from 135 kg per head in 1985 to 112 kg in 1992, and the consumption of pork, other meat and fish, and eggs rose. This growth in the indirect demands for grain had major implications for the mix of grains required, and there was a growing emphasis on the role of feed grains.

Against this background, many observers in China and outside argue that it will not be possible for China to maintain full grain self-sufficiency. It is assumed that the combination of the lack of arable land, the growth in population, increases in demand as income grows and changes in the composition of demand will lead to a greater level of dependency on imports.[48] There is thus a variety of scenarios for China's international trade in grain over the next couple of decades. A sample of the assessments is summarised in Table 7.7.

The outlooks differ significantly. Some project rapid growth in consumption, for example Garnaut and Ma, as well as the OECF study. Others are pessimistic about the outlook for production growth: 500 million tonnes is the upper limit in all the projections for the year 2000. Brown forecasts a dramatic decline in output, mainly ascribed to the loss of arable land associated with salinisation and erosion. Projections differ in the outlook for output beyond the year 2000. Some are optimistic about production growth relative to consumption growth, and others are more pessimistic. The differences in these scenarios are reflected in their ratios of imports to consumption. These range from less than 3 per cent for Mei by 2020 to over 20 per cent for the OECF (at 2010) and around 50 per cent in 2030 in the case of Brown. All of them, however, anticipate some level of dependency on imports.

An important issue in this discussion is the mix of grain imports required. In the early 1990s, the bulk of China's grain imports was wheat. But the studies reviewed above suggest a change in the import mix towards feed grain. This switch is associated with the growth in demand for meat, egg and aquatic products. Once again, however, there are large variations in the projections for import mix. The OECF study suggests that the bulk of the imported grain will be feed grain at the end of the projection period. China will maintain its self-sufficiency in rice, remain a net importer of wheat (but the import volume is projected to remain roughly the same at about 15 million tonnes) while maize imports boom. The IFPRI study notes that the rise in meat and other product consumption will raise the

Table 7.7 Projections of China's grain trade

Source	*Date of publn. and period of projection*	*Consumption at end point (B)*	*Production at end point*	*Net imports at end point (A)*	*A/B %*
Garnaut and Ma	*1992/* 1990–2000	Normal growth (6% pa income growth): 547.2 mt in 2000	Upper limit of 500 mt	Normal growth (6% pa income growth): 50 mt in 2000	9.1
		High growth (7.2% pa income growth): 593 mt in 2000		High growth (7.2% pa income growth): 90 mt in 2000	15.2
Brown	*1994/* 1990–2030	No rise in consumption pc: 479 mt in 2030	272 mt in 2030	No rise in consumption pc: 207 mt in 2030	43.0
		Rise in consumption pc and rise in population: 641 mt in 2030		Rise in consumption pc and rise in population: 369 mt in 2030	58.0
Huang, Rozelle and Rosegrant (IFPRI)	*1995/* Early 1990s to 2000, 2010 and 2020	450 mt in 2000 600 mt in 2020	410 mt in 2000 550 mt in 2020	40 mt in 2000 50 mt in 2020	8.3
OECF	*1995/* 1993 to 2000, 2005 and 2010	508 mt in 2000 571 mt in 2005 645 mt in 2010	484 mt in 2000 502 mt in 2005 509 mt in 2010	24 mt in 2000 69 mt in 2005 136 mt in 2010	 12.1 21.0
Mei	*1995/* 1993 to 2000, 2010 and 2020	511 mt in 2000 593 mt in 2010 695 mt in 2020	500 mt in 2000 578 mt in 2010 675 mt in 2020	11 mt in 2000 15 mt in 2010 20 mt in 2020	 2.5 2.9

Key: mt = million tonnes.

Sources: Ross Garnaut and Ma Guonan, *Grain in China* (Canberra: East Asian Analytical Unit, Department of Foreign Affairs and Trade, 1992).

Lester R. Brown, 'Who will feed China?', *World Watch*, September–October 1994, pp. 10–18.

Jikun Huang, Scott Rozelle and Mark Rosegrant, 'China's food economy to the 21st century', paper presented to a seminar at the Chinese Economy Research Unit, University of Adelaide, January 1996 (summarised in Huang, Rozelle and Rosegrant, 'China and the global food situation', IFPRI 2020 Brief 20, May 1995).

The Overseas Economic Cooperation Fund Japan (OECF), 'Prospects for grain supply-demand balance and agricultural development Policy in China', Press Release, 25 September 1995, Beijing.

Mei Fangquan, 'Sustainable food production and food security in China', paper presented to the FAO 1995 World Food Day Symposium, 16 October 1995, Bangkok.

share of feed grain in total consumption from 20 per cent in 1991 to nearly 40 per cent in 2020. In their projections, feed grain demand rises from 76 million tonnes in 1991 to 108 million tonnes in the year 2000 and 232 million tonnes in 2020. However, the study also reports that by 2020 'wheat will still account for most imports'.

Garnaut and Ma discuss the likely change in the mix of grain demand in China in detail. In their high growth scenario, the share of feed grain in total grain consumption rises from 25 per cent in 1990 to 33 per cent in the year 2000 (30 per cent in the lower growth scenario: see their Table 42, p. 98). They note that the mix of grain output is highly sensitive to shifts in relative prices. They expect, however, that the growth in imports will be concentrated in feed grains and to a lesser extent in wheat and barley.

The overall balance of most studies of this kind suggests that China will continue to be dependent on grain imports into the next century. It also seems likely that while a certain level of wheat imports will be maintained, there is a strong potential for feed grain imports to grow. The environmental and resource limits on the growth of domestic agricultural production, combined with the growth in domestic demand as incomes rise, suggest that such an outcome is very likely. To some extent the eventual level may be influenced by the extent to which the shift towards indirect consumption continues. What is more, as one observer not noted for his excessive optimism towards China's agricultural production argues, there is still capacity within China to make up for some of the demand growth, provided better management, pricing, technology and environmental management can be developed.[49]

In theory, increases in imports should be paid for by the expansion of exports of labour intensive manufactures, which is where China's competitive advantage lies. Such an outcome, however, involves assumptions about China's strategic choices. The priority under the plan system was grain self-sufficiency and food security. The cautious path taken in the reform of the grain marketing system underlines that this is still central to policy concerns. While greater trade in food and raw materials has become a feature of the reform period, the debate in China is about the degree of dependency on imports, and there is a profound concern that there should be limits. Given the size of the population, China's government can be expected to be very sensitive to any dangers of such a situation arising and to the strategic implications of greater dependency on the rest of the world for its food. A higher level of self-sufficiency implies directing domestic resources towards grain production that might, if allocated by market forces, have been used more efficiently elsewhere. The opportunity cost is the lost output of other goods, the higher prices paid for domestic output, and a slower overall rate of economic growth. Despite these costs, however, such policies would presumably be adopted well short of the prospect of international food dependency predicted by Lester Brown.

From the point of view of the rest of the world, the potential size of China in the international grain market means that a large growth in demand from China or major fluctuations in China's trade would be difficult to manage. It is therefore in the interests of the world's grain producers to look for ways of lessening China's strategic concerns so that a stable relationship can grow and the effects of fluctuations in domestic production during the transition to a market system are not perceived within China as a threat to national security.

Energy

China's energy and mineral endowment is extensive and the potential for finding further reserves still remains.[50] According to one study, in 1986 it had around 29 per cent of world reserves of coal, 2.6 per cent of oil and 0.8 per cent of natural gas.[51] Nevertheless, the large population means that its mineral and energy resources per capita are below those of other resource rich countries. Furthermore, the distribution and quality of resources do not always match demands. Coal and oil resources, while abundant, are concentrated in the north and northwest. Hydro-electricity resources are in the south and southwest. The bulk of industrial development, however, is along the coastal zone and often distant from the sources of energy raw materials. In addition, there is an imbalance between resource endowment and processing capacity, so that China's own reserves cannot be extracted and processed at a level demanded by its industrial growth.

China also uses much higher levels of energy than most other developing economies. It also relies primarily on coal as its main energy source. This has consistently accounted for over 75 per cent of consumption, with consequent pollution problems.[52] Drysdale and Huang[53] argue that, if the value of China's GDP is adjusted as discussed in respect of trade ratios above, China's energy intensity ratios (energy consumption per dollar of GDP) move closer to those of other countries, but they also note that the intensity ratio for China is still very high compared to other East Asian developing economies. They argue that this implies substantial scope for improving the intensity with which energy is used in the Chinese economy.[54] Their projections shown in Table 7.8 are therefore based on the assumption that the energy intensity in China falls to slightly below the current average for other East Asian developing economies.

Table 7.8 Energy consumption in China, 1990 and 2010

		1990 Amount mt	*Share %*	*China's share in world cons'n %*	*2010 Amount mt*	*Share %*	*China's share in world cons'n %*	*Annual growth %*
China								
Total		682	100	8.5	2,484	100	19.1	6.7
	Oil	113	16.6	3.7	447	18	9.8	7.1
	Solid fuels	498	73	21.8	1,689	68	43.3	6.3
	Gas	12	1.8	0.7	75	3	2.7	9.6
	Electricity	59	8.7	5.7	273	11	15.0	8
World								
Total		8,059	100		12,990	100		2.4
	Oil	3,061	39.4		4,547	35		2
	Solid fuels	2,286	29.4		3,897	30		2.7
	Gas	1,678	21.6		2,728	21		2.5
	Electricity	1,034	13.3		1,818	14		2.9

Source: Table 6 in Peter Drysdale and Yiping Huang, 'Growth, energy and the environment: new challenges for the Asia Pacific Economy', mimeo, Australia-Japan Research Centre, ANU. The projections are based on the IEA's *World Energy Outlook, 1993* but adjusted by the authors for their own projections of the growth in energy consumption in China and East Asia.

Assuming particular growth rates in China (8.5 per cent a year in real terms over the projection period) as well as the above trends in energy intensity yields, the projections indicate:

- the growth in China's share of world energy consumption;
- the shift in the mix of China's energy consumption pattern towards the world average; and
- the high share of solid fuel consumption in China, with more than twice the world average and low shares of oil and gas.

An implication stressed by Drysdale and Huang is that the projections imply the aggravation of environmental pollution problems associated with the growth and the mix of energy consumption.

Overall, during the 1980s and early 1990s, China was a net exporter of energy and maintained a positive energy trade balance.[55] In terms of particular sectors, however, China is expected to become a net importer of crude oil. Its imports by the year 2005 could be over 40 per cent of Chinese consumption, and it would then account for more than half of East Asia's total crude oil imports, the region itself becoming a large net importer by that time.[56] Over this period the share of the Middle East in the region's oil imports is expected to rise to a range of two-thirds to three-quarters.[57] This potential reliance on the world market, particularly on supplies outside East Asia, is likely to lead to considerable efforts in China to reduce oil consumption, including efforts at energy conservation. There are constraints, however, on further substitution into solid fuel consumption. These include the anticipated growth in demand for liquid fuels by the transport sector, and environmental issues, in which case the application in China of 'clean coal technologies' becomes even more valuable.[58]

Coal is the key sector, accounting for over 75 per cent of primary energy use. China is also a net coal exporter. It exported 18 million tonnes of black coal in 1994–5 (about 8 per cent of world thermal coal trade) and its exports are expected to rise to 22 million tonnes by 2000–1 (about 6 per cent of world thermal coal trade).[59] These export volumes are, however, a relatively small share of total production. Policy changes, including the interaction with developments in other energy sectors, can have significant effects on trade volumes. These projections of coal trade also allow for the growth in consumption of coal in the electricity sector in China.

China's energy trade patterns have been distorted by pricing policies in which domestic prices were capped below world prices.[60] The pricing of both coal and oil has been reformed during the 1990s. This change and the removal of trade barriers contributed to the switch in 1993 from net oil exports to net imports. On the other hand, higher coal prices also contributed to increased coal output and increases in coal exports.

This review of the issues in the energy sector highlights a number of points, including:

- the interaction between sub-sectors and the availability of substitutes for items thought to be in short supply and for which prices may be rising;
- the importance of domestic policy and its influence on trade outcomes and the degree of reliance on world markets; and
- the long-run implications of price changes (as illustrated by the scope for energy conservation in China) which must be noted in assessing concerns about dependency, especially those exacerbated by short-run price changes.

CONCLUSION

The above analysis of China's overall trading position and of particular sectors suggests that it would be a mistake to argue that China has a 'dependency problem'. First, the level of the Chinese economy's openness to trade is less than the official figures suggest. A closer analysis of the data indicates that it is what we would expect of such a large economy and that it is similar to other countries that are both large economies and major traders. While China's involvement in world trade has grown at a faster rate than its economic growth, this has brought great benefits to the economy. Certainly the changes in the composition of China's trade have reflected both the structural changes taking place in its economy as a result of growth and reform and the gains in efficiency achieved by shifting towards China's comparative advantage.

Second, the analysis of particular sectors indicates that a problem, if it exists, is not currently related solely to the size of the Chinese economy and its role in world trade. The data even for the commodities that people indicate are likely to be highly sensitive still show small shares for China.

Problems of dependency are thus more likely to be the consequence of perceptions. In the first place, these are related to swings in domestic policy in China and to the feedbacks from the world market inside China. Swings in domestic policy lead to fluctuations in China's production and consumption which, even at low trade shares, can lead to large fluctuations in world trade and prices. These, in turn, can feed back into Chinese prices and create the impression of a problem caused by reliance on the world market. Further changes in policy to counteract that effect can have a second round of feedbacks, which serves to reinforce the original perception. Exporters, meanwhile, are less likely to gear up to supply China in the face of this sort of uncertainty. In that respect, suppliers also fear becoming dependent on a single market, since a large volume but unstable purchaser can bring grave risks.

Chinese policy makers are not, however, solely responsible for their own perceptions. A second factor is the problem of restricted access to world markets for China's exports, the proceeds from which are used to pay China's import bills for these supposedly sensitive products. If the rest of the world moves to limit China's exports, this will not only affect China's growth pattern but also reduce the volume of China's imports. This outcome will be reinforced by policy initiatives in China that reflect perceptions of the unreliability of the export market.

These are the immediate issues. Over the next decade, however, the shares of China's imports in world trade of some products will rise – grain and crude oil for example. There may be some short-run effects both on the growth of China's trade and on China's terms of trade. Given the volume of effort that is being made now to anticipate China's impact on world markets, however, even this seems unlikely, or at least unlikely to create major problems.

Even if there were a short-run impact on prices, the question then is why China cannot rely on the world market for supply in the longer run. Changes in relative prices can induce:

- diversions of product out of other uses (as suggested by China's still low shares of world output even in products in which China accounts for large shares of trade);
- new sources of supply; and
- economising behaviour in China, since some commodities where dependency is an issue are those whose use has been most severely distorted by the wrong pricing signals.

If there is an issue of 'dependency', therefore, we argue here that it is actually one of 'interdependency'. The careful management of China's trade interdependency is a major issue both for China and for the rest of the world. China's size alone means that world markets need to take account of its behaviour in their own interests. All sides thus have a shared benefit in minimising the risks involved. Apart from the strategic political concerns, it is also important for China's trading partners to build a stable trading framework so that the large fluctuations that sudden changes in China's trading position can bring to world markets are evened out. Policies and mechanisms that reduce China's sense of strategic risk and build stable relationships are thus vital for both sides of the trading relationship.

NOTES

1 We are grateful to Larry Krause for his comments on our chapter and to the discussion at the San Diego conference.
2 For a discussion of the notions of 'adapting' and 'learning', see Alastair Iain Johnston, 'Learning versus adaptation: explaining change in Chinese arms control policy in the 1980s and 1990s', *The China Journal,* No. 35, January 1996, pp. 27–62.
3 See Nicholas R. Lardy, *Foreign Trade and Economic Reform in China 1978–1990* (Cambridge: Cambridge University Press, 1992), 'The role of foreign trade and investment in China's economic transformation', *The China Quarterly*, 144, December 1995, pp. 1065–82, and *China in the World Economy* (Washington: Institute for International Economics, 1994) for an overview of foreign trade reform.
4 Lardy, *Foreign Trade* op. cit., p. 1.
5 *Summary of World Broadcasts, Part 3, Asia-Pacific* (SWB), FEW/0425/WG/1, 6 March 1996.
6 Ho Yin-ping, 'Foreign trade and China's growing international presence', in Lo Chin Kin, Suzanne Pepper and Tsui Kai Yuen (eds) *China Review 1995* (Hong Kong: The Chinese University Press, 1995), p. 23.12.
7 Lardy, *Foreign Trade* op. cit., pp. 29–32.
8 SWB, FE/W0425/WG/1, 6 March 1996.
9 See Anne O. Krueger, 'The role of trade in growth and development: theory and lessons from experience', in Ross Garnaut, Enzo Grilli and James Riedel (eds) *Sustaining Export-Oriented Development: Ideas from East Asia* (Cambridge: Cambridge University Press, 1995), pp. 1–30 and Lardy, *Foreign Trade* op. cit., chapter 1.
10 For a discussion of this issue see Kym Anderson, *Changing Comparative Advantages in China: Effects on Food, Feed and Fibre Markets* (Paris: OECD Development Studies Centre, 1990).
11 Li Peng, 'Government Work Report on the Draft Ninth Five-year Plan', 5 March 1996, SWB, talks of the 'pressure of hegemonism and power politics', FE/2553/S1/3–4.
12 Ibid., SWB, FE/2553/S1/10–11.
13 In an earlier version of this chapter we also examined the fibres and the iron ore and steel markets. See Christopher Findlay and Andrew Watson, 'Economic growth and trade dependency in China', *Chinese Economy Research Unit Working Papers*, No. 5, 1996, University of Adelaide. In the case of these commodities we found that China's size and level of demand are unlikely to cause problems for world markets.
14 Lardy, *Foreign Trade* op. cit., pp. 150–5.
15 Ibid., p. 151.
16 GDP was 4,500.6 billion yuan and the two-way trade value of US$236.73 billion converted at the average exchange rate of 8.6187. State Statistical Bureau, *Zhongguo Tongji Nianjian 1995* [China Statistical Yearbook, 1995] (Beijing: Zhongguo Tongji Chubanshe, 1995), pp. 21, p. 25 and 537.
17 Lardy, *China in the World Economy* op. cit., p. 18.
18 Asia Pacific Economics Group, *Asia Pacific Profiles, 1995* (Canberra: APEG,

1995), Tables 4.2 and 4.4. The exports to GDP ratio in India in 1994 was 10.5 per cent.

19 There is a residual unclassified category of exports so the shares in these tables do not total 100 per cent.

20 See, for example, Australia-Japan Research Centre, *China and East Asia Trade Policy* (Canberra: AJRC, 1995).

21 Ibid., p. 14.

22 Zhang Xiaoguang, 'How successful is China's trade reform: an empirical assessment', Economics Division Working Papers, 4/94 (Canberra: ANU) comments on the use of shares of product groups in exports and imports for this sort of analysis. He presents a more complex measure which takes account of competing imports and shares in world trade. Here we discuss these components separately.

23 Ibid.

24 These data are reported in Pacific Economic Cooperation Council, *Survey of Impediments to Trade and Investment in the APEC Region*, a report by the PECC for APEC (Singapore: PECC, 1995).

25 Australia-Japan Research Centre op. cit.

26 Ho Yin-ping, 'Foreign trade and China's growing international presence', op. cit, pp. 23–41.

27 *China Daily*, 20 November 1995, p. 1.

28 These values of FDI inflows could be overstated as a consequence of 'round-tripping' through Hong Kong. See Chen Chunlai, 'Foreign direct investment in China' (University of Adelaide, *Chinese Economy Research Unit Working Paper*, No. 3, 1996) for a more detailed discussion.

29 Nicholas Lardy, 'The role of foreign trade and investment in China's economic transformation', op. cit., pp. 1074–5.

30 'Zhao Ziyang cong tan yanhai diqu jingji fazhan zhanlüe [Zhao Ziyang discusses the coastal areas economic development strategy], Renmin Ribao [People's Daily], 23 January 1988. See also SWB, FE/00060/C/1–5, 28 January 1988.

31 Lardy, *Foreign Trade* op. cit., pp. 132–6.

32 Australia's experience of the fluctuations in China's wool trade is a striking example of this need. See Australia-Japan Research Centre, *China's Wool Market: Trade and Investment Issues* (Canberra: ANU, 1995).

33 Lardy, *China in the World Economy* op. cit., Table 2.3, p. 41.

34 Richard Pomfret, *China's Trade Miracle*, Seminar Paper No. 96–03, Centre for International Economics Studies, University of Adelaide, February 1996, pp. 13–14.

35 Ibid., p. 14.

36 Australia-Japan Research Centre, *China and East Asia Trade Policy* op. cit., Yang Yongzheng, 'China's textile and clothing exports: challenges in the post-MFA period' (National Centre for Development Studies, mimeo, November 1995) reports that the major part of the expected gain from the Uruguay Round outcome for China (assuming China is not discriminated against as a consquence of its non-membership of the WTO) comes from the MFA reform.

37 The following discussion draws on Andrew Watson and Christopher Findlay, 'Food and profit: the political economy of grain market reform in China', paper presented to the conference on Grain Market Reform and its Implications,

East-West Centre, University of Hawaii, 16–19 September 1995 and Christopher Findlay and Andrew Watson, 'Grain market reform in China: implications for the grain trade mix', mimeo, Chinese Economy Research Unit, University of Adelaide, March 1996.

38 Richard Louis Edmonds, *Patterns of China's Lost Harmony: A Survey of the Country's Environmental Degradation and Protection* (London: Routledge, 1994).

39 Frederick W. Crook, 'Under-reporting of China's cultivated land area: implications for world agricultural trade', *China: Situation and Outlook Series,* United States Department of Agriculture, Economic Research Service, RS-93–4, July 1993, 33–9.

40 Li Ruihuan, 'Guanyu nong-yong tudi de jige wenti' [On some problems of agricultural land], *Renmin Ribao* [People's Daily], 2 July 1994, p. 1, and *Summary of World Broadcasts, Part 3, The Far East* (SWB), FE/2236/S1/3–4, 24 February 1995.

41 Peng Jiahua, 'Wo guo liangshi bozhong mianji di yu jingjiexian' [China's grain sown area is below the danger line], *Jingji Xiaoxi Bao* [Economic Reporter], 19 March 1995, p. 4.

42 Christopher Findlay and Cheng Enjiang, 'Trade reforms and integration of China's domestic and international grain markets since the middle 1980s – the case of wheat and maize', paper presented to the conference on Grain Market Reform and its Implications, East-West Centre, University of Hawaii, 16–19 September 1995.

43 SWB, FE/2169/S1/6, 3 December 1994. These swings in China's net trade positions can have substantial effects on world markets at times when China's share is large.

44 See, for example, the discussion in Guo Shutian (ed.) *Duanque yu Duice: Zhongguo Liangshi Wenti Yanjiu* [Shortage and countermeasures: research into grain issues in China] (Beijing: Zhongguo Renmin Daxue Chubanshe, 1988).

45 For a full discussion of the issues involved see Luo Yousheng and Huang Yanxin, '1993 nian Zhongguo liangshi shichang bodong de yuanyin yu qishi' [The causes of and lessons from the fluctuations in China's grain market in 1993], *Nongcun Jingji Wengao* [Papers on the Rural Economy], No. 5, 1994, pp. 7–15; Chen Xiwen, 'Dangqian Zhongguo de liangshi gongqiu yu jiage wenti' [Current issues in grain supply, demand and prices in China], *Zhongguo Nongcun Jingji,* [China's Rural Economy], No. 1, 1995, pp. 3–8; Wen Jiafang, '1993 nian liangjia shangzhang yinfa de sikao' [Considerations brought about by the 1993 rise in grain prices], *Jiage Lilun yu Shijian* [*Price Theory and Practice*], No. 3, 1994, pp. 14–18; and Zhang Shusen and Sun Wenbo, 'Liangjia fengbo ji qi qishi' [The grain price turmoil and its lessons], *Zhongguo Wujia* [China Prices], No. 4, 1994, pp. 19–21.

46 Ross Garnaut, Cai Fang and Huang Yiping, 'A turning point in China's agricultural development', paper presented to the conference on Grain Market Reform in China and its Implications, East-West Centre, University of Hawaii, 16–19 September 1995.

47 'Quarterly chronicle and documentation', *The China Quarterly,* No. 127, September 1991, p. 663.

48 The Chinese Academy of Sciences Research Team into the National Situation, for example, estimated a shortfall of between 177 and 202 million tonnes by

the year 2000. *Shengcun yu Fazhan* [Survival and Development] (Beijing: Kexue Chubanshe, 1989), pp. 39–50. The estimate was based on a high annual requirement for per capita supply of 500 kg.

49 Vaclav Smil, 'Who will feed China?', *The China Quarterly*, No. 143, September 1995, pp. 801–13.

50 See James P. Dorian, *Minerals, Energy and Economic Development in China* (Oxford: Clarendon Press, 1994), especially chapter 4, pp. 91–106; Yan Changle (ed.) *Zhongguo Nengyuan Fazhan Baogao* [China's Energy Development Report] (Beijing: Jingji Guanli Chubanshe, 1994); and Tatsu Kambara, 'The energy situation in China', *The China Quarterly*, 131, September 1992, pp. 608–36.

51 Peng Zhaoyang, 'Challenges to China's energy market reforms', CERU Working Paper (University of Adelaide, 1996).

52 Yan Changle op. cit., pp. 127–8.

53 Peter Drysdale and Yiping Huang, 'Growth, energy and the environment: new challenges for the Asia Pacific Economy', mimeo, Australia-Japan Research Centre, ANU.

54 See Binsheng Li, James Dorian and Kirk Smith, 'China's energy conservation potential: a preliminary sector-by-sector assessment', East-West Centre Working Papers, Energy and Minerals Series, No. 13, June 1995 (Hawaii: East-West Centre) for a more detailed assessment of the scope for energy conservation in China.

55 Dorian op. cit., p. 145.

56 For more detail of the crude oil outlook for China and the rest of East Asia, see Michael Baugh, 'Factors affecting crude oil production in South East Asia', *Minerals and Energy*, Vol. 3 of the proceedings of the National Agricultural and Resources Outlook Conference (Canberra: ABARE, February 1996).

57 Fereidun Fesharaki, Allen Clark and Duangjai Intarapravich, 'Energy outlook to 2010: Asia-Pacific demand, supply and climate change implications', *Asia Pacific Issues*, No. 19, April 1995 (Hawaii: East-West Centre).

58 See Peng Zhaoyang, 'Challenges to China's Energy Market Reforms', CERU Working Paper (University of Adelaide, forthcoming).

59 This projection is reported in C. Millstead, R. Stuart and A. Kicic, 'Outlook for world seaborne steaming coal trade', *Minerals and Energy*, Vol. 3 of the proceedings of the National Agricultural and Resources Outlook Conference, (Canberra: ABARE, February 1996). They also note that China's national coal trading corporation wants to export about 50 million tonnes by that time.

60 See Peng op. cit.

8 China's role in the WTO and APEC

Stuart Harris

China applied to rejoin the General Agreement on Tariffs and Trade (GATT) in 1986 and negotiations for entry into the successor World Trade Organisation (WTO) are still proceeding.[1] It has participated in regional economic cooperation processes for about the same period. Our interest in China's approach to the WTO and to the Asia Pacific Economic Cooperation forum (APEC) is, in part, in China's interactions with those organisations: its motivations and its approach. We are also interested in how China's participation does or would impinge on the existing members of these organisations, and on the global trading system that those organisations represent. Moreover, the institutions themselves also have interests that are affected.

In assessing what role China might play in these institutions, we need to answer some broader questions: about China's approach to international cooperation in general; and about the extent to which, in its acceptance of the benefits of international cooperation and of economic interdependence, it is willing to meet the obligations and commitments implied in membership of such organisations, including the constraints on domestic policy autonomy. A particular interest is, therefore, how far there has been a learning process (cognitive or adaptive) on the part of Chinese individuals, organisations or the Chinese governing system following China's involvement with these organisations, not only with respect to participation in the international system but also in terms of domestic social and political development.

BACKGROUND

China, then the Nationalist Government, was one of the twenty-three original signatories of the GATT, but the Nationalists withdrew from the GATT in 1950 following their exodus to Taiwan. When, in 1980, China (now the PRC) resumed its seat on the UN's Interim Commission for the International Trade Organisation, which appointed the Director-General of the GATT, this was taken to be an indication of an interest by China in the GATT.[2] In 1981, it started to observe GATT meetings dealing with the renewal of the Multi-Fibre Arrangement (MFA) and became a member of that Arrangement in January 1984. In November 1982, it had started to observe ministerial level GATT meetings, and in December 1984 it became a permanent observer at meetings of the GATT Council and subordinate bodies. In July 1986, China formally applied to resume its status as a contracting party to the GATT. A Working Party was set up in 1987 to consider the terms of China's entry. Negotiations have been proceeding since then on the conditions of China's admission to, now, the WTO. China would also be pressed to join the linked plurilateral agreements, such as the codes on subsidies, antidumping, standards and especially government procurement.

China is already a member of APEC, but in looking at China's participation in that body we need to consider its participation in Pacific economic cooperation as a whole, starting with the Pacific Economic Cooperation Council (PECC), since this was the forerunner, in many respects, of APEC. Discussions about PECC membership had taken place with China on and off over the years following PECC's establishment in 1980. Despite delays involved in working out the respective nomenclatures of Taiwanese participation, China accepted an invitation to join PECC in September 1986, and it joined APEC in 1991.

THE PERSPECTIVE OF CHINA

From the perspective of any country there is usually a mix of reasons for joining an international organisation, based on the presumed benefits of membership. The benefits can be political – such as international status and credibility and national legitimacy, and benefits to particular interest groups – or non-political – such as participation in decision-making processes, the receipt of specific economic benefits, information exchanges or assimilation of technical knowledge and expertise. There are also costs, however, usually related to the commitments and obligations that have to be undertaken, often involving some sacrifice of autonomy over the policy areas central to the organisation's existence.

In China's case, the balance among the various motivations and perceptions has changed over time. While Cold War politics had kept China out of many international institutions from 1949 to 1971, for much of the postwar period the PRC's perspective on the Bretton Woods institutions was that they were instruments of capitalist exploitation. From 1971 onwards, when China resumed its seat in the United Nations, it has sought to resume its position in other parts of the international system, and is now a member of most UN and related organisations. It has been argued that China has entered these organisations largely as a way of countering Taiwan's efforts to extend its diplomatic status internationally.[3] Although this may have been one of several causal factors with respect to the United Nations and related political organisations, a different pattern emerged in the economic-related institutions. Membership competition with Taiwan was not initially a motivation.

In the case of the GATT, competition between the PRC and Taiwan ultimately became important following the 1990 Taiwanese bid for membership, even though Taiwan's bid was made as an autonomous customs territory. This it did in the expectation that its application would not be controversial, especially as Hong Kong had been admitted to the GATT on the same basis in 1986 without objection from China. China has not opposed the Taiwanese membership as such but argued that Taiwan should not become a participant ahead of China. The issue is at the present quiescent. The US and Europe have sought a compromise that would let both China and Taiwan enter together, but the US Congress may also want to push the issue as a further political aspect of the decision.[4] This is also likely to be a point of pressure by Taiwan since the election of President Lee.[5]

When China first applied to rejoin the GATT, it was still at an early stage in the opening up of its economy after a long period of autarky. The technical learning process was seen as important; because of the strategic situation, relations with the US were good; Tiananmen Square had not happened; and the Taiwan Strait situation was more stable. At the same time, the technical aspects of the GATT were less well known to Chinese leaders and officials, and the WTO had not then come into being. Nevertheless, China's decision could be seen as a logical outgrowth of its growing involvement in the world economic system.[6]

Tiananmen Square provided a major set-back to the negotiations for entry and in shaping external attitudes towards China that impinged on them. To a degree, the reassertion of China's interest in the GATT in 1992–3 was a response to recovery from 1989 and to the movement towards establishment of the WTO (eventually established in January 1995), which China hoped, unavailingly as it happened, to join as a founding member. However dominant the economic motivations, political motives behind China's participation may have been a factor, and status an element from the start. Political factors have grown in importance and taken on a different complexion in recent years because of the politicisation of the approach to China's entry, notably by a number of US politicians. China's international status is an important motivating factor for China's leaders and has probably become more so with the establishment of the WTO, especially as the US–China relationship has soured. This has brought back China's national sentiment of being unjustly denied its rightful place in the international system for so long by those more powerful, and its deep sense of historic grievance and ideological vulnerability.

Samuel Kim notes that the UN is a means by which China 'dramatises its national role for domestic and international audiences'.[7] The WTO lends itself less easily to this purpose because, fundamentally, it is a technical treaty involving specific obligations as well as benefits. To a degree, as a largely technical arrangement, the exercise of economic interdependence without the overriding concern of political obligations should make it easier for China to participate, and to use it to establish its economic reputation and status. Nevertheless, there is little doubt that China has come to see prospective membership of the GATT, and more recently the WTO, as consistent with the full acceptance of its part in the international economy and as consistent with what it regards as its new-found international standing.

In addition to such political benefits from WTO membership, there are material benefits that countries gain from membership in exchange for accepting certain obligations. Chinese officials set out some time ago nine such benefits that they calculated they would receive from resuming entry, then, to the GATT.[8] In summary, these were: to contain international protectionism; to expand Chinese markets; to gain for China non-discriminatory access to markets, including unconditional MFN treatment; to gain treatment that developing countries get, such as preferential trade arrangements; to improve China's negotiating capability by having access to multilateral dispute settlement procedures; to encourage Chinese industry to become more competitive internationally; to increase the transparency of China's economy; to increase confidence among China's trade, investment and technology providing partners; and to safeguard China's position in prospective negotiations on new areas such as trade in services, investment and intellectual property rights.

Three overriding reasons can be discerned from this list.[9] First, among the specific national benefits that accrue to WTO members in general is the assurance of non-discriminatory tariff treatment in each other's countries. Since close to 90 per cent of China's trade is with WTO countries, as a member of the WTO, China would be less dependent upon more than ninety bilateral trade treaties it has to manage with trading partners. It would hope to be assured that MFN status would be unconditionally applied to it by all GATT members and in particular that WTO membership would overcome the annual review by the US administration of China's MFN treatment which not only creates great uncertainty but is damaging to China's pride. This has become increasingly important in some respects since the MFN issue has gone up the US political agenda, but, for that reason, more difficult of achievement in the light of constraints of the Jackson-Vanik amendment on the US administration's freedom.

Second, China would have hoped that GATT membership would strengthen its case for access to the preferential arrangements that countries give to developing countries. In particular, it hoped initially to gain from the US the GSP treatment that it receives from many other countries owing to its developing country status. GSP status does not itself flow from WTO membership and, in any case, this aspect has undoubtedly declined significantly in China's concerns today for several reasons, including the diminished benefits from preferential entry following the tariff reduction results of the Uruguay Round.

Third, it would hope to avoid general protectionist measures that might be used to limit China's exports. Membership of the WTO would enable China to participate in the international discussions affecting trade, including its own trade relationships. More generally, China would belong to a formal organisation that coordinates international economic policies and activities of member states and provides rules, procedures and protection against unfair trade practices and discrimination and provides procedures for resolution of other trade disputes. China's experience in the MFA led to their general position being that, despite their substantial bilateral bargaining strength, they prefer the relative predictability of multilateral processes to the somewhat greater uncertainty of bilateral procedures.[10]

As well as these three major interests, for the reformers in China the WTO has been seen as important in order to move the process of domestic economic reform further. WTO membership would, it was judged, strengthen the position of reformers in China, legitimise and promote economic reform and assist in China's management of the reform process and of deregulation.

In the context of regional economic cooperation, for China's membership of PECC, the forerunner and complement of APEC, China's non-ideological attitude to the organisation was important. Unlike the Soviets, China had not voiced a strong anti-PECC position prior to 1986, although the Chinese leadership had viewed the PECC process as primarily a Japan-inspired effort to promote Japanese economic prosperity, national security and political influence. Concern was also expressed about possible Japanese and American domination of the evolving institutional structures.

Nevertheless, in the early 1980s, and particularly after the visit to China of Australian Prime Minister Hawke and Premier Zhao's endorsement of Pacific economic cooperation in 1984,[11] attitudes shifted to where Chinese officials expected, eventually, to participate in the PECC process.[12] China no longer appeared apprehensive about joining a group composed of representatives from industrialised and developed countries, accepting that economic benefits could flow to developing countries in the form of investment, technology, training and market access.[13] It observed the need, as with other countries, to 'seek cooperation to remedy its weakness in order to win respect in the global economy'.[14] More recently, it has seen APEC additionally as a means of pursuing its WTO accession objectives, and especially to put pressure on the US with respect to non-discrimination (MFN). It has not pushed these aspects so strongly as to be disruptive of APEC consensus seeking, however, nor have they been its only objective in APEC.

A further benefit seen by many Chinese analysts from regional economic cooperation is that it will enhance prospects for multilateral security cooperation, since with good economic relations, 'multilateral relations will develop naturally and there will be no conflicts or war'.[15]

COMMITMENTS AND OBLIGATIONS

When China applied for GATT membership, the requirements China had to face were to liberalise its trade policies by reducing tariffs and non-tariff barriers, decentralise trade decisions, phase out import licensing and limit import substitution. China needed to end its own trade discriminating practices by eliminating export subsidies and dumping, and expanding market access by eliminating restrictive and non-competitive processes. It would have to stop treating important parts of its trading system as secret and begin to make fully transparent its trade policies, rules and regulations, its production and trade target levels, its pricing practices, its state foreign trade organisations' practices and operating rules, its foreign trade plan and priorities, and a broad variety of trade data and statistics. It would also have to restructure its two-tiered renmimbi exchange rate (which subsidises exports), loosen accessibility to foreign exchange and revise the Special Economic Zones (SEZs) to ensure a unified national trade regime.

In the bid for WTO membership, China has been adjusting its domestic trading system to meet WTO requirements, starting with the 1985 revision of its customs tariff and regulations. China has since then been progressively lowering its tariffs to meet a variety of international pressures, but notably these of the WTO, as well as doing so for its own benefit. Its trade law changes in May 1994 reflected a marked step forward in ensuring trade transparency and uniformity in a market-based trade policy. China's 1994 financial reforms associated with the unification of the two-tiered exchange rate also largely achieved the convertibility for trade transactions required by the WTO. Bilateral pressures, not only from the US, have been important in these changes. Responses to such bilateral pressures, such as the US market access agreement, were often directly or implicitly foreshadowing the requirements for forthcoming WTO negotiations. Regional influence has similarly been important, notably through PECC/APEC.

Problems with the existing Chinese trade system, particularly the lack of transparency, were acknowledged by some Chinese specialists.[16] Many Chinese administrators saw benefit in the pressure on China to liberalise its foreign exchange regime, eventually to full convertibility (more from the US than from the WTO or the IMF, since the WTO does not require full convertibility but only convertibility for trade activities). These reforms have already put pressure on China to liberalise in other areas important in terms of WTO accession, especially the service sector (including transport and banking) and state enterprise reform, and this is proceeding, if slowly, despite the problems that it requires China to face and the costs it must thereby incur. Accession to the WTO, rather than to the GATT, has added to the requirements China has to meet, including on agriculture (notably questions of market access, domestic support and export subsidies), other services and intellectual property.

The question of what constitutes costs is, of course, ambiguous. In the economic field what are costs to some Chinese will be benefits to others or to the economy as a whole. For example, under the pressure of the WTO negotiation process, the SEZs have been losing some of their competitive benefits. For the Zones, this is a cost; for the economy as a whole, while acknowledging the short-term learning gains from the Zones, it is probably a significant benefit.

Nevertheless, the commitments and obligations China must accept involve substantial political and short-term economic costs, in terms of the necessary domestic adjustments and in overcoming domestic opposition. In this sense, accession to the WTO is different to its participation in other international organisations.

China has sought to emphasise its developing country status as a means of enabling it to avoid many of the more onerous aspects of membership (e.g. through sustained infant industry protection, balance of payments motivated import restrictions and government development subsidies). This is a contentious issue to outside observers: on the one hand, China is now among the top ten trading nations; yet, on the other, it is the only one that is a developing country (if Hong Kong is excluded).[17] China's size and economic importance do make it a 'one off' case, but in any event, such issues are normally tackled on an issue-by-issue basis on their specific merits.[18] Whatever concessions might be negotiated to reflect its developing country status, its overall control and flexibility in managing its economy and foreign trade regime would still be diminished, and there would be significant costs for certain sectors of the economy.

The benefits for China from the processes associated with involvement in regional economic cooperation and accession to the WTO have already been significant. It has achieved greater competitiveness in many of its industries, as its export performance shows. Its financial and trade reforms have encouraged lenders – public and private – and investors, and have increased investor and lender confidence. They have also encouraged among Chinese elites a deeper understanding of the market processes that have been largely responsible for the rapid growth rates of the national economy. In that process, China has been able to draw upon valuable foreign professional economic expertise to analyse the strengths and weaknesses of its economy, draft economic blueprints and train substantial numbers of officials.

Not everyone in China has seen it all this way. Many in China still oppose the reforms for ideological reasons; others see major costs in the dependence they imply on a hostile international community; others are concerned at the massive social costs involved in dismantling the welfare support from state enterprises. Even among those accepting the need to open up the economy there have been concerns. Some Chinese interests saw the pressure to free the exchange rate as moving too fast and therefore as a costly move, as do some external commentators.[19] For many Chinese officials, particularly those in the engineering and electronics industries, foreign competition and the liberalisation of the economy that has already taken place are worrying. 'They view Chinese entry to GATT as a "disaster (that) will soon befall them".'[20] To overcome the political opposition that these various objections generate, it will be increasingly important to relate the benefits from the continuing liberalisation of the economy to more reliable access to the global market which would be delivered through WTO accession.[21] That argument will become stronger in the future as the reform pressures facing China, particularly state enterprise reform, become even more complex and more politically contentious than those already undertaken.

China's membership of APEC is consistent with its opening up to participation in the international economy but it is also consistent with its aspirations for a greater regional role. Again, it strengthens the position of economic reformers within China as part of the price it has to pay both for participation and for its gains from the reforms undertaken by other countries. Although it is towards the more conservative end of the spectrum of member economies, wanting to move slowly, voluntarily and flexibly, it has supported APEC moves on trade and investment liberalisation. China has come increasingly to link its participation in APEC with its WTO accession request, both because it participated in the Uruguay Round negotiations and, although not a binding commitment, signed up to the Uruguay Round outcome, and because of the pressures for trade reform now coming from APEC. This has become a matter of some comment by Chinese officials. For example, after the Osaka APEC meeting a senior Chinese official said that whether a WTO member or not, China would 'continue to take a constructive attitude towards participation in economic cooperation in the region', but in the absence of WTO membership it would be at its own pace and within its own timetable.[22] At this stage, these two are not greatly divergent, but they could become so in the future.

PECC/APEC commitments have been less specific than for the WTO but they have generally required constructive and cooperative participation in those institutions' activities, and this has been the Chinese approach. In response to the requirements of the APEC commitments, the Chinese have been careful to act constructively, as their actions at the Bogor and Osaka meetings in 1994 and 1995 indicate. China was part of the 1994 Bogor consensus committing APEC members to the goal of free and open trade in the Asia-Pacific region by the year 2010 or, for developing economies, 2020. The Osaka meeting put in place a plan of action to achieve that goal.

Although China was among a number of economies that wanted to exclude agriculture from the commitment, it showed itself willing to work towards the APEC compromise. China supported the Osaka Action Agenda, in spite of its concerns over the principles of comprehensiveness, comparability and non-discrimination (essentially the US MFN issue). Its downpayment was one of the more impressive tabled at Osaka and, although that represented a downpayment of part of the WTO tariff cut accession offer, if the programme is implemented the tariff cuts will be substantial; it also reflected added reforms in other areas including financial, foreign investment and trading regulations.

China has increasingly stressed in APEC its developing country status, as in the timing of its commitment under the Bogor consensus and in its stress on flexibility. In part this is to bolster its objective to accede to the WTO with developing country concessions, or at least to improve its bargaining position when the final accession arrangements are agreed upon.[23]

PERSPECTIVE OF OTHER TRADING NATIONS

Among the other members of both the global and the regional organisations, there is a strong interest in principle in China's participation. This was in the belief that it would subject China, already a large but a rapidly growing player in global markets, and deeply integrated in the global economy, to the rules of the WTO, with the associated benefits of lower tariffs, increased transparency and greater predictability of China's regulatory regime. Moreover, it is in the interests of the trading world that China not only be locked into the commitment it has made to reform, but also that it do so having access to the benefits of the system that provides it with a more confident basis in its dealings with other nations and would therefore underpin its reform process. China's reforms have already made a substantial contribution to world trade growth; not only have Chinese imports nearly doubled by 1992 as a result of the reform process, but estimates suggest that they would grow more rapidly with WTO accession.[24]

Japan has been more sensitive than most to not excluding China from the international community and has shown a particular interest in China's membership of the WTO for this reason and because of its large and growing investment stake in China's economy. Hence the special interest it has shown in investment-related trade issues in the accession negotiations. At the same time, it is cautious in its approach to the negotiated outcome. While, in its response to China's seeking Japanese assistance in the negotiations, it has sought to be helpful, it is still careful to ensure that the balance finally reached is compatible both with the international system and with Japanese interests.

The general support for China's accession is not unqualified since it offers potential problems for the major trading nations. For the US, but less so for the Europeans, China is viewed as both a non-market economy and an East Asian producer of low-cost competitive products. The concern about the continued central planning of parts of the Chinese economy poses problems for some countries. At the same time, some countries, notably the United States, know that once China accedes to the WTO they will be unable to exert the same degree of unilateral economic pressure on China as they currently can.[25] Some developing countries, including India, were also concerned in the initial years following China's application about its prospective competition as a member of the WTO, but this concern seems to have diminished.

Nevertheless, given the importance of China's future trade prospects, and the credibility of the liberal international trading system, the need for China to comply fully with WTO disciplines is a matter of urgency if the Organisation is to continue to be an effective basis of international trade. To do this, however, China has to be given appropriate WTO entitlements, and this some trading nations are reluctant to do. A balance also needs to be struck between what is expected of China, consistent with undertakings by other WTO members of similar trade importance and development level, and what targets might be set for the future, consistent with Chinese aims in developing its economy on market principles and its administrative capacity to achieve those targets. Just where that balance comes is hard to determine, and precedents elsewhere, such as for Eastern European countries, are little help given China's present and potential size.

Judgements of this kind are more difficult to make now that the WTO has become a major political issue for the US in two ways: the trade policy conflict with China and the broader policy conflict between the US Congress and China. In respect of the first, Mickey Kantor considered China's WTO accession as a bargaining tool in enforcing US trade policy. At one stage, he described WTO accession as a 'tool' at his disposal.[26] The second is unlikely to be helped by the US Congress's interpretation of events surrounding the Taiwanese presidential election. A particularistic approach seems also to be illustrated by the desire to have China involved in bodies like the WTO, while 'rejecting demands for special concessions'[27] – which would of course make China almost unique among countries in or acceding to the GATT or WTO over the years.

Regionally there was clear desire among most PECC members to have China, a significant regional economic actor, become a member of PECC, to engage China in regional economic diplomacy, and to note that, although Indonesia blocked entry for a while on other grounds (continuing antipathy towards China), PECC was not just for market economies. There has been an interest in subjecting China, through the PECC/APEC process, more directly to the views of other regional members on trade and investment (and more general economic) questions. Moreover, PECC/APEC processes now represent the only area where China, Taiwan and Hong Kong participate together and this will become increasingly important in the years ahead.

Similarly, the original members, again with Indonesia initially the coolest, sought China's participation in APEC for much the same reasons as applied for the WTO with the addition of specific regional benefits. For example, in the case of APEC, China's entry provided a forum for high-level Sino-US dialogue.[28] A positive political aspect is the Leaders' meetings which bring together regional heads of government once a year. This has considerable potential in several respects but in particular it has brought the Chinese leader into more regular contact with other regional leaders, including the US President. The inclusion of China, however, has its critics such as, characteristically, the *Asian Wall Street Journal*.[29]

PERSPECTIVE OF THE ORGANISATIONS

It was evident that the GATT Secretariat was keen to see China enter the GATT. Several missions went from Geneva in the 1980s, including two visits by Director-General Dunkel, to explain the benefits of GATT membership to the Chinese leadership. One reason for wanting China's membership of the WTO, in its most expansive form, is that its participation would legitimise the WTO's claim to be managing a truly global economic order, with Russia the only major outsider. For an organisation looking to maintain and advance a liberal trading system and to ensure the widest possible coverage of the rules and procedures of the WTO, participation by China would be a great step forward.

China's application also raised the credibility of the GATT in the eyes of other developing countries. In particular, it further undermined the New International Economic Order (NIEO), and virtually put paid to any remaining hopes of UNCTAD as an alternative forum to the GATT for negotiations on international trade matters.[30]

For APEC, and for PECC, there is no comparable institutional structure to support their function as regional cooperation institutions. For those concerned in an organising role, however, China's participation was critical to its ability to be effective in expanding regional cooperation. Considerable effort was therefore made to involve China and to resolve the nomenclature problems relating to Taiwan.

THE WTO ACCESSION PROCESS TO DATE

There are three phases of the accession process that China has to pass through: examination of its foreign trade regime; drafting a protocol outlining its rights and obligations within the WTO; and negotiations over its specific tariff concessions. Considerable progress had been made on the first under the GATT Working Party, and a start made on the drafting of the protocol by the time of Tiananmen Square, and it was some little time before the hiatus was surmounted. Considerable progress was then made but it was only in 1993 that the hard bargaining began over, in particular: a unitary national trade policy in which imports receive the same treatment at every entry point; full transparency for all regulations, requirements and quotas; elimination of non-tariff barriers; a commitment to move to a full market economy; temporary safeguards against Chinese export surges,[31] and, more recently, broader WTO issues such as agriculture, services and intellectual property.

On many of the major issues that fall within the realm of the accession process proper, leaving aside, for example, the US pressures outside that process for complete freedom of the Chinese exchange rate system, progress has been substantial and hard bargaining is proceeding. The issues are gradually being narrowed down and agreement reached on the large number of technical issues that are involved, many of which cover new ground now that the WTO is in place. There is frequent criticism of the US approaches to China's WTO accession outside the negotiations themselves. 'That the US is the predominant negotiator on China's accession in many ways is unfortunate because US/China trade relations have peculiar systemic problems of their own.' This was in 1989 and there now need to be added the 'peculiar systemic' political problems of the relationship.[32] The US approach within the enormously complex negotiations, however, is generally accepted by those involved as basically very professional and the belief exists that the issues can be negotiated through. Although the Chinese are similarly judged to be approaching the issues on a workmanlike basis, their recent approaches have been judged as increasingly unhurried, suggesting the strength of domestic bureaucratic constraints or the difficulties of obtaining high-level decision-making attention to the issues.

The implicit issues, however, are likely to be even harder than the explicit ones. These include: a growing US–China trade imbalance; the problem of US MFN and the Jackson-Vanik amendment; the question of transitional arrangements, and the safeguards regime to be adopted.

The US rhetoric on its trade imbalance with China has been growing. What is commonly overlooked is that the imbalance with the three Chinas (PRC, Hong Kong and Taiwan) has changed substantially less; while China's surplus grew from US$3.4 billion in 1987 to US$32 billion in 1994, the surplus of the three 'Chinas' over the same period rose substantially less, from US$25.1 billion to US$39.7 billion. While China's trade surplus was growing, Hong Kong's large surplus with the US shifted to a substantial deficit, much of its export activity moving to China; Taiwan has similarly moved significant levels of export production to the mainland. Nevertheless, the question of quantitative growth in China's imports is likely to be a major discussion point, and not without precedent in other GATT arrangements with non-market countries.

The basis of the WTO is non-discrimination and this is certainly one of the objectives that China has consistently pursued in seeking WTO membership. The US is the one major trading country not unconditionally applying MFN treatment to China, and its capacity to do so is limited by the Jackson-Vanik amendment that requires that the President extend MFN treatment annually to communist countries, which is then open to the Congress to overturn. Thus, under existing legislation, the US cannot extend MFN treatment to China unconditionally. There has been talk of the US applying Article XXXV of the GATT (now Article XIII of the WTO) to China. Such a step was applied by a number of countries to Japan when it joined the GATT in 1955 but it would now be seen as retrograde in the light of where the trading world, including China, has moved to. Given the importance of this issue to China, it would also mean that much of what it hoped to gain from membership would be negated.

It would also mean that the US would need to develop a bilateral arrangement for US–China trade relations outside the WTO reflecting much of the WTO arrangement but accepting the continuation of Jackson-Vanik. One of the consequences is that, because in current circumstances the US cannot offer permanent MFN treatment to China, 'the United States may be shut out of key WTO closing negotiations . . .'.[33] While this is not a good time to seek Congressional changes in legislation affecting China, the annual review of China's trade status is 'a relic of a past era and is counterproductive generally and in particular to US interests in the modern environment'.[34] Such measures can contribute only to reducing the competitiveness of US business efforts in China.

Although China continues to stress its developing country status, and in large degree that is self-evident in much of its social and political as well as economic infrastructure, its size makes the normal developing country treatment more problematic. There is general agreement that membership issues of this kind should be dealt with on an issue-by-issue basis.

The question of safeguards will be a complex one but there will no doubt be some form of special safeguards arrangement introduced to deal with potential surges of Chinese exports. There have also been suggestions for commitments by China for annual growth in imports in total and from the US. Although earlier GATT accession arrangements with other non-market economies provide only a limited guide to what might be suitable to China, such commitments were part of the deals with Eastern European countries when they joined the GATT in the late 1950s and early 1960s.

Although China is still a substantial way from being a full market economy there may be a need for such arrangements in areas under central administrative control. An easy ride for China, in this as in other areas, would be in no one's interest, quite apart from its potential impact on implementation of the Uruguay Round commitments by existing WTO members or with respect to Russia's application for membership. There is also a need, however, for reasonably objective guidelines to be set for their removal as market systems come into place – and to ensure that such issues do not become yet another political plaything.

Many of the WTO benefits are already in place because of the changes China has already made. Many of the outcomes, however, will be commitments with transitional arrangements. Despite the noise from the US trade negotiators about China's non-compliance with bilateral agreements, there is less concern among those familiar with the negotiations about China's intention to adhere to any commitments than there is about its administrative ability to do so. This is where the developing country nature of its economy is real, but it is also accentuated by the process of economic decentralisation that has been underway, in response among other things to the advice of experts from the international economic organisations.

DISCUSSION

The question that remains is how China will respond or how it will fit as a member of the WTO. We cannot of course know what China's approach will be when, assuming it does, it becomes a member of the WTO. We can draw some conclusions, however, by asking three questions: what approach has China taken in regional economic cooperation institutions and in other international economic organisations; has it undergone learning or value changes (cognitive learning) with changed conceptions of its national interest, or is it simply adapting to the new international circumstances while its objectives remain the same; and how does WTO membership contribute to interdependence and the understandings commonly associated with that.

China's participation in PECC/APEC has been basically cooperative and constructive. Its interests have tended to be closer to those of the developing countries, with interests in human resource development and, more particularly, science and technology, and it has played an organising role in the task forces in these areas, without any particular problems. Within the agreed guidelines for the basis of Taiwan's membership it has cooperated effectively with Taiwanese participants, even at APEC leaders' meetings, despite the continuing pressure from Taiwan to widen the guidelines. 'Since the entrance into APEC, China and Taiwan have sometimes clashed on protocol and procedural issues but rarely on substance.'[35]

As far as other organisations are concerned, we noted earlier that China accepted conditionality on part of its 1981 drawings from the IMF and in so doing not only tacitly supported conditionality but accepted international organisational constraints on its domestic decision making.[36] A study of international economic organisations showed that China's involvement in the World Bank and the IMF, rather than supporting various fears that China would bring its own agenda and ideas to its membership and try to impose them, was basically to accept and work within the existing framework.[37] It concluded that 'the Chinese posture has been to facilitate the work of the World Bank and the International Monetary Fund by espousing and adhering to their norms'.[38]

Although we looked at China's role from the perspectives of China, of other trading nations and of the organisations, a further perspective, that of the developing countries, has been suggested as important.[39] Certainly, China from time to time proclaims itself as the leader and protector of developing country interests. China's presence could from that perspective have impacts: positive impacts, such as advancing developing country interests; or negative impacts, in the case of the international financial institutions (IFIs), such as competing for the institutions' resources. The developing country interest could be important in the WTO. The experience in the IFIs is that China has argued for changes affecting developing countries which have been adopted as appropriate by those organisations. At the same time, it has been constructive in reducing North–South tensions at times within those organisations.[40]

For the WTO, this has not been an issue so far. In other organisations, China has generally supported the position of the developing countries on such issues as world debt relief, easing up on conditionality and giving developing countries more weight in decision making in international organisations, but China has joined no developing country groupings, and it follows the norms and expectations of the international institutions. Like other countries, it seeks generally to maximise the benefits it can receive from these institutions, but in doing so it generally adopts a pragmatic rather than a strident or ideological stance.

With respect to our second question, China had been a member of a number of economic institutions well before it sought GATT or WTO membership. In some cases these may not have been of major significance;

in other cases the change in principle – although not necessarily of basic beliefs – was great. This can be illustrated, first, by China's willingness not only to borrow money from a Western institution but also to accept the conditions that were imposed by the IMF, and, second, by the learning process involved for, and seemingly internalised by, Chinese decision makers. Nevertheless, perhaps more than anything else, the changes required of China in order to accede to the WTO membership involve a major commitment to the capitalist trade and economic order.

The initial interest of China in GATT membership had a substantial technical component: it reflected its change in policy in opening up to the world. It joined the Multi-Fibre Arrangement, after observing its operations, for the rational economic reason that it would expect to gain in terms of increased textile exports. The establishment of research and training institutions to analyse and assess GATT processes and mechanisms indicates an interest at the time in developing the necessary technical expertise to support its membership. Jacobsen and Oksenberg concluded that China's participation in international economic organisations had led to changes in policy, policy processes and institutions in China.[41]

The process of learning is complex and there are different views and concepts in the literature on the subject, mostly related to the Soviet Union.[42] It does seem clear, however, that China did undergo a major learning process over this period at each of the three levels specified earlier. The idea of global interdependence, which was starting to enter into the discourse of China's leaders at the time of its application to rejoin the GATT, and since espoused often by Chinese leaders and scholars, is contrary to what has been Chinese political culture for many centuries and the world view which that reflected. The changes that occurred did not simply come from an adaptive decision from the top: there was an extensive internal economic debate in China which moved towards a new 'world view'.

Chinese policy thinkers and leaders abandoned many deeply rooted assumptions about the nature of the international economic environment. They now saw the old and new world orders as historical categories in a relative sense and the GATT-based international trade order as 'in conformity with the objective needs of the development of modern productive forces'.[43] Acknowledging this higher stage of economic development that needed more than national markets, they came to accept and internalise the reality of one world market with capitalism as the prevalent force, and with a need for economic cooperation globally and in the Asia-Pacific region, including the need for socialist regimes to cooperate with capitalist ones. It also involved an acceptance, following intensive study of Ricardo (a major source of Marx's economic ideas, notably on the labour theory of value, although not on international trade), that trade, rather than being exploitative, could be mutually beneficial.[44]

Not all of this change in understanding necessarily stems from fundamental beliefs in global interdependence, although Samuel Kim accepts that international organisations can be said to have played a variety of global socialisation roles in Chinese foreign policy learning processes.[45] China's shift to be part of the international order through its membership of international organisations, however, has been rapid. Moreover, China does seem willing to accept the costs of global interdependence as well as the benefits, even if, like the other countries, it sometimes argues about the costs.

The decision to apply to re-enter the GATT was undoubtedly a political one but only in the same sense that that is true of membership of major institutions for any country. Whether it had originally major 'foreign policy' aspects, as has been suggested,[46] is less clear than that after 1989 it moved much more into the foreign policy field in both China and the US. It was not only the global response to Tiananmen Square but the changed US policy towards China that pushed WTO up the political agenda. Certainly, China now sees WTO membership as a major issue in the bilateral relationship with the US, since that country was able, and perhaps willing, to withhold benefits from economic interdependence.

China's view of the US–China relationship is relevant because of its implication for its overall motivation. It is possible to see China's national security concerns as less of a military kind than 'resting on its economic and technological edge'[47] and that threats to that security would then come from the pressure that can be put on it in economic terms. Consequently,

> China is more concerned with the role that the United States plays in the course of its modernisation, whereas the United States is more interested in China's strategic position in the Western Pacific region and the role it may play with respect to US security interests there.[48]

The conclusion that cognitive learning has taken place in the economic field is important in that it supports liberal rather than realist views of the world, including the possibility of cooperative international behaviour not only among 'liberal' societies, but also among liberal and non-liberal (in the Western sense) societies. Several questions emerge from this conclusion. The first relates to conclusions that in some other areas, such as arms control, learning of a cognitive nature seems not to have occurred.[49] On the other hand, in its association with the International Labour Organisation, learning does seem to have taken place; and it has been argued that cognitive learning in the economic field has occurred among all the economies participating in the regional economic cooperation process.[50] Second, the Chinese, as with many other Asian countries, have been able to pursue economic interdependence without necessarily being involved in social and political change of a Western liberal kind. This is less critical for those who accept, with Kant, that the process of evolution of an international society does not require the homogenisation of domestic political forms (e.g. democracy),[51] than for those, such as Fukuyama, who believe it does.[52]

Third, it raises the question, not addressed here, as to what precisely leads to cognitive learning and where the lessons come from. While the West would want China, and Asia, to learn the lessons of Western liberalism, what is privileged in Western liberalism is possessive individualism. In China (and other Asian states) it has been argued that group conformity, collective welfare and defence to authority are more valued[53] and that it is nation building, in which the value of individuals is assessed 'in terms of their compatibility with the task of achieving freedom for the state as an actor in international society', that is privileged.[54] The Chinese learning on this argument comes more from the Japans and Singapores of this world than from Europe or North America. It does not of course tell us what specific form China's participation in global society would be, although the evidence suggests that it is looking for equality and respect above all. If learning is possible, however, presumably so is relearning. If the Chinese assumption that trade is mutually beneficial is found wanting, such as through undue US or other politicising of WTO membership, or in other ways, China's cooperative behaviour in the international economic field could change.

NOTES

1 The GATT was a contractual agreement rather than an organisation: participants were contracting parties, not members. We use the terms organisation and members here for simplicity, and because they are more appropriate for the WTO.

2 Harold Jacobsen and Michel Oksenberg, *China's Participation in the IMF, the World Bank and GATT: Towards a Global Economic Order,* Ann Arbor: University of Michigan Press, 1990, p. 84.

3 Richard Cooper, 'The PRC and International Economic Organisations', in Richard Holton and Wang Xi (eds), *U.S.–China Economic Relations: Present and Future*, Berkeley: Institute of East Asian Studies, University of California, 1989, p. 311.

4 See the exchange between Senator Robb and Assistant Secretary of State Winston Lord, Hearings of the East Asian and Pacific Affairs Subcommittee of

the Senate Foreign Relations Committee on US Policy Toward Taiwan, *Federal News Service* (US), 27 September 1994.

5 Leslie Chang, 'Election in His Pocket, Taiwan Leader Says Lowering Tensions is up to China', *Wall Street Journal*, 27 March 1996.

6 William Feeney, 'China and the Multilateral Economic Institutions', in Samuel Kim (ed.), *China and the World: Chinese Foreign Relations in the Post-Cold War Era*, Boulder: Westview Press, 1994, p. 242.

7 Samuel Kim, 'China's International Organisational Behaviour', in Thomas Robinson and David Shambaugh (eds), *Chinese Foreign Policy: Theory and Practice*, Oxford: Clarendon Press, 1994.

8 Li Zhongzhou, 'China's Foreign Trade Policy Problems', in H. Edward English (ed.), *Pacific Initiatives in Global Trade*, Vancouver: Institute for Research on Public Policy for PECC, 1990, pp. 265–71.

9 I have used WTO throughout this chapter except when historically GATT is more appropriate. In many cases, WTO needs to be read as 'WTO and the GATT before it'.

10 Jacobsen and Oksenberg, op. cit., p. 127.

11 Akira Chiba, 'Pacific Cooperation and China', *The Pacific Review*, 2(1), 1989, p. 49.

12 Dick Wilson, 'The Pacific Basin is Coming Together', *Asia-Pacific Community*, 30, 1985, pp. 1–12.

13 Lawrence Woods, *Asia-Pacific Diplomacy: Nongovernmental Organisations and International Relations*, Vancouver: UBCPress, 1993, p. 131.

14 *Reuters Textline (South China Morning Post)*, 27 November 1990.

15 Cited in Banning Garrett and Bonnie Glaser, 'Beijing's Views on Multilateral Security in the Asia-Pacific region', *Contemporary Southeast Asia*, 16(1), 1994, p. 22.

16 Wang Lingshen, 'Comment' in Holton and Wang, op. cit., p. 334.

17 *Reuters Textline* (Kyodo News Service) citing Li Enheng, 6 October 1995.

18 Accession conditions are normally negotiated on an issue-by-issue basis according to the level of development, their ability to meet specific requirements and the time needed for this, and the commitments negotiated with comparable countries.

19 'The Trouble with a Convertible', *The Economist*, 2 March 1996.

20 Susan Shirk, *How China Opened Its Door: The Political Success of the PRC's Foreign Trade and Investment Reforms*, Washington: Brookings, 1994, p. 70, citing Pi Zi from FBIS, 4 February 1993, p. 28.

21 Peter Drysdale and Song Ligang, 'China's Trade Policy Agenda in the 1990s', paper to Australia-Japan Research Centre Conference on China and East Asia Trade Policy, Australian National University, September 1994.

22 Kuang Mei, 'APEC vs China's Reforms and Opening Up', in Ippei Yamazawa and Akira Hirata (eds), *Papers and Proceedings of a Symposium*, September 1995, Tokyo: Institute for Developing Economies, 1996.

23 Greg Mastel, *Trading With the Middle Kingdom*, Washington: Economic Strategy Institute, September 1995.

24 Drysdale and Song, op. cit.

25 James Feinerman, 'The Quest for GATT Membership: Will Taiwan be Allowed to Enter before China?', *The China Business Review*, May–June 1992, p. 24.

26 Cited by Kim Changsoo from remarks prepared for delivery by Kantor; see Kim Changsoo, 'Terms of Endearment: The United States' China Policy and China's Accession to the World Trade Organisation', *Journal of East Asian Affairs*, X(1), 1996, p. 94.
27 Gideon Rachman, 'Containing China', *The Washington Quarterly*, 19(1), 1996, p. 137.
28 Yoichi Funibashi, *Asia Pacific Fusion: Japan's Role in APEC*, Washington: Institute for International Economics, October 1995, p. 76.
29 'Communist China Hopes to Muscle in Cheap on the Respect Earned by Hong Kong and Taiwan' *Reuters Textline*, 1 August 1990.
30 Jacobsen and Oksenberg, op. cit., p. 131.
31 Feeney, op. cit., p. 244.
32 John McDonnell, 'China's Entry into the GATT', in English (ed.), op. cit., p. 256.
33 Mastel, op. cit., p. 36.
34 Mastel, op. cit., p. 37.
35 Funibashi, op. cit., p. 75.
36 Richard Cooper, in Holton and Wang, op. cit., pp. 311–16.
37 Jacobsen and Oksenberg, op. cit., p. 127
38 Jacobsen and Oksenberg, op. cit., p. 136.
39 Nai-Ruenn Chen, 'Comment', in Holton and Wang, op. cit., p. 334.
40 Jacobsen and Oksenberg, op. cit., p. 135.
41 Jacobsen and Oksenberg, op. cit., pp. 139–52.
42 See, particularly, Philip Tetlock, 'Learning in US and Soviet Foreign Policy: In Search of an Elusive Concept', in George Breslauer and Philip Tetlock (eds), *Learning in US and Soviet Foreign Policy*, Boulder: Westview, 1991, pp. 20–61.
43 Wang Dinyong, 'On Tariffs and the General Agreement on Tariffs and Trade (GATT)', *Social Science in China*, 15(1), 1994, p. 121.
44 Ma Shu-yun, 'Recent Changes in China's Pure Trade Theory', *China Quarterly*, 106, 1986, pp. 291–305; Jacobsen and Oksenberg, op. cit., p. 143.
45 Samuel Kim, op. cit., pp. 433–4.
46 Shirk, op. cit.
47 You Ji, 'Interdependence and China's Economic Security', paper to Workshop on Economic-Security Interactions in the Asia-Pacific, Australian National University, December 1995.
48 Zi Zhongyun, 'A Multidimensional Approach to Sino-US Relations', in Holton and Wang, op. cit., p. 18.
49 Alastair Johnston, 'Learning versus Adaptation: Explaining Change in Chinese Arms Control Policy in the 1980s and 1990s', *The Chinese Journal*, 35, 1996, pp. 27–61.
50 Ann Kent, 'China, International Organisations and Interdependence: the ILO as a Case Study', Department of International Relations, ANU, Seminar paper; Stuart Harris, 'Policy Networks and Economic Cooperation: Policy Coordination in the Asia-Pacific Region', *The Pacific Review*, 7(4), pp. 381–95.
51 John MacMillan, 'A Kantian Protest Against the Peculiar Discourse of Inter-Liberal State Peace', *Millennium*, 24(3), 1995, pp. 549–62.
52 Francis Fukuyama, *The End of History and the Last Man*, London: Penguin, pp. 276–84.

53 Steve Chan, 'Regime Transition in the Asia/Pacific Region: Democratization as a Double-Edged Sword', *Journal of Strategic Studies*, 18(3), 1995, p. 58.
54 Christopher Hughes, 'China and Liberalism Globalised', *Millennium*, 24(3), 1995, pp. 425–45.

9 China in Southeast Asia

Interdependence and accommodation*

Michael Leifer

> The top priority of China's foreign policy is to maintain a stable peripheral environment so as to safeguard normal economic circumstances at home. China regards the establishment of long-standing and stable good relations with ASEAN as an important factor in attaining this goal.
>
> Qian Qichen, 30 July 1995

The relationship between China and the states of Southeast Asia has displayed features of interdependence from the outset. From China's perspective, its regional interests have been invariably linked to a wider global dimension. An illuminating example of such linkage very early in the relationship was the contentious issue of the national status of ethnic Chinese resident in the countries of Southeast Asia.[1] Its resolution served to demonstrate the extent to which an autonomous Chinese policy entailed opportunity costs in the case of the emerging post-colonial governments of the region. The prospect of their alienation in a Cold War context became a matter of some concern in Beijing, leading to an attendant clarification of policy.

Despite this important example of political sensitivity, the relationship between the People's Republic of China and the states of Southeast Asia has long been problematic.[2] With the end of the Cold War, that relationship has changed for the better in many important respects, in part at China's initiative, but has remained replete with difficulties nonetheless. At the centre of those difficulties is the fact of geopolitical life that China, which shares and disputes common land and maritime borders with Southeast Asian states, is a rising and potentially dominant regional power.[3] A successful policy of economic reform has given it the resources with which to begin to take advantage of the transformation in strategic environment

*A version of this chapter has been published separately by the Chinese Council of Advanced Policy Studies, Taipei as CAPS Papers No. 14, January 1997

within Asia-Pacific after the end of the Cold War. Indeed, the People's Republic of China has come to enjoy a unique regional latitude because for the first time in its troubled history of international relations, it is free of the persistently hostile attentions of a global power.

Despite a conscious attempt to cultivate the Association of Southeast Asian Nations (ASEAN) states which dates from the mid-1970s, China continues to cast a shadow over the states of Southeast Asia because of its huge size, enormous population, close geographic proximity and considerable economic potential. It does so, in addition, because it asserts an irredentist agenda in the South China Sea with a steely and self-righteous nationalist determination underpinned by a programme of military modernisation. That modernisation, involving the replacement of antiquated equipment with an upgraded order of battle, holds out a worst-case prospect that in the early twenty-first century China may be in a position to pursue that irredentist agenda by superior force of arms. The realisation of that agenda in full would enable China to command the maritime heart of Southeast Asia, with hegemonic implications for its resident states as well as for all states concerned with the safety and freedom of navigation.

INTERDEPENDENCE AND A UNITED FRONT POLICY

China is not a totally free agent in its dealings with Southeast Asia. Its government has embarked on a process of economic reform from which there would not seem to be any turning back because of the likely domestic political consequences for the ruling Communist Party. That process depends for its success on an important measure of external confidence. China has a continuing need to attract direct foreign investment, including capital from enterprises controlled by members of ethnic-Chinese communities in Southeast Asia. In addition, although the end of the Cold War has permitted China an unprecedented regional latitude, its relationships with major Asia-Pacific powers are sometimes tense and those tensions have a bearing on policy towards Southeast Asia. The Chinese relationship with the United States has lost the degree of shared interest and strategic convergence that were present when confronting the Soviet Union and its regional allies during the second phase of the Cold War. Especially since the bloody events in Beijing in June 1989, the relationship has come to be distinguished by mutual mistrust. Issues of trade and intellectual property, transfers of arms and military technology as well as human rights violations have continued to cause trouble. Major security disputes include the unresolved issue of Taiwan and the matter of freedom of navigation in the South China Sea. Moreover, Beijing's perception that the United States has begun to renege on its commitment to recognise only one China, implicit in the terms of the Shanghai Communique of 1972 and two others and in the agreement to establish diplomatic relations in 1979, has generated nationalist fury as a weak political leadership grapples with the problem of transition from the rule of Deng Xiaoping.

Relations with Japan have also not been trouble-free. An underlying tension, in part a legacy of Japan's militarist past, has been aggravated by a progressive diplomatic assertiveness on the part of the government in Tokyo, exemplified by an openly expressed objection in May 1995 to China's resumption of nuclear testing soon after the extension of the Non-Proliferation Treaty. Japan was also conspicuous in protesting at China's acts of military intimidation in the Taiwan Strait during March 1996.

The problem of managing relationships with the United States and Japan, both of which possess capabilities to affect Chinese interests, means that China's latitude in pursuing its interests within Southeast Asia would seem to be subject to a measure of constraint. China has been consistent, in the main, in seeking to avoid provoking a united front against itself within Asia-Pacific and to that end has taken some care to differentiate between its various regional relationships. Up to a point, this degree of care on China's part has been to the advantage of Southeast Asian states. It should, of course, be pointed out that China is not an embattled state either globally or regionally. As a rising power in Asia-Pacific, it has not found itself in the predicament of Japan before the onset of the Pacific War. China has been committed to economic modernization for nearly two decades but has not been impeded in that aspiration by other global or regional powers. China has not been denied access to the international economy. On the contrary, the world has opened up to China concurrently with China opening up to the world. China has been able to develop in tune with the prevailing economic temper of the times and has been a party to the so-called East Asian Miracle. That said, Southeast Asia is an integral part of the economic constituency towards which China has looked from the late 1970s to help expedite its economic reform process. To that extent, China's policy of economic reform would seem a hostage to its fortunes as a rising regional power.

For its part, Southeast Asia in the form of an expanding ASEAN has not shown any intention of mobilising countervailing military power against an assertive China. But ASEAN is a diplomatic community of some international standing which China would not wish to alienate unnecessarily in the light of its economic interests and its recurrent problems with the United States and Japan. Moreover, there is a legacy of political interference by Beijing in Southeast Asia which lingers on in the region and which ensures that whatever the public rhetoric there about China being an opportunity and not a threat, the People's Republic's declarations of good intent are not taken totally at face value.

China's agenda in Southeast Asia has changed radically over the years, making possible, for example, a restoration of diplomatic relations with Indonesia in August 1990. Singapore and Brunei then followed suit in October 1990 and October 1991 respectively, but it meant that it had been over forty years after the establishment of the People's Republic before China had been able to enjoy diplomatic relations with all ten states of the region. Communism as an ideology is no longer at issue; nor is support for revolutionary movements. The problem of the relationship with resident ethnic-Chinese communities has not disappeared completely, however, despite the long-resolved issue of dual nationality. As China exhibits a growing sense of nationalist feeling in place of a moribund ideology, there is always the possibility of a resented diplomatic intervention should an ethnic-Chinese community in the region appear to have been ill-treated, as was the case in Medan in Indonesia in April 1994.

For China, however, policy towards Southeast Asia after the initial wave of revolutionary enthusiasm that followed the establishment of the People's Republic has been mostly pragmatic and selective (discounting the turbulent fall-out from the Cultural Revolution). For example, in the case of Myanmar (Burma), border concessions were made in order to curry political favour as China contended with India over territorial issues. China's policy may be said to have followed a standard united front practice whereby potential alignment partners, irrespective of political identity, were cultivated to the extent that they were considered useful in helping to cope with hostility from major powers.[4]

Such united front practice was an implicit admission of the vulnerabilities of interdependence and an attempt to come to manage them. The relationship with Cambodia during the rule of Prince Norodom Sihanouk was a notable example of such practice during the 1950s and 1960s, while the tacit alliance with ASEAN during the Cambodian conflict in the 1980s was even more striking. The Cambodian conflict provides a useful point of reference for assessing such practice in a post-Cold War context. During the Cambodian conflict, China's priority was to deny Vietnam (viewed as an agent of the Soviet Union) the prospect of achieving an undue dominance in Indochina and so revising the distribution of power in the peninsula to Beijing's disadvantage. To that end, its government engaged in a united front policy with the states of ASEAN among others in a successful attempt to reverse the outcome of Vietnam's invasion of Cambodia in December 1978. Although that alignment was problematic and a source of some discord within ASEAN because of differences of strategic perspective over the identification of primary external threat, it held together during the course of the conflict because of a particular correspondence of interests. With the end of the Cambodian conflict, that correspondence of interests no longer obtained. ASEAN no longer served the function of diplomatic agent of China, while China was no longer required to help contain Vietnam. The degree of divergence of interests was signalled towards the end of the 1980s when China clashed with Vietnam in the South China Sea, so registering a new phase of maritime assertiveness. Such divergence was confirmed in February 1992, when China promulgated a law on territorial waters and their contiguous area which reiterated extensive territorial and maritime claims in the South China Sea.

THE PROBLEM OF THE SPRATLYS

ASEAN's attempt to secure a commitment to moderation on China's part through a Declaration on the South China Sea at a meeting of its foreign ministers in Manila in July 1992 produced only an equivocal response from Beijing. Concern at such equivocation turned to alarm in February 1995 when it became known that Chinese forces had seized control of a reef in the Spratly Islands claimed by the Philippines, as well as by Vietnam, and had erected naval-support structures on them. Moreover, China's participation in a series of unofficial regional workshops on managing potential conflict in the South China Sea, which had been convened by Indonesia with Canadian financial support, has not provided any indication of compromise beyond an ambiguously expressed willingness to engage in joint development.[5]

The issue of the Spratly Islands has served to divide ASEAN from China, despite a growing economic engagement. Apart from shared geopolitical concerns, three of its founding members are also claimant states to some of those islands. Accordingly, the long-standing irredentist objective of China began to harm the relationship with members of the Association which was put on a formal basis in July 1992 when China's Foreign Minister, Qian Qichen, attended the annual meeting of his ASEAN counterparts as a guest. It was that meeting in Manila that issued the Declaration on the South China Sea. China had been consistent in its territorial claims in the South China Sea ever since Japan had renounced its sovereign jurisdiction there in the San Francisco Peace Treaty of September 1951 after having surrendered Taiping (Itu Aba), the largest of the Spratly Islands, to the forces of the Nationalist government of Chiang

Kai-shek after the end of the Pacific War. Direct confrontation over competing maritime claims had arisen before the end of the Cold War only with Vietnam: first with the former Republic of Vietnam in 1974 over the Paracel Islands and then with a united Socialist Republic of Vietnam over the Spratly Islands soon after unification in 1975. The issue had been set aside in China–ASEAN relations during the greater course of the Cambodian conflict, reviving only towards its end.

The issue of the Spratly Islands has highlighted the problem of interdependence for China in its dealings with the states of Southeast Asia. It turns on how Beijing seeks to reconcile conflicting priorities of irredentist goals and good regional relations. In the case of the Spratly Islands, an untrammelled pursuit of irredentist ambition could run counter to the promotion of economic interests and the management of relations with the United States and Japan. The Chinese political and military establishment is in no self-doubt about the legitimacy of the People's Republic's claim to island territories in the South China Sea. Underlying the strident manner in which entitlement to sovereignty has been represented as both indisputable and irrefutable has been the conviction that the territories in question have been Chinese from time immemorial and that other regional claimants that have seized a good number of the Spratly Islands have engaged in unacceptable acts of trespass which are said to date only from the 1970s.[6] Their ability to encroach on China's rightful domain has been regarded as just one more example of how China's past weakness has been exploited in the face of constraints on its action imposed by the nefarious policies of major powers. China in its rising nationalist mood is determined in time to rectify the historical record. A full rectification would, of course, move China's jurisdiction and potential reach southward some 1,000 nautical miles from its mainland in a historic and revolutionary act of geopolitical fusion between Northeast and Southeast Asia. Such a prospect was indicated by an article in China's army newspaper in March 1995 which pointed out that 'After years of active probes, a South Sea Fleet naval base has successfully integrated into a systematic whole the procurement, transport and supply of materials to islands and reefs in the *Nanshas* (Spratlys) . . . treating it as a strategic problem under conditions of high-tech war.'[7]

At issue is to what extent will China's relations with the countries of Southeast Asia be allowed to stand in the way of the People's Republic asserting its historical title in the South China Sea. It is here that considerations of interdependence interpose. Such an irredentist objective would seem to be in direct conflict with China's more immediate economic priorities and also its united front interest of generating good relations with the ASEAN states. For the time being, that particular conflict of interests may be deferred as China's government temporizes over the Spratly Islands.

Another conflict of priorities has been pointed up by the problem posed for China of separating its policies towards Southeast Asia from those in Northeast Asia, especially in the case of Taiwan over which national feeling is much stronger than over the Spratly Islands. The protracted problem of Taiwan has proved continuously frustrating for Beijing, despite recurrent acts of intimidation designed to influence the political process within the so-called renegade province, as well as serving a domestic political function within a People's Republic beset by a rising nationalism. Those acts of intimidation, especially the displays of armed force in the run-up to Taiwan's presidential elections in March 1996, in addition to the way in which China has conducted itself at times over the terms of recovery of Hong Kong, have not served the cause of confidence-building and united front practice with Southeast Asian states. For example, in March 1996, Singapore's Senior Minister, Lee Kuan Yew, who occupies a special position as an interlocutor between the mainland and Taiwan, was so disturbed by the escalation in military display by China that he interceded publicly in the cause of moderation without directly criticising China's conduct. He expressed the view that 'The countries of the region will not understand why China cannot be patient and resolve the matter peacefully when using force will damage both China and Taiwan and also hurt third parties, the countries of ASEAN and East Asia.'[8] In reflecting regional concerns, Singapore's elder statesman was making the obvious point that Chinese policy in Southeast Asia cannot be separated from its conduct in Northeast Asia and indeed that the two were then at odds with one another.

Despite the emotive nationalist priority of Taiwan, China's leaders have been obliged to take into account the important interest of sustaining the momentum of economic and diplomatic cooperation with Southeast Asia. They would not willingly wish to manoeuvre the People's Republic into a position of diplomatic isolation whereby an alienation of regional states compounds difficulties experienced with the United States and Japan over Taiwan and other matters. At issue is the requirement of sustaining a viable relationship with ASEAN which has expanded significantly with the membership of Vietnam in July 1995 and which is expected to include all ten Southeast Asian states by the turn of the century. An additional and related problem has arisen as ASEAN's heads of government concluded a treaty in Bangkok in December 1995 with the declared object of making Southeast Asia a nuclear weapons-free zone. The geographic terms of reference of that treaty include the exclusive economic zones and continental shelves of the signatory states. China has refused to sign a protocol to the treaty endorsing its terms for fear of prejudicing its territorial claims in the South China Sea.

CHINA, ASEAN AND THE ASEAN REGIONAL FORUM

It would be an oversimplification to see China's relations with the states of Southeast Asia solely in terms of its dealings with ASEAN as a unit. Individually, China enjoys mixed relationships within Southeast Asia. It much prefers to deal with ASEAN's members on a bilateral rather than on a multilateral basis so as to limit the constraints arising from interdependence. For example, relations with Vietnam have remained chequered despite the restoration of party-to-party ties expressed in reciprocal visits by respective party secretaries general. Sino-Vietnamese contention over disputed territories has continued to disturb the association. China has no interest in displacing the regime in Hanoi which shares its model of political economy. But it is seemingly determined to make the point diplomatically that Vietnam should heed the 'lesson' that its armed forces taught it through their intervention in February 1979, and give due recognition to the seniority of the People's Republic's position. To that end, Vietnam's Foreign Minister, Nguyen Manh Cam, has given assurances that his government will not develop ties with its neighbours at the expense of relations 'with third countries' (namely, China) or enter into an alliance 'with some country' (namely, the United States) to oppose 'another country' (namely, China). China has not recorded any public displeasure at Vietnam's entry into ASEAN. However, China's unilateral action in seizing Mischief Reef could have been inspired by the timing of Vietnam's entry which had been announced a year in advance in July 1994. A practical demonstration of Sino-Vietnamese accommodation was the reopening of cross-border rail links in February 1996 after an interruption of seventeen years. Bilateral tensions revived visibly in April 1996, however, when Petro-Vietnam granted exploration leases for two blocs some 400 kilometres southeast of Ho Chi Minh City to Conoco, the American oil major. China entered a formal protest in response to the grant which covered half of the zone that Beijing had leased to America's Crestone Corporation in May 1992.[9] Those tensions had moderated sufficiently by the following June for China's Prime Minister Li Peng to attend the Eighth National Congress of Vietnam's Communist Party.

The relationship with the Philippines has become correspondingly testy because of the direct conflict of interests over competing claims in the

Spratly Islands. Matters came to a head when, in response to the revelation in February 1995 that Chinese naval forces had seized Mischief Reef, Philippine naval units began to blow up Chinese markers on nearby unoccupied reefs and also conveyed journalists to the vicinity of Mischief Reef. China's Foreign Ministry responded with an explicit warning before tensions moderated.[10] Tensions have arisen also with Indonesia over the ambiguity of China's clarification of maritime claims within that part of the Republic's exclusive economic zone extending from the Natuna Islands at the western periphery of the South China Sea. Indeed, such tensions are believed to have had a bearing on Indonesia's willingness to enter into an unprecedented security agreement with Australia in December 1995. By contrast, for example, the relationship with Singapore has been exceedingly good, with the island-state acting as a key economic partner in a joint venture to create a satellite city in Suzhou, near Shanghai, modelled on its own successful experience of urban development. Equally, Malaysia has also opened up to China with great enthusiasm, with Prime Minister Dr Mahathir Mohamad espousing the view that 'It is high time for us to stop seeing China through the lenses of threat and to fully view China as the enormous opportunity that it is.'[11] Moreover, China's relationship with Myanmar has burgeoned because of extensive economic cooperation and military assistance which has been a critical factor in maintaining the ruling State Law and Order Restoration Council (SLORC) in power. Indeed, the nature of that relationship has been a factor in ASEAN pursuing a policy of 'constructive engagement' towards the government in Rangoon designed to counter China's influence.

China's relationship with ASEAN as a corporate entity has been of paramount importance, however, because of the leading role that the Association has played in transposing its model of regional security dialogue onto a wider Asia-Pacific canvas.[12] In May 1993, ASEAN took the initiative to employ the vehicle of the annual conference between its foreign ministers and their counterparts among major trading and investment partners as a structure for multilateral security dialogue within Asia-Pacific. At an unprecedented meeting of senior officials in Singapore, it was agreed to augment the membership normally in attendance at the ASEAN Post-Ministerial Conference (ASEAN-PMC) by inviting China and Russia as well as Vietnam, Laos and Papua New Guinea to participate in a novel enterprise called the ASEAN Regional Forum (ARF). A meeting of the respective eighteen foreign ministers in Singapore in July 1993 then agreed to convene the first working session of the ARF in Bangkok in July 1994, concurrent with the annual meeting of ASEAN's foreign ministers. That enterprise in cooperative security, as opposed to either collective defence or collective security, attracted China's membership from the outset, albeit not without some misgivings which were expressed at a preliminary meeting of senior officials in Bangkok in May 1994.

From China's perspective, multilateralism beyond the United Nations was viewed as a risky enterprise because of a concern that it would provide a context in which undue pressure could be brought to bear. It was well understood in Beijing that a prime purpose of the initiative was to address the uncertainty in the regional strategic environment in which rising Chinese power was a matter of prime concern. The Chinese government was apprehensive at being locked into an institutionalised expression of interdependence. It was not in a position, however, to avoid participation because of the Asia-Pacific-wide scope of participation and remit of the new Forum. The pragmatic judgement was made that such a Forum would be better influenced from the inside than from an isolated outside. Moreover, a very important consideration was that the formal initiative for the security dialogue had come from ASEAN rather than from any major regional power such as Japan or the United States which would have aroused even greater Chinese suspicions. In addition, it became quite clear early on that ASEAN was set on assuming a diplomatic centrality within the embryonic venture. Interestingly, objections to that role have come not, so far, from China but from countries like Australia, Japan and the United States which have resented the assertive diplomatic centrality of a body whose experience is limited to Southeast Asia, while the critical problems of regional security are located primarily in Northeast Asia.

Misgivings about participation in the ARF may well have been sustained as a result of the first working session in Bangkok in July 1994 at which the issue of the South China Sea was raised briefly. However, after the second working session in Brunei in August 1995, it would appear that China's view had softened somewhat. In the interim, China had been confronted with the diplomatic ire of ASEAN at an initial security dialogue between senior officials of members' foreign ministries which was held in April 1995 in Hangzhou. At an informal dinner, the evening before the meeting, ASEAN's permanent secretaries registered their common position in reproaching China for its unilateralist action in seizing Mischief Reef. In addition to that collective admonition, the ASEAN side took great pains to explain the consensual culture and modalities of the Association. To the extent that ASEAN was determined to transpose its own model of security dialogue to the wider framework of the ASEAN Regional Forum, the Chinese officials had their initial apprehensions of multilateralism reduced. Moreover, when the ARF convened for its second working session in Brunei in August 1995, a diplomatic crisis had arisen between China and the United States over the ostensibly private visit to Cornell University by President Lee Teng-hui of Taiwan in spite of prior American assurances that a visa would not be granted. In addition, a testiness had arisen in relations with Japan over China's resumption of underground nuclear tests close to the extension of the Non-Proliferation Treaty. Circumstances were such that it would not have been politic to have risked a clash with ASEAN either over the issue of the South China Sea or the modalities of the ASEAN Regional Forum. China showed itself willing to be constrained up to a point by the degree of interdependence in its regional relationships.

ASEAN's approach to the norms and procedures for governing the workings of the ARF were set out in a Concept Paper that was discussed by the assembled foreign ministers in August 1995. That paper stressed that a gradual evolutionary approach to managing regional security was required, with two complementary approaches recommended. The first of these drew on the practice and experience of ASEAN in reducing tensions and fostering regional cooperation through its characteristic informal processes. The second was to be based on concrete confidence-building measures that were to serve as the first stage in an evolutionary process moving through preventive diplomacy to ultimate conflict resolution mechanisms. The paper stipulated that the rules of procedure of the ARF should be based 'on ASEAN norms and practices' and that decisions should be made by consensus and without voting after careful and extensive consultations. It also recommended that the ARF should progress 'at a pace comfortable to all participants'. Despite the measure of reserve over the diplomatic centrality of ASEAN, the meeting endorsed the substance of the Concept Paper's recommendations. An essentially consultative security role was identified for the ARF which was not to be used to impose solutions. Moreover, China had its way in the Chairman's final statement in changing the ultimate goal of conflict resolution mechanisms to that of the elaboration of approaches to conflict. China also succeeded in having a distinction drawn in nomenclature between two categories of inter-sessional activities, with the object of reducing the impression that continuous institutionalised working groups had been set up.[13]

INTERDEPENDENCE AND ACCOMMODATION

This brief discussion of the initial workings of the ASEAN Regional Forum has not been intended to turn the subject of this chapter on its head by addressing Southeast Asian relations with China. The point at issue is the diplomatic context of interdependence. China showed itself to be comfortable to a degree with its participation in the ARF as part of a general strategy towards its Southeast Asia component. During the ARF session in Brunei, Foreign Minister Qian Qichen indicated the strong degree of convergence between his government and those of ASEAN over how the ARF ought to proceed.[14] Moreover, at a meeting between Qian Qichen and his ASEAN counterparts in Brunei shortly before the ARF convened, a number of concessions in form were made which indicated the priority placed by China on its relationship with the Association. Without offering any compromise on the issue of sovereignty, he registered his government's recognition of international law, including the basic principles and rules of the United Nations Convention on the Law of the Sea, as a basis for negotiating a settlement of the Spratlys issue. This was a modification of position from a rigid insistence on the historical foundations of China's claim.[15] He also revived the prospect of shelving the dispute in favour of joint development as well as reiterating the great importance that China attached to safe and free passage in international sea lanes in the South China Sea. Qian Qichen departed from a previous insistence on addressing the matter of the Spratly Islands on a solely bilateral basis between contending parties by indicating a willingness to having it discussed on a multilateral basis between Chinese and ASEAN officials. Close to that time, Qian Qichen also held a bilateral meeting with Domingo Siazon, the Secretary of Foreign Affairs of the Philippines, at which he promised that China 'will not take any action towards the complication of the situation in the region as both China and the Philippines are concentrating on economic construction which needs a peaceful and stable peripheral and international environment'.[16]

Such concessions were of form only, particularly as China had then yet to ratify the Law of the Sea Convention and had also failed to clarify publicly the precise extent and nature of its maritime claims in the South China Sea, including the relevance of a dotted median line drawn in 1947 by the Chiang Kai-shek regime which overlapped with Indonesia's exclusive economic zone from the baselines of the Natuna Islands. Such concessions, however, indicated an undoubted willingness to accommodate the concerns of ASEAN governments about the perceived creeping assertiveness of China aggravated by the Mischief Reef episode. Indeed, it is instructive to note the way in which China's government subsequently took pains to distance itself from any responsibility for naval clashes that took place off the coast of the Philippines in January and February 1996. In the first case, Philippine naval gunboats intercepted and clashed with two foreign vessels, initially identified as flying the People's Republic flag, off Zambales Province close to the former American naval base of Subic Bay. That incident was described in Beijing and by China's embassy in Manila as having 'nothing to do with the Chinese side'.[17]

China has continued in its cooperative mode, albeit in its own interest. In May 1996, the Standing Committee of China's National People's Congress announced the ratification of the United Nations Convention on the Law of the Sea. Baselines for the territorial sea were defined for China's mainland and for the Paracel Islands (disputed with Vietnam) but no mention was made of the Spratly Islands towards which four ASEAN states have differing claims.[18] Strong individual protests followed from Vietnam and the Philippines but not from ASEAN as a whole. Moreover, a second security dialogue between senior officials of China and ASEAN states convened in Indonesia in early June 1996 at which the Spratly Islands and the nuclear weapons-free zone treaty were addressed without undue contention and with a tentative agreement on an exchange of views between respective legal advisers.

The Mischief Reef episode in the Spratly Islands would seem to have been a defining diplomatic moment for China in ordering its priorities with the states of Southeast Asia. China demonstrated a vulnerability to the workings of interdependence. But it is too early to say that a line has been drawn under further acts of unilateral territorial revisionism in the South China Sea, especially as a revival of political turbulence within China in the context of a struggle for leadership could find an external nationalist expression beyond Taiwan. That said, the more rational strategy, and the considered view of China's Foreign Ministry, would seem to be that it is in the People's Republic's continuing interest to cultivate good relations within Southeast Asia.[19] The Association is no longer regarded as a compliant client of the West but is seen as an increasingly autonomous entity with international standing and with its own agenda. On the issue of the sanctity of national sovereignty and a resentment of foreign interference in domestic affairs on the grounds of human rights violations, China has found common cause with ASEAN in resisting the imposition of Western values.

China's policy within Southeast Asia has become largely governed by a rational ordering of national priorities in the interdependent context of economic interests and continuing tensions with the United States and Japan. Such a policy, which requires self-restraint in asserting perceived legitimate territorial objectives in the South China Sea, is based in part on a recognition of the lack, so far, of a decisive military capability for projecting power to the south of Hainan Island.[20] Correspondingly, China has been obliged to take into account the air and maritime force modernisation on the part of some ASEAN states, which are also claimants to islands in the Spratly group, and which could make the irredentist task of even a strong China in the future exceptionally difficult. A cautious calculation would seem to have been made, for the time being. A more assertive alternative would not be practical in current regional circumstances in which the most pressing priorities are to sustain the pace of economic development and to secure the reunification of Taiwan with the mainland. But should those regional circumstances change to China's strategic advantage, then it may become less cautious and accommodating.

The states of ASEAN would seem in the main to have based their overall relationship with China on a corresponding rational basis, in part because they lack the collective resources and resolve to do otherwise. The vehicle of the ASEAN Regional Forum enjoys their strong support in the interest of inducting China into habits of good regional citizenship, underpinned by the nexus of economic incentive and the fail-safe expectation of engaging the United States in a balance of power role. In encouraging such a policy of constructive engagement, the states of Southeast Asia have become a party to helping China's government to realise as historical ambition of creating a strong state of truly global significance. They may also therefore be a party to China escaping the constraints of interdependence. In consequence, a pessimist might wish to quote Lenin's aphorism that the capitalist will even sell you the rope with which you intend to hang him. The more optimistic calculation in Southeast Asia, based on the premise of interdependence, is that if China is given enough economic rope it will tie itself down and behave differently from the way in which rising powers have conducted their international relationships in the past. It is this kind of calculation that has caused ASEAN's governments to respond positively to China's request to become a formal dialogue partner and to join in the ASEAN-PMC.

As the Chinese like to say, only history will decide. For the time being, China's policy would seem to be to avoid engaging in practices likely to generate political alienation within Southeast Asia so as to be able to focus on the more critical priorities of economic development and managing relationships with the United States and Japan. To that end, Southeast Asia has been allocated the role of a component of a united front. From China's perspective, the costs of interdependence in Southeast Asia have not been high, and accommodation as opposed to compromise over the Spratly Islands has been a small price to pay for advancing the prime ends of its regional policy.

NOTES

1 See Stephen Fitzgerald *China and the Overseas Chinese: A study of Peking's changing policy, 1949–1970*, Cambridge University Press, Cambridge, 1972.
2 See Michael Yahuda *The China Threat*, Institute of Strategic and International Studies, Kuala Lumpur, 1986 and also his general discussion in this volume 'How Much Has China Learned about Interdependence?'.
3 A survey of the relationship with the ASEAN states which highlights their attitudes towards China may be found in Leszek Buszynski 'China and the ASEAN Region' in Stuart Harris and Gary Klintworth (eds) *China as a Great Power: Myths, Realities and Challenges in the Asia-Pacific Region*, Longman, Melbourne and St Martin's Press, New York, 1995.
4 See Peter Van Ness *Revolution and Chinese Foreign Policy: Peking's Support for Wars of National Liberation*, University of California Press, Berkeley, 1970 and J.D. Armstrong *Revolutionary Diplomacy: Chinese Foreign Policy and the United Front Doctrine*, University of California Press, Berkeley, 1977.
5 See Mark J. Valencia *China and the South China Sea Disputes*, Adelphi Paper No. 298, Oxford University Press for International Institute for Strategic Studies, London, October 1995, pp. 20–2 and also *The Straits Times*, 12 October 1995 for an account of the inconclusive outcome of the sixth workshop in October 1995.
6 For a representative view, see Pan Shiying 'The Nansha Islands: A Chinese Point of View' *Window Magazine*, Hong Kong, 3 September 1993. See also Chen Jie 'China's Spratly Policy' *Asian Survey*, Vol. 34, No. 10, October 1994 and Sheng Lijun 'Beijing and the Spratlys' *Issues and Studies*, Vol. 31, No. 7, 1995.
7 Cao Baojian and Ding Feng 'Years of Effort by a South Sea Fleet Naval Base Results in Integrating the Procurement, Supply and Transport of Materials to *Nanshas* into a System' *Jiefangjun Bao*, 17 March 1995 in BBC *Summary of World Broadcasts*, FE/2260/G 1–2.
8 *The Straits Times*, 4 March 1996.
9 Adam Shwarz and Matt Forney 'Oil on Troubled Waters' *Far Eastern Economic Review*, 25 April 1996.
10 Its spokesman advised 'the Philippine side not to misinterpret the Chinese side's restraint. The Philippine side had better return to the correct course of settling the relevant dispute through peaceful talks. If the Philippine side continues to act wilfully and recklessly, it should be responsible for all consequences arising therefrom.' *Xinhua News Agency*, 16 May 1995.
11 *New Straits Times*, 21 January 1995.
12 For a representative benign Chinese view of ASEAN, see Lu Jianren 'Characteristics of the Present Security Situation in the Asia-Pacific Region' *Foreign Affairs Bulletin*, Beijing, September 1995.
13 See Michael Leifer *The ASEAN Regional Forum: Extending ASEAN's Model of Regional Security*, Adelphi Papers No. 302, Oxford University Press for the International Institute for Strategic Studies, London, July 1996, Ch.3.
14 He pointed out that

> The Chinese side advocates the development of regional cooperation in security matters in stages in the spirit of dealing with issues in ascending

order of difficulty, and of seeking common ground while reserving differences. For some time to come, the countries concerned may hold preliminary informal discussions and consultations on the principles, content, scope and method of cooperation in security matters. Meanwhile, they should carry out specific activities of cooperation on which the parties have reached a consensus or which are not highly contentious, and institute some practical and feasible confidence-building measures in a practical manner.

Xinhua News Agency, 1 August 1995

15 Op. cit., 30 July 1995.

16 Ibid.

17 *The Straits Times,* 30 January 1996. Note also reports that electronic equipment had been added to the naval-support structures on Mischief Reef, *The Straits Times*, 2 March 1996.

18 For a graphic depiction of the baselines, see *Window Magazine*, Hong Kong, 24 May 1996. The press announcement stated that 'The Government of the People's Republic of China will announce the remaining baselines of the territorial sea of the People's Republic of China at another time' *Xinhua News Agency*, 15 May 1996.

19 See Shi Min 'Background and Impact of a "Greater ASEAN"' *Foreign Affairs Bulletin*, December 1995.

20 It has been widely noted that China has entered into a US$2 billion licence-production agreement with Russia to produce SU-27 long-range fighter aircraft (of which it has already taken separate delivery of twenty-six, with another twenty-four on order). Deployed from a base being developed on Woody Island in the Paracels, the SU-27 could patrol over the Spratly Islands for at least an hour on each mission. See *International Herald Tribune*, 8 February 1996.

10 'Enlitening' China?

Gerald Segal

The rise of China poses perhaps the most far-reaching challenge to the international status quo. While there is much that can be done to engage China, it is unclear what policies might constrain China's undesired activities. China is, and increasingly will be, constrained by the need to become interdependent with the outside world, but interdependence is not enough. In the long term the only effective constraint on great powers is a wider process of liberalism that turns them into Lite powers. If China is to be 'enlitened', then it will be through some of the features of interdependence, but also through a firm constraint on its unwanted activity while it is in the long and uncertain process of turning Lite.

LEARNING TO ADAPT

There are a number of different ways in which we can attempt to understand Chinese behaviour. Alastair Johnston's struggle with the distinction between 'learning' and 'adaptation' in Chinese policy is a valiant attempt to tackle what is essentially the question of whether China has come to see the common sense of real interdependence, or whether it has merely been forced to adjust to superior force while it is still relatively weak.[1] There are, of course, a number of problems in any such attempt to divide Chinese action into 'learning' or 'adaptation'. It can be argued that even those states which now seem to embrace the post-modern sense of interdependence and reduced sovereignty did so initially out of a sense of the futility of confronting superior force. Do the states of the Atlantic like having their economies swept by the force of the global financial markets and do they not wish they could restrain those forces? Do they enjoy being Lite powers which can barely use military power, even in their own backyard? It is far from clear that the states of the developed world accept their post-modern condition because they have learned to see that it is a better system.[2]

What seems most likely is that the developed world has learned to adapt to seemingly inexorable realities. Modern great powers have become Lite powers in the sense that they have undergone deep structural change because of powerful social, economic and political forces. They adapted to the forces of change in advanced capitalist and pluralist democratic systems. If they were to prosper and remain free, they had to open their economies and social systems to outside influences and surrender key aspects of control over their economic, social and foreign policies. These changes are not just manifest in open trading economies or global media companies, but are also evident in the aversion to the use of military force and the development of small, professional armed forces. The former heavyweight powers of the Atlantic world (and Japan) have become Lite powers in what looks like the inevitable path of development for rich and free people.

This apparent digression is relevant to China. The most obvious connection is the conclusion that if other great powers eventually learned to adapt and became Lite, then we should expect no less from China. It is unlikely that China will embrace the powers of economic interdependence and enjoy the loss of sovereignty that is part of the process, but in the long term it cannot have prosperity without becoming Lite. If China wants to become rich it will eventually not only be forced to adapt to interdependence, it will also become enlitened.

Before the critics erupt in cries of 'Western determinism' and denounce this view as 'pidgin scholarship', let us acknowledge that each country adapts somewhat differently to the process of modernisation and democratisation.[3] As Francis Fukuyama has noted, some 20 per cent of the character of the modern political economy of developed states is probably the result of 'culture'.[4] But the overwhelming determinants of the character of developed states are the result of the deep structural forces of modernisation and democratisation. The lesson for China, as it was for Japan, is that if it is to modernise, it will democratise, and as it does both, it will be forced to adapt to the international system.

Nevertheless, it may be that China, by virtue of its size and grand traditions, has a greater ability to change the international system as it joins, and therefore a greater ability to resist the deep structural forces.[5] When Japan, with its population a tenth the size of China, became a major player in the global economy, it accounted for less than 10 per cent of world GDP. As China joins the international economy, it is somewhat larger, although still roughly the size of the modern Japanese economy (in purchasing power parity terms). In terms of military power, China is far less impressive than the Soviet Union when it tried, and failed, to transform.

ADAPTATIONS SO FAR

Clothing

The *clothing* worn by Chinese leaders and many of the Chinese people has changed out of all recognition in the past twenty years. The days are long gone when China could be described as the 'nation of blue ants'. Also long gone are the days when the 'Mao suit' was *de rigueur* for Chinese leaders and even many others in the developing world.[6] Although we should avoid the temptation to get carried away with the significance of these sartorial adjustments, they do signify a degree of surrender to forces of global socialisation. To be sure, there still are some world leaders, most notably in the African and Arab worlds, who attend international gatherings in local dress, but East Asians (less so in South Asia) have more or less abandoned the practice. The batik shirts on display at the APEC meeting in Bali were so much derided because they were obviously unconvincing symbols of a supposedly common Asianness (and informality). The standard dress for these leaders, whether around a conference table or on the golf course, is best described as mid-Atlantic in origin. When Chinese leaders choose, as they still do from time to time, to wear a 'Mao suit', they are well understood to be making a statement about conserving basic values, usually of a Marxist kind. Thus the change in dress is still symbolically important, still resisted in some quarters, and yet still unavoidable for Chinese leaders in the modern world.

The standard dress for Chinese in China is probably less explicable in such overtly political terms. What seems to have happened is that urban Chinese are more able to break the once rigidly applied strictures of a Communist Party state. As their incomes rise, and they come into greater contact (mostly through the media) with the outside world, they seek to express their individuality in their clothes, and they have the income to afford new attire and hairstyles. The process is far from universal in China, for the majority of the people still live in the countryside and their habits (although perhaps no longer their tastes) in clothing have barely changed. But what is clear is that there is a process of modernisation in the way the Chinese people appear, and it is in the direction set by the forces of globalisation.[7]

One hastens to add that because so much of developed East Asia has already adopted these styles, most Chinese think of the styles as more modern-Asian than derived from the Atlantic world. Indeed, the strength of the process of modernisation is probably attributable to an important extent to the fact that other Asians are more easily accepted as role models and that these wealthier Asians have no particular problem in wearing designs set in some distant way by the fashion houses of the global market economy (including the designers of Tokyo). In short, as Chinese modernise, they become more like the rest of us in the developed world. At least as far as clothing is concerned, they do it because they want to, not because they are forced. Such is the power of the forces of global society.

Tourism

A second adaptation is the extent to which China has opened itself to international *tourism*. China is now the world's most popular tourist destination, and even though there has been much exaggeration about the impact of tourism on local culture, there is a steady drip of influence from constantly seeing richer and very different people behaving in distinctive ways. Most tourism is packaged, and often tightly, so risks of 'contamination' are reduced. The activities of tall, bearded, big-nosed foreigners may be dismissed as zoological oddities, but the swarms of ethnic Chinese visitors who behave like other middle-class big noses makes a greater impact in the long term. When the ethnic Chinese visitor speaks in support of economic choice and political pluralism, it is harder for mainland Chinese to dismiss the powerful forces as decadent Western exports.

Is China forced to accept tourists? In truth they willingly did so because it was a way to attract foreign investment. Deng Xiaoping was not terribly worried about the 'flies' that come in through open doors, and he was persuaded of the financial benefits of investments in the service sector. Building better hotels and allowing more 747s ensured that the even more important business investors would be happier to come to China. Foreign investment does not depend on tourism, but it is part of the climate that makes foreigners confident about China. If China were suddenly to restrict the numbers of tourists, the business climate would be adversely affected. In that respect, China, with all its grand history that is so attractive to foreigners, had to open up to tourism if it wanted to modernise.

Foreign culture

A third, essentially social, transformation is China's relative openness to foreign culture. Of course, China is much less open than the OECD countries, but then openness, even in developed countries, is relative and still the subject of much debate (viz. France or Japan). Nevertheless, in comparison to twenty years ago, Chinese can see more foreign films, television, music and art. As we have already suggested, the impact is perhaps greatest from the portion of foreign culture that comes from modernised and wealthy Asians, and especially those who are ethnically Chinese. Canto-pop is more popular than heavy metal. But even the hedonism of modern East Asian Chinese culture undermines authoritarian values and Marxist economics.[8]

The power of the challenge posed by foreign culture is well understood in Beijing, even if the nature of the challenge is harder to grasp. Hence the periodic efforts to clamp down on the Chinese artistic scene, including dissident writers and film makers. Hence also the attempt to restrict access to the Internet or to limit satellite broadcasting. Even economically developed states like Singapore still try to restrict the power of external cultural influences. While some restrictions are possible, especially if Chinese authorities can work with the foreign broadcasters (such as Rupert Murdoch), the long-term trend is that the process is unstoppable and powerful. Beijing can succeed in bumping BBC Television news from foreign satellites, but *Baywatch* and soap operas are let through and in the end are far more corrosive of authoritarian values.[9]

Was China forced to accept such limits on its ability to determine the culture and values of its citizenry? To a large extent the answer is yes. The Internet is increasingly a necessary tool for companies operating in the global economy or intellectuals keeping abreast of global trends, ideas and data. Access can be restricted, but not for long or with an effective comprehensiveness. Satellite broadcasters can be stopped from making much money if they are unable to work with local cable companies and arrange for payment. But where foreign broadcasts can change local tastes, for example in southern China which receives Hong Kong and Taiwanese influences, the local broadcasters must respond to popular demand. As these 'pernicious' demands spread to neighbouring and eventually most other major cities, then local broadcasters do become anxious to strike a deal with foreigners. These forces worked in Eastern Europe and the Chinese autocrats are right to fear that they are no more successful in limiting the power of foreign ideas and values.

The law

Despite the signs that China's civil society is gradually changing under the relentless pressure of these foreign forces, progress in entrenching deep structural change is often uneven. One key area is the possible emergence of *new legal systems*. In some technical areas, such as methods of accounting and measurement, China has made good progress in reaching international standards. There are often serious reasons to doubt the reliability of Chinese data, and the inclination to 'cook the books' and produce bogus figures is clearly very high. Chinese officials know that foreign investors want reliable indicators of results, productivity and profit. They need a real sense of trends in inflation, unemployment or the money supply. There can be little doubt that China has become more transparent in this respect, but there is still a long road to travel. China's inflation figures do not add up, even using official data. Corruption has grown so rife that international rankings of such ills now put China among the top three.[10]

The cheekier economists will tell you that corruption can be seen as merely a useful market mechanism at a time of major economic transformation. But foreign investors are increasingly worried that there is much more sham than reality to China's supposed move to a more regular international legal standard. Compare India and China. Both are well known for official corruption, but at least Kentucky Fried Chicken in India had recourse to the courts to rein in corrupt or arbitrary officials, while McDonald's in Beijing had to succumb in a system essentially without recourse to law.

The key test of China's adaptation to international legal norms is not so much whether they adopt Western laws, for other East Asians have adapted legal systems in much more subtle ways. The real test is whether there is blind justice – whether there are clear rules objectively adjudicated. In this respect, China has so far resisted significant change. Where it has adopted foreign rules and norms, it has clearly done so because that is what is required by foreigners to do business. China has been forced to adapt, but there are still severe limits to the process of adaptation.

International trade

Of course, China has become far more open to *international trade*. In the first decade of reform, from 1978, China's foreign trade more than tripled (GNP increased by 2.5 times). Total trade in 1995 was ten times that in 1980. Trade as a ratio of GDP has roughly doubled since the economic reforms began in earnest fifteen years ago. Whether or not the ratio of trade to GDP continues to increase depends primarily on the extent to which barriers to internal trade come down fast enough to allow China's internal market to develop. So far, it has often been easier, especially for coastal provinces, to trade with the outside world than with the rest of China.[11]

Total foreign investment in 1978–82 was about $1 million, and increased to $4 million in 1991. But by 1993 the level of foreign investment also increased ten-fold, with some 85 per cent coming from ethnic Chinese outside China. For much of the 1990s China received more foreign direct investment than any other developing country, and in 1995 it ranked second in the world to the United States as a host country for foreign investment. Foreign-funded enterprises account for more than 14 per cent of total Chinese industrial output (1994) and they produce 40 per cent of Chinese exports. According to the Chinese Ministry of Trade, nearly half the Chinese economy is 'related to the international market'.[12]

China was not forced to open up to international trade in the sense that it was in the Opium Wars, but China has grown to understand, in large part because of the trends in its home region in East Asia, that autarky could not be a route to prosperity. China was not compelled to learn that lesson or draw those implications (viz. North Korea and, for a time, Albania), but once it decided that it wanted greater prosperity, it was 'forced' to open up. There was no necessary recipe for how, or how much, it would open itself to international trade and finance.

It is important to remember that the degree of connection with the outside world varies a great deal in different parts of China. The growth in GDP and trade and investment are far from synchronous, with some regions doing well with relatively less foreign investment. The decentralisation of economic policy has meant that different parts of China have different degrees of commitment to interdependence, and those which are interdependent are tied to very different trade partners. Thus it makes little sense to discuss the impact of interdependence on China without understanding that, in many important respects, there are different Chinas and different forms of interdependence.[13]

The results of these economic reforms, the new foreign connections and the decentralisation are well known. Coastal China grew faster than the hinterland, setting up major disputes over resources and uneven prosperity. Different regions integrated more closely with their foreign neighbours and in some cases trade grew faster with the outside world than with other Chinese provinces. Central government lost important levers of economic control as regions and entrepreneurs were newly empowered by their access to the outside world. These risks of decentralisation are sometimes exaggerated, but what is clear is that they result from an economic reform strategy that was necessary in order to open up effectively to the outside world. Beijing is reaping what it sowed. Although Beijing tries to portray itself as in strategic control of this process and working to a blueprint, in reality it is often merely pretending to rule.

Few can doubt that the opening of China to the global economy has had far-reaching consequences for the way in which China is governed.

Important elements of sovereignty have irrevocably slipped from the grasp of a once far more centralised authoritarian government. Beijing has serious difficulties controlling the money supply, fiscal policy, reform of state-owned industries and various other key aspects of policy because of this decentralisation. China's foreign policy is also affected, for Beijing cannot implement international accords, such as on intellectual property rights, because it does not control those parts of the economy. For the time being, it still pretends to make such solemn agreements (as do foreigners), even though all concerned know that China cannot make them reality. Neither China, nor even the outside world, seems ready to start dealing with a China that has changed shape.[14]

This is not so much a China learning to lose sovereignty, as one that is not yet ready to acknowledge the consequences of having lost sovereignty by virtue of its decision to engage in economic reform and to open to the global market economy. This is evidence for neither learning nor formal adaptation, as much as it is an attempt to pretend that it can have the benefits of openness without the consequent loss of control. Real learning and formal adaptation will come later.

Security

In the security sphere China has also made some far-reaching changes of policy. But a change is not necessarily the same thing as accepting the constraints of interdependence. Take, for example, the issue of China's *cessation of support for revolutionary movements*. This change of policy is often considered a sign of China's acceptance of the constraints of interdependence. But the evolution of Chinese policy can be read in a different way. China used to support revolutionary movements around the world, and especially in Southeast Asia. When China improved relations with the capitalist world because of its fear of the Soviet Union, it began to dump old revolutionary comrades. The initial motive was geo-strategic and only secondarily reinforced by an appreciation that the benefits of international economic relations were unlikely to come if Beijing was trying to foment revolution in its neighbours. It might also be recalled that none of these revolutionary movements was on the brink of success and therefore their abandonment carried few costs. Also, at a time when China was reforming its own view of markets and capitalism, it was illogical to be supporting 'Maoist' radicals.

The change in Chinese policy was in fact far more an assertion of China's new-found faith in a system of sovereign states. Support for revolutionary movements had been an expression of a Marxist world view.

The problem with China's conversion to nineteenth-century state sovereignty was that this modernism was increasingly anachronistic in a post-modern world where sovereign states were said to be of fading importance. To be sure, many other states in East Asia that had only recently gained full sovereignty were (and still are) loath to move into the post-modern world.[15] But the truth remained that the abandonment of revolutionary movements, beneficial as it undoubtedly was, was not so much a sign of the acceptance of the constraints of interdependence, as it was the precise opposite.

Arms control

What about *arms control*? It is said that China is learning to accept the constraints of interdependence and the need to surrender sovereignty because it has signed important arms control agreements. China joined the NPT, the Chemical Weapons Convention and the Biological Weapons Convention, takes part in the United Nations conventional arms register and signs confidence-building measure agreements with India and Russia. Is China learning that true security is interdependent and that it must agree to international inspections and in fact a surrender of sovereignty?

Alastair Johnston's careful study of this issue revealed little in Chinese behaviour that could be accurately described as learning.[16] Of course he found much evidence of Chinese adaptation to the realities of power in international security. China will sign arms control agreements with neighbours when the agreement is in its favour. India accepted the line of control as China had wanted. Where Russia and China have reached agreement, it has been on Chinese terms. Nothing surprising or difficult here.

Less tractable territorial disputes have not been the subject of arms control agreements. In the South China Sea, China refuses to accept international arbitration or even to accept that anyone else has a claim to sovereignty. The notion of shared sovereignty is nowhere to be found. This is a situation where China feels it has the power to take what it wants, and will do so in time. In 1995 it made more explicit commitments to apply the UN Convention Law of the Sea to the South China Sea, but this was done while asserting that UNCLOS terms would be applied only on the basis of Chinese assertions of sovereignty.[17] And then of course there is Taiwan, for which China refuses to contemplate any form of sovereign status. Once again, the picture is of a nineteenth-century approach to sovereignty.

China's signature on multilateral arms control accords offers more support for the notion that Beijing is learning to see security as divisible.[18] For example, the NPT imposes real restrictions on Chinese behaviour. Is this learning, or just China seeing, in good old-fashioned balance of power terms, the virtue of being inside rather than outside the NPT system? What was most notable about the timing of China's decision to join the NPT, or to join a moratorium on nuclear weapons testing, was that it was the last of the declared nuclear powers to do so. Is it too cynical to suggest that China did not want the opprobrium attached to being the only power seen to be standing in the way of arms control? If so, things could be worse. China could decide to stand outside the system no matter what – that would be the action of a confident non-status quo power. But China is less confident and more worried about being seen to be a bad citizen. That is not a wholly admirable spirit, but it is better than sheer cussedness.

This sullenly pragmatic spirit of accommodation to the flows of international power is also apparent in the way in which China comports itself on the United Nations Security Council. Being a supporter of the Victorian value of sovereignty, China does not like the notion that the international community, through the Council, can intervene in the domestic affairs of states. When the Council sanctions such intervention, China regularly grumbles, does not participate in the detailed discussions, and then does not block the action through its veto. It regularly expresses qualifications and makes it plain that the international community should not take such intervention as a change in the definition of acceptable international practice. The conclusion could not be more obvious: China is the rearguard great power when it comes to the erosion of state sovereignty. Nevertheless, China does follow where others lead, for fear of being left behind. Amid the cynicism, there should be reason for some optimism about China's ability to change when given no other option.

AN AGENDA FOR INTERDEPENDENCE

The story so far is of a China that has changed in very important ways because of its far-reaching decision to seek prosperity through economic reform. But that need for economic reform has also required growing interdependence with the outside world. This is also a story of reluctant change, for China has resisted the constraints imposed through interdependence. Chinese leaders know full well that the changes they are forced to make are changing their society and the way in which China is governed. And yet they seem to be locked into a process that requires increasing concessions to the outside world, even as China grows rich. As is the case with already much more Lite powers, China is finding its state power weakens, even though it is growing more prosperous. Chinese leaders had long assumed that as they grew wealthy they would grow stronger in their ability to resist the outside world. It has been the experience of all other modern great powers that eventually they grow to be Lite powers bound by the constraints of being a democracy and living in an interdependent world. The challenge for the non-Chinese world is to ensure that China follows the same path of enlitenment.

The key to enlitening China is a determination to continue to urge it down the path that will lead to economic, social and political liberalisation. Chinese leaders often complain that the West keeps 'moving the goal posts' for acceptance into the international system. Beijing asks (to change the metaphor) for a road map. What follows is a sketch of a road map that should lead both to China's further acceptance into the international community, and the enlitenment of China. But as we work our way through the map, it is important to remember that should China stray from that path, then it will need to be constrained. If China is left unconstrained, it is more likely to undergo the dangerous nationalist stages of enlitenment as seen in earlier phases of German or Japanese power.

Economic challenges

The main method of enlitening China has been, and will continue to be, the lure of economic prosperity. A weak and weakening Communist Party knows that it needs to produce the economic goods for its essential legitimacy. China knows that it cannot sustain economic growth without continuing to open up to the outside world. It needs the access to foreign markets on favourable terms that comes, for example, from membership in the World Trade Organisation. China must export to the developed world in order to pay for imports of technology, and increasingly the imports of vital food and fuel.[19]

An organisation aspiring, as the WTO does, to be a 'World' body, can see the virtue of Chinese membership. But if only because of the scale of the potential Chinese economic challenge, it is obvious why the developed world wants China to join the WTO under a strict set of rules with an effective dispute settlement mechanism to ensure that China is more changed by the rules than the rules are changed by China. Therefore a key starting point for the enlitening of China is the desire to see it *reduce its current average tariff level* from 23 per cent to at least 16 per cent (the average level for developing countries).[20] But this is not a one-time concession to the West, the WTO or even to common sense. The opening of the Chinese economy is an ever-demanding and perhaps even never-ending process. As the nature of the Chinese and global economies change, the pressure will always be there for further opening to the outside world. Indeed, it may be that one of the reasons for the seeming softening in the Chinese desire to join the WTO is the recognition that a deal is not a one-time negotiation and the pressure to reform will be constant and intense, even when it is inside the WTO. For those Chinese leaders who feel that concessions to the outside world are just short-term necessary evils, the WTO issue begins to look increasingly like a major trap. Chinese planners are beginning to make more explicit their desire to see international trade bodies, including APEC, as 'non-binding'.[21]

There are already plenty of signs that China is increasingly torn between the need to bend to the global economy and the desire to make the outside world bend its knee to China in order to enjoy the benefits of the Chinese market. Consider the question of the restrictions China imposed in early 1995 on the operations of providers of global financial information such as Reuters and Bloomberg, or its attempts to restrict use of the Internet.[22] China may have been merely trying to ensure that *Xinhua* reap the profits of such services, or this might have been just a foolish decision taken at a relatively low level; but even if these were the more benign explanations (rather than a desire to censor the outside world), then it is a clear violation of WTO rules. It is a sign either that China is determined to resist the logic of economic interdependence, or that, as Hu Yaobang once said, 'the main foe of the Chinese communists is their own ignorance and their main task is to overcome that ignorance'. Whether the explanation is greed, ignorance or political fear, the result is resistance to the strategy of opening China up to external constraints.

The free trade in financial service information is merely a recent prominent example of a much wider problem concerning China's attempt to resist the power of the global economy in shaping its domestic system. Similar motives lie behind China's imposition of quotas on items that can be imported and even on the number of companies which can import specific goods. Therefore a key challenge is to *reduce the myriad (formal and informal) regulations on how foreigners can access the Chinese market*. Many of these regulations are subject to arbitrary and changing rules by corrupt officials.[23] A China that joins the international economy will find all these activities subject to intense external scrutiny. As the Chinese economy continues to grow, and its exports continue to do well in American, EU and Japanese markets, the pressure will increase, not decrease, for further reform.

A related challenge for China is the need to *move to a fully convertible currency*. By remaining outside the stormy seas of the global financial markets, China believes it can avoid the buffeting of national policy by international pressures. China was only too aware in 1994–5 of how the Mexican economy was forced to conform to external dictates, and China can see how even developed economies in Europe or East Asia are upset by the power of the global market economy. It is therefore not surprising that China has slowed its move to a fully convertible currency. China has just accepted a convertible currency for current account transactions (i.e. trade in goods and services) in the near future, but will resist full convertibility (including for capital account transactions). Full convertibility is probably not sustainable without far-reaching reform of the dinosaurs of state-owned industry, and reform of state-owned industries obviously requires far more progress in building a welfare system and in breaking through powerful political logjams.[24] In short, China recognises that opening its economy to the constant and powerful scrutiny of the international money markets will reduce the power of the Chinese state, help push China down the road to being a Lite power subject to the whims of outside forces, and even help re-shape its society and lay the basis for a pluralist civil society. The stakes could hardly be higher.

Convertibility of the currency, like the notion of free trade, in the end will require China to abide by internationally agreed standards and accords. In the days when China had hardly signed any international agreements, it used to be said that when it did sign something, it was good at keeping its promises.[25] But since China has opened up to the outside world, there has developed far more doubt about whether it can be trusted. What concerns Western business leaders is *whether China can be trusted to abide by agreements* and what pressures can be brought to bear in case it breaks the rules.

The reasons for China's deteriorating record in abiding by agreements are as myriad as the features of its economic and social reform. The complexity of the problem is well evident when assessing why, for example, China has violated the intellectual property rights agreement with the United States in 1995.[26] Even before the accord was signed, it was clear that the central government would have great difficulty in ensuring compliance. Those parts of the Chinese economy that were violating intellectual property rights were in the free-wheeling entrepreneurial sector, often with good connections to the children of senior leaders or key parts of the establishment such as the armed forces. In a chaotically decentralised economy, Beijing found that it had little control and therefore its solemn pledges to the United States could not be implemented, even if there was the will to do so.

It is obvious that there is a great need for China to implement agreements already reached and there are growing doubts about its ability to ensure compliance on its own territory. Chinese public security units are engaged in piracy and other crimes. Smuggling is so rife, often with official sanction, that the likes of Motorola find that more of their products are smuggled into China (and sold at a cheaper price) than are produced within China. Chinese authorities are unable to provide effective help in controlling the swelling drug trade, nor are they able to stop thugs closing the anti-intellectual piracy office established in China. The list could go on and on, but even a Chinese paper reported in 1995 that China had more trade and investment disputes with foreigners than any other country.[27]

Without a better record of implementation and control over what goes on in its territory, China's signature on a WTO entry accord is equally meaningless. Of course, part of the problem is political. A Beijing that admitted it was having trouble controlling its economy and society, and sought help and understanding from the outside world, might get a more sympathetic hearing than one that pretends to rule but cannot. Beijing is disinclined to be realistic because to do so would be to admit just how much it is constrained by its own reforms and the process of interdependence with the outside world. The result is a China that is harder for the outside world to handle. But it is difficult to see why the outside world should believe the fiction that Beijing tries to sell when it claims to be abiding by international accords. The outside world has an interest in seeing Beijing recognise its more Lite reality and come to terms with its diminished ability to act like an authoritarian state.

Security challenges

The international economic agenda will obviously be the most important battleground in the effort to ensure that China becomes enlitened. China can see the benefit of economic interaction and therefore will be more willing to make concessions in order to bring prosperity. A much more difficult battleground will be in the security realm, where a China that is growing strong will see less reason to be constrained through interactions with the outside world.

A key concern for the world outside China will be to *ensure China does not use force to settle territorial disputes*. In 1994 China ejected Filipino fishermen from Mischief Reef and established a military facility on the disputed territory. In 1995–6 China closed air and sea lanes and conducted major military exercises in its attempts to scare Taiwan into backing away from seeking a greater international status. While the specific rights and wrongs of Chinese claims to such territory remain in dispute, what is of concern to the international community is the right to have these issues settled without the resort to force. In the case of the South China Sea, China has agreed not to use force, but it used coercion when ejecting the fishermen. In the case of Taiwan, China refuses even to pledge not to use force.

These issues are crucial tests of the extent to which the world is prepared to constrain China and therefore defend the long-term strategy of enlitenment.[28] It will take time for Chinese society and politics to be changed by the liberalising forces; in the meantime, a firm line needs to be held against the use of force. The outside world need not defend Taiwanese independence or the claims of ASEAN states to the South China Sea, but it does seem more necessary to defend the right to settle such issues peacefully. If no defence is offered, then China will feel that it can use, or threaten the use of, force in order to manage its neighbours. It was in part concern about such a future that led Indonesia and Australia to sign a defence accord in December 1995, and led Japan to formalise its claims under the UN Law of the Sea, and include territory disputed with China, in 1996. It was similar concerns that led the United States to take a firm line against Chinese pressure on Taiwan in 1996 and to reconsider the wisdom of its previous policy of 'strategic ambiguity'. In short, there is a growing concern that China will use force to settle territorial disputes, and that its neighbours need to resort to the balance of power as well as a long-term trust in economic interdependence in order to constrain Beijing.[29]

In theory there are also possibilities of *tying China into arms control accords* that might limit its propensity to use force. While China refuses to discuss any such accords in its maritime disputes, much has been made of its willingness to sign confidence building measures with India and Russia. Yet what is instructive in both these cases is that China has done little to constrain its behaviour and nothing to constrain its realistic territorial claims. India has essentially accepted the 'line of control', as China has long demanded.[30] Russia has given up only its absurd claims that the frontier should run along the Chinese bank of the river, but all other major issues remain unresolved. Where tiny bits of territory have changed hands, it has always been Russia giving up land to China.

The pattern seems to be that where China is strong, it finds it easy to accept accords that confirm its superior position. Where China feels it will grow in relative strength, it sees little point in being constrained through arms control. This pattern is also evident when we consider current arms control negotiations such as the Comprehensive Test Ban Talks. After France and Russia agreed to a zero-level CTBT, China at first demanded exemptions for peaceful nuclear tests, and then capitulated when it was clearly the last power holding up an accord. As was the case in previous arms control accords, China eventually signs once it is clearly the last power standing in the way.

The case for the virtues of the interdependence of security, which is often used in discussing arms control, has also motivated some attempts to get China to agree to schemes for military transparency. China does comply with the United Nations Conventional Arms Register and it published a 'White Paper' on arms control.[31] The latter revealed nothing that had not appeared in *Xinhua* press releases, and adherence to the UNCAR was hard to avoid when other arms importers and exporters already provided embarrassing detail concerning China. Where transparency measures would really show that China understood the need to be more interdependent about security – for example on the defence budget – it has been particularly unhelpful.[32]

Neither has China been helpful in international efforts to deal with piracy, illegal migration or control of the drug trade. These are all areas of increasing concern because Chinese, and even Chinese officials, have become increasingly involved. The causes of these problems, as with the issue of violation of intellectual property rights accords, lie deep in the social, political and economic reforms in China.[33] Decentralisation of authority has made Chinese more able to operate in these illegal manners and more difficult for the authorities to get a grip. Once again, the unwillingness of the Beijing authorities to admit the extent to which they have lost control is part of the reason why China is so uncooperative in dealing with the challenge. Just as an IPR accord is worthless under these conditions, so would be arms control with China, or even bilateral cooperation, for example in drug control. Only when China can implement such arms control, or seeks the outside world's help in dealing with problems that have internal origins, will China be truly said to have accepted the logic and constraints of interdependence. For the time being, China's resistance is a sign of its refusal to face the consequences of social change, and the need to recognise the consequences of its *de facto* surrender of important powers.

A related testing ground of China's approach to international security continues to be how it reacts to the role of the United Nations. Like the United States, but unlike any other permanent member of the Security Council, China is very wary about putting its soldiers under UN command. It is a difficult decision for any great power to allow foreigners to put its troops into harm's way, and China refuses to do so. Although its non-combat units have been used in UN operations (for example in Cambodia), they have yet to be put into circumstances where foreigners would command Chinese troops at times when deadly force would be used. The

United States does put its troops under these conditions when it is working with allies, but China has none. One trusts allies (and friends), but because China trusts no one with its security, it finds it very difficult to take serious steps that suggest it sees the value of interdependent security.

When issues of Chinese national security are at stake in the UN, China even abandons its relatively passive role of allowing the Security Council to intervene in other countries' affairs. Consider the case of the UN mission in Haiti in March 1996. China blocked, and then had amended, the efforts to alter the UN mandate, not so much because it disagreed with the operation, but because the Haitian authorities dared to have ties with Taiwan.[34] The old pattern reasserts itself: China takes an active part only if its direct interests are involved. Otherwise it is content neither to block nor to support the wider will of the international community as expressed through the United Nations (or arms control).

Making enlitenment work?

China is on its way to enlitenment. It may still be ruled by a communist party, but it is a much weaker party in far less control of the country. The Chinese economy is less than half state-owned. Economic and social power has been decentralised throughout a far more complex society. Chinese citizens have far more contact with the outside world than they have ever had before. Contact with foreigners helps feed the processes of reform, because it both helps provide economic incentives and offers alternative models of governance.

So far so good. But while enlitenment works its spells, in the meantime there are also the inevitable difficulties and risks in sustaining reform. It is clear that human rights in China will not substantially improve until there is a far more plural civil society, and that will take generations.[35] In the meantime, as is often the case in times of rapid modernisation, elites are shattered and old leadership structures shudder. When those who made the previous so-called revolution pass from the scene, the shudder turns to judder and the system can become even more unstable. Weak leaders, as so often in the past, find that dead ideologies can be replaced with nationalism as a way of building unity. The result is often simultaneous social and economic reform, accompanied by a very conservative political system. This picture of China is well within the experience of other rapidly modernising but destabilised societies.

The actions of outsiders can have an impact on such societies. There are groups within China who want the developed world to help them get beyond nationalism. There are groups outside who do not want confrontation with China and would prefer just to wait for the forces of enlitenment to take their course. Of course, there are also those within and outside China who would relish confrontation. Can these diverse views be accommodated in a policy towards China?

A sensible strategy towards China requires four components – all of which are necessary but none of which is sufficient on its own. China needs to be:

1 given more space in the international system;
2 engaged with the international society, economy and patterns of security;
3 kept to a rules-based international system; and
4 constrained when it undertakes unwanted action.

Until recently, much of the debate about policy towards a rising China has been foolishly based on the notion that one or two of these components would suffice as a policy. The puerile 'containment' versus 'engagement' debate was a symptom of this underdeveloped thinking about policy towards China.

Where there is common ground is in the view that it is good that China should be engaged with the outside world. While the motives behind such engagement undoubtedly differ, the policy output looks similar.[36] Some hope that engagement will hasten the enlitenment of China, while many Chinese expect that engagement will provide them with the tools better to resist the outside world. The correctness of one view or the other depends on how long enlitenment takes and how resistant China and its society are to liberalism.

It also depends on the policies adopted while we are awaiting to see how long enlitenment takes. While China grows Lite, will the outside world resist China's unwanted actions? Unconstrained authoritarians can resist liberalism for far longer than those who are constrained and forced to submit to liberal forces. The challenge for the world outside China is both to persist with the agenda for enlitenment, and to continue constraining China until it works.

NOTES

1 Alastair Iain Johnston, 'Learning Versus Adaptation: Explaining Change in Chinese Arms Control Policy in the 1980s and 1990s' *The China Journal* No. 35, January 1996.
2 These issues are discussed in Barry Buzan and Gerald Segal, *Anticipating the Future* (London and New York: Simon & Schuster, 1997).
3 On pidgin scholarship see 'Intellectuals: The Self and the Other', *China News Analysis* No. 1556, 15 March 1996.

4 Francis Fukuyama, *Trust: The Social Virtues and the Creation of Prosperity* (New York: The Free Press, 1995).
5 W.J.F. Jenner, *The Tyranny of History* (London: Allen Lane, 1992).
6 Raymond Cohen, *Theatre of Power* (London: Longman, 1987).
7 These trends are described in nearly every popular book about modern China, but an early and still entertaining analysis is Orville Schell, *Discos and Democracy* (New York: Pantheon, 1988).
8 Jianying Zha, *China Pop* (New York: The New Press, 1995).
9 Gerald Segal, 'Asians in Cyberia', *The Washington Quarterly* Vol. 18, No. 3, summer 1995; Kim Gordon, 'Riding China's TV Dragon', *Prospect* April 1996, pp. 76–8.
10 On various aspects of these issues see *Financial Times* 18 July 1995, *The New York Times* 20 August 1995, *China News Analysis* 1 June 1995, *The Economist* 14 October 1995, and more generally 'China', *Strategic Survey* (Oxford: Oxford University Press for the IISS, 1996).
11 See various chapters in Gerald Segal and David Goodman (eds), *China Deconstructs* (London: Routledge, 1994).
12 Statistics based on *China Statistical Yearbook 1995* (Beijing, 1995). Other statistics from *The Economist* 'Business in Asia Survey' 9 March 1996 and *Xinhua*, 3 March 1996 in BBC/FEW/6425/WG/1.
13 Segal and Goodman op. cit.
14 Gerald Segal, *China Changes Shape* (London: Adelphi Paper No. 287, Brassey's for the IISS, 1994).
15 Michael Yahuda, *The International Politics of Asia-Pacific* (London: Routledge, 1996).
16 Johnston, op. cit.
17 Mark Valencia, *China and the South China Sea Disputes* (Oxford: Adelphi Paper No. 298, Oxford University Press for the IISS, 1995).
18 Banning Garrett and Bonnie Glaser, 'Chinese Perspectives on Nuclear Arms Control', *International Security* Vol. 20, No. 3, winter 1995–6. See also Robert Mullins, 'Chinese Missile Proliferation', *The Pacific Review* Vol. 8, No. 1, 1995.
19 *Financial Times* 7 November 1995 and *The Economist* 2 August 1995.
20 On 1 April 1996 China reduced its tariff level from 36 per cent to 23 per cent. World Bank research showed that numerous exemptions and rampant smuggling had reduced actual import revenue to 6 per cent. By bringing formal tariff levels to more realistic rates, the hope was that the actual import revenue figure would rise. See *Financial Times* 7 December 1995 and *International Herald Tribune* 1 April 1996.
21 For example, Lu Jianren, 'APEC's Objectives and China's Position'. An unpublished CASS paper.
22 *The Economist* 20 January 1996, *International Herald Tribune* 17 January 1996, and *Zhongguo Xinwen She* 14 February 1996 in FE/2537/G/6, *The Straits Times* 29 March 1996.
23 *The Economist* 2 December 1995 and *The Far Eastern Economic Review* 21 December 1995.
24 *The Economist* 2 March 1996.
25 Harold Jacobsen and Michel Oksenberg, *China's Participation in the IMF, the World Bank and GATT* (Ann Arbor: University of Michigan Press, 1990).
26 *Financial Times* 25 January 1996.

27 *Asian Wall Street Journal* 17 July 1995, *Far Eastern Economic Review* 13 July 1995, 8 February 1996, *Newsweek* 29 January 1996, *International Herald Tribune* 14 December 1995, *United Press International* 20 June 1995, *Financial Times* 21 March 1996, citing the *Shanghai Business News.*

28 Gerald Segal, 'East Asia and the "Constrainment" of China', *International Security* Vol. 20, No. 4, spring 1996.

29 Douglas Stuart and William Tow, *A US Strategy for the Asia-Pacific* (Oxford: Adelphi Paper No. 299, Oxford University Press for the IISS, 1995) and more generally Paul Dibb, *Towards a New Balance of Power in Asia* (Oxford: Adelphi Paper No. 295, Oxford University Press for the IISS, 1995).

30 For a more positive spin see Rosemary Foot, 'Chinese-Indian Relations and the Process of Building Confidence', *The Pacific Review* Vol. 9, No. 1, 1996.

31 Malcolm Chalmers, *Confidence-Building in South-East Asia* (Bradford: Department of Peace Studies, distributed by Westview Press, 1996).

32 'China's Military Expenditures' in *The Military Balance 1995–96* (Oxford: Oxford University Press for the IISS, 1995).

33 Greg Austin, 'The Strategic Implications of China's Public Order Crisis', *Survival* Vol. 37, No. 2, summer 1995.

34 *Xinhua* 1 March 1996 in FE/2551/G/1 and the *International Herald Tribune* 2 March 1996.

35 An American government study not surprisingly reports that there is little evidence that economic reform in China has made an appreciable difference to the poor state of human rights. See the *International Herald Tribune* 7 March 1996.

36 See a careful study of these issues in James Shinn (ed.), *Weaving the Net: Conditional Engagement with China* (New York: Council on Foreign Relations, 1996).

Index

Note: Page numbers in *italics* refer to tables. Page numbers followed by 'N' refer to notes.